Literacy Across Communities

Literacy Across Communities

edited by

Beverly J. Moss
The Ohio State University

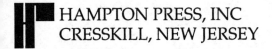
HAMPTON PRESS, INC
CRESSKILL, NEW JERSEY

Second printing 1997

Printed in the United States of America

Library of Congress Cataloging-in-Publication Data

Literacy across communities / edited by Beverly J. Moss.
    p.   cm. -- (Written language)
    Included bibliographical references and index.
    ISBN 1-881303-61-6 (cloth). -- ISBN 1-881303-62-4 (paper)
    1. Literacy--United States. 2. Socially handicapped children-
-Education--United States--Language arts. 3. Non-formal education-
-United States. I. Moss, Beverly J. II. Series: Written language
series.
LC151.L465   1994
302.2'244'0973--dc20   94-7395
                                                   CIP

Hampton Press, Inc.
23 Broadway
Cresskill, NJ 07626

Contents

Series Preface

This series examines the characteristics of *writing* in the human world. Volumes in the series present scholarly work on written language in its various contexts. Across time and space, human beings use various forms of written language—or writing systems—to fulfill a range of social, cultural, and personal functions, and this diversity can be studied from a variety of perspectives within both the social sciences and the humanities, including those of linguistics, anthropology, psychology, education, rhetoric, literary criticism, philosophy, and history. Because writing often is used concurrently with oral language and/or with reading, many volumes in this series include other facets of language and communication, though writing itself receives primary emphasis.

This volume of studies views the use of written language across diverse cultural communities, and primarily in nonschool settings. Churches, neighborhood organizations, homes, stores, and workplaces provide the contexts in which language, both oral and written, is fashioned and used for various purposes. What is distinctive about this volume, in contrast to much other work on writing, is the ethnographic, or insider's perspective; that is, the meanings concerning written language in these studies are understood from the perspectives of those studied, not simply from the points of view of particular researchers. Significantly, they provide very different conceptions of written language from those usually assumed in school contexts and, as such, can be used to inform educational practice.

Thus, while the study of writing is absorbing it its own right, it is an increasingly important social issue as well, as demographic movements occur around the world and as language and ethnicity accrue more intensely political meanings. Writing, and literacy more generally, is central to education, and education in turn is central to occupational and social mobility. Manuscripts that present either the results of empirical research, both qualitative and quantitative, or theoretical treatments of relevant issues are encouraged for submission.

Acknowledgements

I have been most fortunate over the past several years to have worked with wonderful graduate assistants who helped me with this project. They have done everything from transcribing numerous sermons to corresponding with contributors to preparing the subject index. To those former graduate assistants—Carole Clark Papper, Juanita Comfort, Victoria Dunn, Robyn Lyons—I thank you. I also thank Marcia Farr, Andrea Lunsford, and Jacqueline Royster for their helpful comments and support. Finally, I thank my parents for their unconditional love and support.

Introduction

Beverly J. Moss
The Ohio State University

Dan McLaughlin (Chapter 3, this volume) argues that "the analysis of Navajo reading and writing in one isolated corner of the Navajo reservation, although far removed from mainstream concerns, provides a window to understandings of literacy in theory and practice." The aim of this volume is to provide a "window to understandings of literacy" as literacy is defined in theory and practice within varied cultural settings in the United States. More and more, questions arise as to the literacy and language practices of students in communities outside the classroom. Our success as educators depends a great deal on our ability to understand what literacy and language resources our students, particularly those from nontraditional or nonmainstream communities, bring as part of their cultural backgrounds into the English classroom. These understandings can only be achieved with more focused attention on literacy in nonmainstream (non-middle class and often, though not exclusively, non-white) settings. Studies such as Philips's (1983) ethnography of the language use and literacy practices of Warm Springs Indians, Heath's (1983) ethnography of three Piedmont Carolina communities, Taylor and Dorsey-Gaines' (1988) ethnography of the types of literacy of Shay Avenue families, and other similar studies have provided great insight into what literacy practices occur outside the schools and has led to a call for more qualitative studies of literacy in nonmainstream communities. Thus, *Literacy Across Communities* is a response to this call.

This call for more qualitative research on literacy outside the academy comes as the academy begins to turn its attention toward the

1

needs of its growing diverse student population. Many of us in the academy have begun to recognize the limits of our knowledge about our students who come from nonmainstream backgrounds. We have come to understand that there is no monolithic student and that to continue in this vein only leads to the miseducation of scores of students, generally of the working class and minorities. Included, then, in this call for more qualitative research is the need to open up the academic conversation about literacy to the people who seem to have the most at stake—our students, particularly those from "powerless" communities. This collection of chapters, then, extends and expands on the growing interest in literacy in nonmainstream communities. The chapters in this volume highlight both mainstream and nonmainstream literacy practices in nonmainstream communities, three of which are bilingual communities where the need to juggle two languages and two literacies places more demands on its members. Equally important, however, the chapters in this volume expand the parameters of educational settings beyond the school. Just as there is no monolithic notion of student, there is no monolithic notion of an educational setting. The chapters in this volume point to homes, churches, sports associations, and other nonschool locations as important and often powerful educational settings that extend the work of the schools or come in conflict with the work of the schools.

The five studies discussed in this volume contribute to the academic conversation on literacy by complicating our notions of literacy—that is, by pushing us to look at how literacy is defined, valued, and used by people in their home communities. In that sense, this volume adds voices to the conversation—not just the voices of the researchers, but the voices of those who are the object of much discussion and debate—members of nonmainstream communities where literacy practices may or most likely may not match literacy practices in mainstream academic communities. These are the voices that have been missing from so much of the previous research on literacy. These voices articulate the contradictions, tensions, vulnerability, pride, and empowerment that generally can be associated with literacy. These voices also articulate the difficulty of characterizing literacy.

The chapters in this volume were chosen because, as a collection, they argue for the concept of literacies rather than literacy. It is the collection as a whole rather than any one single chapter that provides a multidimensional picture of literacy. In attempts to define literacy, the debate has progressed from a focus on the dichotomy between orality and literacy (Goody & Watt, 1963; Olson, 1977; Ong, 1982), which associated higher order cognitive abilities with literacy and cognitive deficiencies with orality, to a discussion that links literacy to a complex web or network of social practices (Heath, 1983; Scollon & Scollon, 1981; Scribner

& Cole, 1981). There is still much discussion and disagreement on definitions of literacy, but that discussion has, for the most part, moved away from "great divide" theories to a need to understand more about how literacy is learned and used in communities and institutions outside the mainstream (see Farr, Chapter 1, this volume, for further discussion on literacy controversy). This is not to ignore the importance of defining literacy. As Farr (in press) suggests, "what is at stake are the political implications" of the definitions of literacy. That is, how one defines literacy as well as who defines it has as much to do with who has political and economic power as with the way one uses language. Political and economic power, social status, and other "desirables" are most often attributed to those who are labeled literate. In other words, defining literacy is a complicated task which has far-reaching consequences.

Guerra (1992), in the course of conducting a literature review on literacy, found no fewer than 43 definitions of literacy which ranged from defining it as the simple encoding and decoding of graphic symbols (the ability to read and write) at a basic level to the more complex acquisition of knowledge and skills which allows one to use language according to community norms. According to the latter definition, everyone is literate as it is defined by a particular community. Heath (1987) uses the terms *literacy skills* and *literate behaviors* to distinguish between those two definitions of literacy. Yet, many argue that literacy cannot be defined without examining it in the social contexts in which it occurs along with the social practices that surround it (Street, 1984; Szwed, 1981). Although this latter argument suggests no fixed definition of literacy, it also points to the importance of examining how literacy (however it is defined) fits within the social structure of the community or group in which it functions.

This volume is concerned not so much with offering a fixed definition of literacy as it is with focusing on nontraditional literacy practices and uses, informal (outside of school) ways of learning literacy, and peoples' interactions with literacy(ies) in their nonmainstream communities and/or community institutions. Thus, although the authors in this volume define literacy, explicitly or implicitly, differently from one another, each does examine literacy (and/or literate behavior) as it fits within the social structure of a particular community or group. The communities and institutions represented in this volume—a Chicago *Mexicano* (immigrants born and/or raised in Mexico) social network, Philadelphia's Hmong community, Mesa Valley's Navajo community, an African-American Youth Basketball Association in a Chicago YMCA, and three African-American Chicago area churches— offer rich examples of literacies that "we don't see" (Mahiri, Chapter 4, this volume), ways of learning literacy that have indirect or no links to school, and ways in which people interact with literacies in their communities and institutions. In short, this volume focuses on nonschool and school contexts for literacy and/or literate behaviors.

The five chapters in this volume rely on ethnography to provide a methodological framework, and ethnography of communication to provide a theoretical framework for examining literacy and language use in communities outside the formal academy. It is this ethnographic perspective that allows readers to see the connections among a community's literacy practices, events, and behaviors and its participants' everyday lives. Because ethnography is holistic in nature, these ethnographies of literacy, by necessity, focus on language and literacy practices in the larger sociopolitical contexts of their communities or groups. Ethnography, a qualitative research methodology whose aim is to provide a descriptive analysis of a community, focuses on the daily routines, social interactions, values, beliefs, and behaviors of the members of a community (Agar, 1986; Moss, 1992; Spradley, 1979). In other words, ethnography is concerned with describing the culture of a community.

The ethnography of communication looks at "communicative behavior in specific cultural settings" (Saville-Troike, 1982, p. 9) and has as a basic tenet that language must be studied in the context in which it occurs. Saville-Troike (1982) suggests that:

> the ethnography of communication extends understanding of cultural systems to language, at the same time relating it to social organization, role-relationships, values and beliefs, and other shared patterns of knowledge and behavior which are transmitted from generation to generation in the process of socialization/enculturation. (p. 9)

Several particular ethnographies of communication have had a tremendous impact on how we currently view language use and literacy. Studies such as Philips's (1972, 1983) ethnography of language use on the Warm Springs Indian reservation, Scollon and Scollon's (1981) ethnography of the Athabaskan of Alaska, Heath's (1983) ethnography of three communities in the Piedmont Carolinas, and Fishman's (1988) study of an Amish community have forced scholars to examine the incongruities between language use and literacy practices in mainstream schools and nonmainstream communities. Studies such as these have pointed to an understanding of the speech communities from which students come as crucial to a more comprehensive understanding of how literacy works within a society such as the United States, which has multiple speech communities.

In keeping with the ethnography of communication's focus on examining communicative events within specific cultural settings, the researchers in this volume have conducted studies that connect literacy to social relationships, schooling, religious practices, and individual voice in an effort to emphasize how literacy works within the social structure of a community and vice versa.

In Chapter 1, "*En Los Dos Idiomas:* Literacy Practices Among Chicago *Mexicanos,*" Farr looks at how literacy is learned and used by members of a social network within a Chicago *Mexicano* community. Her study shows how literacy functions within the everyday lives of the families within this social network. By examining the public and private domains in which literacy is used, Farr focuses on how these families learn literacy through formal schooling and especially on how members learn literacy *"lirico"* (outside of formal schooling). She notes, however, that regardless of how literacy is learned, it is linked to schooling.

Like Farr, Weinstein-Shr examines literacy in social networks. In "From Mountaintops to City Streets: Literacy in Philadelphia's Hmong Community" (Chapter 2), Weinstein-Shr examines the functions and uses of literacy for three Hmong refugees who function within separate social networks in Philadelphia. In examining the role of kinship and other social relationships with literacy, Weinstein-Shr offers readers a portrait of three very different Hmong refugees and what they do with literacy rather than what literacy does to them. This chapter provides insight into how individuals and groups interact with and adapt to literacy to "make it their own."

Chapter 3, "Toward a Dialogical Understanding of Literacy: The Case of Navajo Print," successfully gives "voice" to individuals in this Navajo community as they struggle with the cultural, social, and political forces that shape their decisions for and against vernacular Navajo literacy and English literacy. In this chapter, McLaughlin sees an irrevocable link between how a community defines literacy and "individuals' struggle for voice." This unique focus on the attitudes and perceptions of Mesa Valley Navajo residents toward Navajo print literacy emphasizes McLaughlin's position that literacy cannot be defined fully unless the struggle for individual voice (against and/or within political and social contexts) takes place.

Whereas the first three chapters examine literacy through a broader look at particular communities, the final two chapters examine literacy in specific community institutions within Chicago's African-American communities. In Chapter 4, "Reading Rites and Sports: Motivation for Adaptive Literacy of Young African-American Males," Mahiri examines literacy practices in a sports setting among one of the highest "at-risk" groups in our schools—preadolescent African-American males. He looks at how sports promote print and computer literacy as well as literate behaviors in both the Youth Basketball Association and the home. Mahiri argues that the sports-related literacy practices that occur in this Youth Basketball Association serve to empower these young men and to motivate them in ways that school normally does not.

In the fifth chapter, "Creating a Community: Literacy Events in African-American Churches," I report on literacy events in three African-American churches, focusing especially on features of the major literacy event in this institution—the sermon. My analysis of African-American sermons points toward a model of a literate text that differs greatly from the academic essay—the traditional model of the literate text. Although this discussion of the sermon as a literate text focuses greatly on textual analysis, it also focuses on how the sermon fits within the social structure and within the literacy tradition of this community.

In the final chapter, "World Travelling: Enlarging Our Understanding of Nonmainstream Literacies," Chiseri-Strater considers the educational implications of the five studies in this collection. She examines how these discussions of cultural-based literacy practices help us better understand our students from nonmainstream communities. More specifically, Chiseri-Strater addresses how these discussions translate into classroom practice. Her chapter not only synthesizes and reconsiders the data provided in the previous five chapters, but it moves us toward action—the next important step.

Each of these chapters contributes much needed knowledge to the ongoing scholarly conversations about literacy and language. More importantly, each chapter provides an opportunity for communities generally considered the "other" to have a voice (even though filtered through the ethnographer) in the scholarly debates that concern them.

With the increasing focus on diversity and multiculturalism in American education comes a more urgent need to understand more about how people generally labeled "nonmainstream" learn and use language and literacy outside of school settings. This kind of knowledge allows educators to begin to understand what kinds of resources their students bring to the classroom in the hope of learning from and making use of those resources. This knowledge also broadens our notion of literacy beyond the scope of academic "essayist" literacy. This newly acquired knowledge and broadened perspective may be a major step toward making our schools and academic literacy more accessible to those groups who do not use the mainstream model.

REFERENCES

Agar, M. (1986). *Speaking of ethnography*. Newbury Park, CA: Sage.
Farr, M. (in press). Biliteracy in the home: Practices among Mexicano

families in Chicago. In D. Spener (Ed.), *Biliteracy in theory and practice.*

Fishman, A. (1988). *Amish literacy: What and how it means.* Portsmouth, NH: Heinemann.

Goody, J., & Watt, I. (1963). The consequences of literacy. *Comparative Studies in Society and History,* 5(3), 304-345.

Guerra, J. (1992). *An ethnographic study of the literacy practices of a Mexican immigrant family in Chicago.* Unpublished doctoral dissertation, University of Illinois at Chicago.

Heath, S.B. (1983). *Ways with words: Language, life and work in communities and classrooms.* Cambridge: Cambridge University Press.

Heath, S.B. (1987). Foreword. In H. Graff (Ed.), *Labyrinths of literacy.* Cambridge: Cambridge University Press.

Moss, B. (1992). Making the familiar strange: Ethnography in one's own community. In G. Kirsch & P. Sullivan (Eds.), *Composition research: Methods and methodology.* Carbondale, IL: Southern Illinois University Press.

Olson, D. (1977). From utterance to text: The bias of language in speech and writing. *Harvard Educational Review,* 47, 257-281.

Ong, W. (1982). *Orality and literacy: Technologizing the word.* New York: Methuen.

Philips, S. (1972). Participant structures and communicative competence: Warm Springs children in community and classroom. In C. Cazden, V. John, & D. Hymes (Eds.), *Functions of language in the classroom* (pp. 370-392). New York: Teachers College Press.

Philips, S. (1983). *The invisible culture: Communication in classroom and community on the Warm Springs Indian Reservation.* New York: Longman.

Saville-Troike, M. (1982). *The ethnography of communication.* New York: Basil Blackwell.

Scollon, R., & Scollon, S. (1981). *Narrative, literacy and face in interethnic communication.* Norwood, NJ: Ablex.

Scribner, S., & Cole, M. (1981). *The psychology of literacy.* Cambridge, MA: Harvard University Press.

Spradley, J. (1979). *The ethnographic interview.* New York: Holt, Rinehart, and Winston, Inc.

Street, B.V. (1984). *Literacy in theory and practice.* Cambridge: Cambridge University Press.

Szwed, J.F. (1981). The ethnography of literacy. In M. Farr (Ed.), *Writing: The nature, development, and teaching of written communication,* (pp 13-23). Hillsdale, NJ: Erlbaum.

Taylor, D., & Dorsey-Gaines, C. (1988). *Growing up literate.* Portsmouth, NH: Heinemann.

1

En Los Dos Idiomas: Literacy Practices Among Chicago Mexicanos

Marcia Farr
University of Illinois at Chicago

INTRODUCTION

Background

Most studies of Mexican-origin people in the United States have taken place in the southwest, especially in the border states of California, Texas, New Mexico, and Arizona. Although these states have by far the largest numbers of Mexican-origin people in the United States, the midwest, and particularly Chicago, has experienced remarkable growth in this population within the last several decades. Unlike the southwest, Chicago and the midwest were never part of Mexico; consequently, the Mexican-origin population here originated and has increased largely from immigration, not through incorporation as a result of war.

This historical fact may account for a difference in orientation between many midwestern and southwestern Mexican-origin people, a difference primarily reflected in an "immigrant" orientation. In terms of Ogbu's cultural ecological theory (1987), most Mexican-origin people in Chicago would constitute an "immigrant minority" (i.e., people who have moved, more or less voluntarily, to the United States) rather than a "caste-like or subordinate minority" (i.e., people who were originally brought into the United States involuntarily through slavery, conquest, or colonization). In the southwest, of course, both types of Mexican-origin groups currently exist, those whose predecessors were incorporated into the United States through war, and those whose families migrated more recently from Mexico. Recent immigrants in California (Delgado-Gaitan, 1987), for example, evidence the same qualities of optimism and belief in the future that I have observed in my fieldwork among Mexican immigrants in Chicago.

In this fieldwork, at least three major subgroups of the Mexican-origin population in Chicago have been identified: *mexicanos* (immigrants born and/or raised in Mexico), Mexican Americans (those born and/or raised in the United States, primarily in Chicago or elsewhere in the midwest), and *tejanos* (those whose families came to Chicago from Texas). The terminology used here for these three groups is in keeping with local usage (Elías-Olivares & Farr, 1991). The data reported in this chapter are part of a study of one social network within the first group, *mexicanos*; it is hoped that future studies will focus on Mexican Americans and tejanos in Chicago.

A study of these latter two groups would be able to determine, among other things, whether these Chicago groups see themselves as belonging to Ogbu's "castelike" or "immigrant" minorities, that is, whether their orientation is more reflective of one group or the other. There are some indications (D. Horowitz, 1985) that Mexican-origin people in the midwest share characteristics (e.g., voting and residential patterns) with other immigrant groups in the United States, rather than with African Americans, whom Ogbu refers to as a "castelike" minority. Another study of Mexican Americans in Chicago (R. Horowitz, 1983), however, examined gang activities, a feature some would consider more reflective of castelike status. It may be that different subgroups of the larger Mexican-origin community in Chicago hold either castelike, immigrant, or, indeed, other types of orientations; that is, those who were born and/or raised (and enculturated) in Chicago (especially second and third or later generations) may hold different beliefs, values, and attitudes from those who were born and/or raised (and enculturated) in Mexico or in the U.S. southwest. Because these are questions that can be answered empirically, future studies can either validate or invalidate these assumptions.

This chapter focuses on one aspect of a study of *mexicanos*, or Mexican immigrants, in Chicago[1]. The research program of which this

[1]We are grateful to the National Science Foundation, Linguistics Program, for supporting the first year and a half of this study. I am additionally grateful to the Spencer Foundation for continued support through August 1993 and to the Office of Social Science Research at UIC for both financial and administrative support during the entire course of the project.

analysis is a part was initiated by Lucía Elías-Olivares and me and carried out by the two of us and Juan Guerra, while he was an advanced PhD student in the English department (Language, Literacy, and Rhetoric specialization) at the University of Illinois at Chicago.[2] The larger research program is exploring both oral language patterns (Elías-Olivares, 1990; Farr, 1993) and literacy practices (Farr, 1989, 1990, 1994; Guerra, 1992) among one social network of families living in the two most concentrated (and contiguous) Mexican-origin neighborhoods in Chicago.

As indicated above, Chicago has experienced tremendous growth in the Mexican-origin population within the last several decades. A study of the history of this population (Kerr, 1977) dates the first large-scale Mexican immigration to Chicago in 1916, with a recruitment of railroad workers. In ensuing years, Mexicans came in increasing numbers to work in the railroad, steel, and meat-packing industries. By 1930, there were 20,000 Mexicans and Mexican Americans in Chicago, thereby establishing it as a major city for Mexican settlement in the United States. By 1940, this population was somewhat smaller (16,000) due to repatriation (both voluntary and involuntary) during the Depression years. During and after the Second World War, however, Mexican immigration (and Mexican American in-migration) again increased, resulting in a second major wave of migration. The third large wave of migration has occurred in the last several decades.

The 1980 Census showed Chicago to have the fourth largest Hispanic population in the United States and the third largest when only a central city's population (as opposed to an entire metropolitan area's population) is counted: 422,061 out of 3,005,072 (Acosta-Belén & Sjostrom, 1988; Chicago Fact Book Consortium, 1984). Out of the total "official" number of Hispanics in Chicago, Mexican-origin people constitute 60% (*Al Filo*, 1986). In addition, estimates of the undocumented Mexican-origin population in Illinois, most of which is in Chicago, range from 135,000 (Warren & Passel, 1987) to 300,000 (Juárez-Robles, 1990), which adds a substantial number of "uncounted" persons to the official count. In terms of the official count alone, the Hispanic population in Chicago *doubled* from 1970 to 1980, and preliminary results from the 1990 census indicate that between 1980 and 1990 it may have doubled yet again in the Chicago metropolitan area (*La Raza*, 1991). There is every indication, moreover, that this population will continue to grow due to both migration and immigration patterns, as well as to fertility rates (*Al Filo*, 1986).

---

[2] I would like to thank Susana Bañuelos, Maria Tristán, and Mayra Nava, undergraduates at UIC, for their long-term assistance on this project, especially for transcribing many hours of audiotaped discourse and for organizing and managing the office.

Rationale for Study

What has been termed the "literacy crisis" in U.S. society was part of the stimulus for initiating this study. Definitions of literacy vary markedly over time and across contexts, and studies have reported a range of "illiteracy," generally between 23 and 30 million adults in this country. A variety of claims and research reports is reviewed by Kozol (1985, pp. 7-12) that lead him to conclude that 1 of every 3 adults (60 million out of an adult population, in 1984, of 170 million) is "illiterate in terms of U.S. print communication at the present time" (p. 10). Depending on how literacy is defined, this estimate may be excessive, especially in view of the wide range of literacy practices used by the families in this study. This issue is discussed more fully in later sections of this chapter.

On a variety of standardized measures, however, culturally nonmainstream groups show higher "illiteracy" rates than do middle-class "mainstream"[3] populations. For example, the Mexican-origin population (approximately 57% of the national Hispanic population), like other "minority"[4] populations, consistently scores lower than the "white" population on literacy scales (NAEP, 1986, 1989a, 1989b). It should be noted that in the above reports, *all* members of these ethnic groups are reported together, regardless of socioeconomic class or mainstream orientation. Because socioeconomic class, which includes educational level in most scales, may be a more decisive indicator of literacy attainment than ethnicity, these analyses misleadingly suggest that ethnicity itself is the correlate and possible explanation for the low rates of literacy. As more members of non-white ethnic groups join the middle-class mainstream, class differences will become even more apparent in this situation.

Currently, high school dropout rates, which correlate with low literacy achievement rates, are extremely elevated in high schools serving working class, culturally nonmainstream populations; at Benito Juarez High School in Chicago, for example, which has a 98% Hispanic

---

[3]I use the term *mainstream* following Heath (1983, p. 392): "Mainstreamers exist in societies around the world that rely on formal educational systems to prepare children for participation in settings involving literacy. Cross-national descriptions characterize these groups as literate, school-oriented, aspiring to upward mobility through success in formal institutions, and looking beyond the primary networks of family and community for behavioral models and value orientations."

[4]Both the term *minority* and the term *white* are increasingly problematic because of ongoing and expected demographic changes in this country, including growing numbers of persons of mixed ethnicity. The meanings of these terms at the level of various local communities is a question to be answered empirically. For a description of problems with the race and ethnicity questions on the Census questionnaire among Mexican-origin populations, see Elías-Olivares and Farr (1991).

(and over 90% Mexican-origin) student body, the drop-out rate is over 50%. Student language problems are often cited as a factor in high dropout rates (Kyle, Lane, Sween & Triana, 1986). Language problems, of course, can refer to a lack of fluency in English or to other, more subtle differences between the ways a nonmainstream cultural group uses language (both oral and written) and the ways standard English is used in formal schooling.

Because even those who speak English fluently often have education and literacy problems (e.g., working-class African Americans and Native Americans), it clearly is not simply a lack of fluency in English that is at the heart of language problems. A number of studies have shown, in fact, that differences in the way language is learned and used, especially if those ways differ from language use in formal schooling, provide one explanation of low achievement levels in literacy and other aspects of schooling (Heath, 1983; Philips, 1983; Scollon & Scollon, 1981; among others). Thus it is crucially important to identify the cultural and linguistic differences between the standard English of formal schooling and the ways of communicating of particular nonmainstream groups; few studies have investigated what Hymes (1974b) called "ways of speaking" (or writing and reading) among Mexican-origin people in the United States, and none have been done in Chicago or the midwest.

Methodology and Focus of Study

The present study is carried out within the framework of the ethnography of communication as conceptualized by Hymes (Hymes, 1974a; Saville-Troike, 1989). This type of linguistic research emphasizes the importance of context and holistic analysis, and its aim is to understand meaning from the point of view of the members of a particular cultural group. Consequently, long-term participant-observation is deemed necessary for a valid understanding of cultural and linguistic patterns. My participant-observation so far has included five years in Chicago (primarily on weekends) and six weeks in Mexico. In addition to participant-observation, we carried out informal, open-ended interviews with the adult members of the families in the study and audiotaped informal discourse in the homes of members and in public settings in the neighborhood.

The families in the study comprise one social network of *mexicano* immigrants (approximately 45 people) who in the United States would be designated working class by virtue of their blue collar occupations and limited formal educational levels (years of schooling range from 0 to 8). The concept of a social network has been developed within anthropology and used in sociolinguistic research (Hannerz,

1980; Milroy, 1987); a social network consists of one center person or family—the latter in this case—and all immediate intimates in terms of kin and friendship. For linguistic research, one advantage of studying a social network is that normal group rules for interaction tend to prevail, thus minimizing the effect of the participant-observer and yielding more natural language data (Milroy, 1987).

Social networks have been studied in various working-class communities around the world, and although they are probably important for many U.S. immigrant groups (as a support and survival mechanism), they seem to be particularly important for *mexicanos* because of *compadrazgo*. *Compadrazgo* refers to the Mexican system of godparentlike relationships that function as a reciprocal exchange network to facilitate economic survival and provide emotional and social support. This phenomenon is described by Horowitz (1983), and it matches that from my own participant-observation:

> *Compadres* and relatives usually make up an emotional and social support group. Women move freely back and forth between homes— cooking together, talking, taking care of one another's children, shopping, and going out together for entertainment. . . .
>
> Holidays, birthdays, and other special occasions are usually celebrated with *compadres*, relatives, and their children. A special dinner is prepared, and people eat in several shifts if no table is large enough to accommodate all the guests. . . .
>
> The strong network of intergenerational relationships provides a means by which traditions can be readily passed on (Horowitz, 1983, pp. 58-59).

According to Horowitz's references (Gibson, 1966; Mintz & Wolf, 1950), the *compadrazgo* system originated in 6th-century Mexico and was widely adopted during the colonial period, "when an epidemic caused significant depopulation and compadres became accepted as substitute parents" (Horowitz, 1983, p. 243, n. 5). There is some evidence that this system, although important in rural areas, becomes even more crucial (for economic survival) in urban areas such as Chicago (Lomnitz, 1977).

The present network of about 45 people is only a subset of a larger group of kin and *compadres* which numbers over 100 people; these 45, then, are the closest kin and *compadres* with whom interactions are much more frequent (at least weekly and, for some, daily) than they are with other members of the larger group (whom we met infrequently on various occasions). One interesting aspect of this network is that it is essentially binational. Movement is almost continual in both directions between Chicago and the two *ranchos* (small rural communities) in Mexico, one in Guanajuato and one in Michoacán, from which the center family's husband and wife emigrated. Some network members live in Chicago (visiting Mexico from time to time), some live in Mexico (and visit Chicago every few months), some live for years in Chicago and then for years in Mexico, and others come to Chicago annually (for up to half a year) to earn income. Moreover, whereas both men and women have emigrated to Chicago from the Michoacán *rancho*, only men from the Guanajuato *rancho* have emigrated to Chicago (their wives and children, up to this point in time, have remained in Mexico and receive financial support sent from Chicago).

Before turning to a description of literacy as learned and used by the members of this social network, I would like to consider briefly how literacy has been variously defined, both by theorists and by empirical (primarily ethnographic) researchers.

Conceptions of Literacy

One goal of this study has been to identify the uses of written language, both Spanish and English, among Mexican immigrant families in Chicago. This necessarily involves a consideration of what "literacy" is. Guerra (1992) located no fewer than 35 different definitions of literacy from a range of literature. In general, though, literacy is seen in two primary ways; Heath (1987) terms these two ways *literacy skills* and *literate behaviors*. In the first view, literacy is seen as "the ability to read and write," that is, the ability to use the writing system (alphabet, syllabary, or other script) of a language. This, in fact, is the definition most linguists use because, as Graff (1981) has pointed out, it is the only definition that can be used universally, both over space (cross-culturally) and over time (historically). The second major way of viewing literacy involves ways of thinking, or cognitive style (Scollon & Scollon, 1981, for example). In this view, literacy (in Western cultural contexts) usually means thinking critically, "objectively," or analytically; scholars who take this view of literacy disagree on whether or not the definition should be tied to the use of written language, that is, some claim that one can be "literate" with oral language alone (e.g., Gee, 1989; Vasquez, 1989), whereas others see literacy talk as occurring around written texts (e.g., Heath, 1987).

I have argued (Farr, 1994) for the "linguistic" definition of literacy (knowledge and use of a writing system) that spans cultures and historical periods and have suggested that "cognitive" definitions (i.e., literate behaviors), especially those that focus on oral language use, can result in either denigration or patronization, rather than a more egalitarian respect for differences that may exist. This is not to deny that literacy is used in particular ways of thinking, nor even to argue against instruction in Western literate behaviors, but to avoid labeling people who in fact have literacy skills as either "illiterate" or "semi-literate" (Miller, 1988).

Given the cognitive importance many have attributed to literacy (Goody, 1977, 1986, 1987; Goody & Watt, 1963; Olson, 1977; Ong, 1982), the controversy that has surrounded the literacy "crisis"—and, particularly, the attempts to define literacy—is not surprising. To sum up this controversy briefly: Some scholars argue that literacy itself, particularly alphabetic literacy, changed, over the long term, human cognitive processes (see especially Goody 1977; Goody & Watt, 1963; Ong, 1982). This theory has been criticized for privileging the Western "literate" cognitive style over other cognitive styles (Street, 1984). Moreover, evidence from anthropological studies has shown aspects of the Western "literate" cognitive style in nonliterate peoples (Finnegan, 1988). Finally, Finnegan (1988) has demonstrated that it is not the technology itself that causes change in a culture but, rather, how the technology is used in particular social and historical contexts (see also Scribner & Cole, 1981; Street, 1984), as well as what other social factors (e.g., the production of paper from trees) are present along with a particular technology (e.g., writing).

Hence, the use of literacy over many centuries (e.g., in Europe, China, and India) may act as an "enabling factor" (Finnegan, 1988) which, along with other social factors, can stimulate significant changes in a culture. Writing, then, although no "great leap," especially in the development of individuals, nevertheless is a significant human invention, primarily because of its ability to extend communication over space and time. Hymes (1980), in fact, pointed out that writing (in this sense the use of written symbols to represent speech) is quintessentially a cultural creation, a human invention, in contrast to oral language, which was not "invented" but presumably evolved over time. Because it is a cultural construct, writing is consciously learned, and oral language (one's native language, that is) is unconsciously acquired. In a linguistic sense, then, writing, or literacy, is a technology, a system that can be abstracted from its contexts of use (see Coulmas, 1989; Sampson, 1985). Although Street (1984) and others have argued convincingly that literacy is never an autonomous technology in its *use*, that is, it is always a cultural practice embedded in particular social and historical (and political) contexts[5], there is nevertheless a sense in which writing systems *are* "something apart," cultural tools that are taught and learned explicitly. This conception of literacy, in fact, is held by the members of the Mexican immigrant families with whom I have been working.

Literacy, among these families, is seen as connected to schooling,

---

[5]In this sense written language is no different from oral language, which also always is used in a particular social, historical, and political context. Many descriptions of literacy in the literature, in fact, ascribe qualities to literacy that are actually characteristic of humanistic discourse in general, whether oral or written, for example, the ability to raise consciousness, or empower.

either directly or indirectly. That is, those who read and write are respected for being especially "intelligent" and usually for being more formally educated, although a number of the men from one of the *ranchos* in Mexico learned how to read and write outside of school from those who did learn literacy in school. Thus, whether literacy is learned in school, with books, or *lírico* (informally, orally, without books), it is ultimately connected with schooling and is seen as a cultural tool, like mathematics.

Thus far I have provided an overview of the larger study of which this chapter is a part—background information relevant to the particular group of people whose literacy has been studied—and a brief discussion of conceptions of literacy. In the rest of this chapter I focus on some results of the study, first dealing with the learning of literacy by different network members, both as a part of formal schooling and *lírico*, or outside of formal schooling. Then I turn to a description of the literacy practices of network members within both the public and private domains of their lives.

LITERACY LEARNING

Most members of this social network learned how to read and write as part of formal schooling. Others, however, experienced very little formal schooling (in some cases virtually none at all), either because when they were young their *rancho* in Mexico did not yet have a school or because they had to work in order to help support their families. These individuals, in this case the adult males over 35 years old from the Guanajuato *rancho*, learned to read and write, as they say, *lírico*, or on their own outside of formal schooling. In what follows I describe patterns in both kinds of literacy learning, paying most attention to the interesting *lírico* phenomenon.

The level of formal schooling among those who learned literacy in school is largely a function of generation, which in turn is related both to the availability of schooling and to the opportunity to attend. For the older adults, schooling usually meant attendance (variously from 2 to 6 years) at the public elementary school in their *rancho*; for the younger adults, it meant either public schooling in Mexico (sometimes including both *primaria*, grades 1 through 6, and *secundaria*, grades 7 through 9) or a combination of schooling in Mexico and in Chicago.[6] For the youngest generation, it usually meant schooling, often through high school, almost entirely in Chicago. Among the older adults, older female

---

[6] It is important to point out that *secundaria* is sometimes referred to as "high school" and that education beyond that level (*preparatoria*) prepares one for a specific career or for college. Thus, not continuing one's formal education after *secundaria*, or ninth grade, may not be seen as "dropping out," but simply as "finishing."

siblings often had fewer years of schooling because they had to help their mothers maintain their homes; older male siblings, similarly, often had to work on the land to help support the household. Younger siblings in this older generation, in contrast, frequently were more expendable in terms of household labor and thus were able to attend school for more years.

The subsequent "one and a half" generations (younger adults and the first generation born and/or raised in Chicago) have increasingly higher levels of formal schooling, as the opportunities for attending increased, again for reasons of availability and sufficient household income. After "finishing" their formal schooling, a number of the younger adults, in addition to working full time and frequently being parents as well, have attended English, literacy, and GED (general equivalency diploma) classes at a community-based organization or at the church they attend, which often houses an educational program in the basement. In the youngest generation, most are finishing high school, although some have not done so, and some are attending college; one young woman has attended graduate school.

In general, literacy skills correlate with the number of years of schooling, as would be expected, but there are interesting exceptions, all of which have to do with personal motivations to learn and use literacy. These motivations include the use of literacy for religious reasons (discussed in a later section on literacy practices in the religious domain) and for "personal obligations" to maintain correspondence with network members in Mexico. The latter motivation led a number of men to learn how to read and write *lírico*, outside of formal schooling. In these cases especially, literacy skill has little correlation with years of formal schooling.

Learning Literacy Lírico

Lírico es. . . puro hablado. . . que no hayan libros ni nada.
Lyrical is purely spoken. . . there are no books or anything.

Puede ser tambien con maestro, pero que no haya nada de libros.
It also can be with a teacher, but with no books.

La voz, pues, nada mas pura voz.
The voice, then, nothing more than pure voice.

La voz y la palabra.
The voice and the word.

As often happens in ethnographic studies, an interesting but unexpected phenomenon emerged early in the study. A number of the men in their mid-30s and beyond from the Guanajuato *rancho* became functionally literate essentially without formal schooling. They report that they learned literacy *lírico*; that is, they "picked it up" informally from others who used only spoken language—not printed materials—to pass on knowledge of the writing system. The teaching and learning process, then, proceeded through oral language, from one person to another, in informal arrangements.

This pattern of learning literacy *lírico* is not restricted to the families in the network under study; I have been told basically the same story by other men in this community—who are not part of this network—from other *ranchos* in Mexico. The pattern is not, however, typical of the men in this network from the *rancho* in Michoacán. The differences between the two *ranchos* account for the fact of informal education in literacy in the one case and school-learned literacy in the other. The *rancho* in Michoacán is located immediately off a highway, and the local *municipio* (township center) is less than 2 kilometers away—a walkable and easily drivable distance; during recent decades, moreover, the growing of avocados has brought this area increased prosperity (Damien de Surgy, Martínez, & Linck, 1988). The rancho in Guanajuato, in contrast, is over 13 kilometers from the nearest city, and there is infrequent (once a day) public transportation to and from it—without a car, it's a very long walk; moreover, this rancho has only benefited from electricity within the last decade and as of 1991 did not yet have running water. In contrast, the *rancho* in Michoacán has benefited from both of these services for some time. As a recent study of another *rancho* in "Jalmich" (the border area between the states of Jalisco and Michoacán) has shown (Barragán López, 1990), proximity to modern roads can make a significant difference in a Mexican rural community's social and economic life.

Even after a public school was established in the more isolated *rancho* during the 1950s, some of the children who were "of school age" had to work rather than attend school. The center family husband estimates that he went to school for a "maximum of about three months" at two different ages, first when he was 8 (for a month and a half) and some time later when he was put in third grade (for another month and a half). He says the reason he could not go to school was that he had to work (his mother had died and his father worked for long periods in the United States):

> *Es que teníamos que trabajar. Mira, como no había la jefa, mi papá siempre estuvo acá en Estados Unidos. Entonces pues, teníamos que trabajar para comer. . . o sea que a los ocho años ya empieza uno a trabajar en México. Desgraciadamente allá, tienes ocho años, ya puedes caminar bien, tienes que ir a ver los animales. . .*

> It's that we had to work. Look, since our mom [the boss] was not around, my dad was always in the States. Well, we had to work to eat . . . in other words, already at the age of eight one starts to work in Mexico.

Unfortunately, there, when you are eight and can walk well, you have to go look over the animals. . .

This description is strikingly similar to Spufford's (1981) discussion of literacy among working-class rural Englishmen in the 17th century; in both cases literacy, at least that learned through formal schooling, was inextricably linked to the economy, in that only children who could be spared from other labor were able to attend school. Like the 17th-century spiritual autobiographers whom Spufford studied, these men from the Guanajuato *rancho* learned to write and read outside of school. Someone else who had been schooled, usually a friend, taught them their "letters." As one man explained it:

> *Bueno. . . te voy a decir la pura verdad. Mira, no hay persona que se enseñe por su mismo a nada. Tiene que haber una base, tiene que haber un, ¿Cómo te dijera? Nosotros decimos un pie. O sea, una base para empezar, porque, simplemente, para que tú te enseñes a algo, tienes que aprenderlo de otro.*

Well . . . I'm going to tell you what it is really like. Look, there isn't a person who can teach himself anything on his own. There has to be a base. There has to be a, how can I tell you? We say there has to be a leg to stand on. In other words, a base for beginning, because, simply, for you to teach yourself something, you have to learn from someone else.

When this man was 9 or 10 years old a teacher began to give classes in his *rancho*, but he could not go to school for more than a few months because he had to work. According to him, those who did not go to school learned some of the letters from those who did go to school. Later, during his second few months at school, he learned more letters and how to put them together to form his name. After that, he built on what he had learned by reading and writing by himself ("in the street"), practicing with such things as empty cigarette boxes, which he used both for reading and for writing. Here is how he describes the way he learned:

> *Por ejemplo, tú traes una cartilla de cigarros. . . . Ves las letras y dices, "pues, esta es esta, y esta," así, verdad, y las vas juntando, entonces ya después te vas empezando a practicar tú mismo, y hasta que llega el día que ya conociendo todas las letras, las puedes juntar. Entonces yo después empecé a escribir solo, a escribir. Y cuando les platicaba a mis amigos, "Mira, fíjate que ya sé escribir, y esto ya se escribe así de este modo, de este otro." Entonces seguí practicando y practicando. . .*

> *Algunos amigos allí ya mayores tenían revistas, cuentos, sí, revistas de historietas. Y me las prestaban. Entonces, como en esas revistas me gustaba leer, yo creo fue la base de donde aprendí yo más también, porque ya cuando empiezas a leer una revista, cuando terminas una revista y la leés completa, ya allí ya vienen casi todas las palabras. Entonces se me fue mejor, o sea, sí fui*

mejorando la lectura mía. Para escribir pues, eso sí batallé más, pa' eso sí era, era más complicado. Pero, cajetilla de cigarros que me encontraba por allí tirada y toda la dejaba rallada. Yo trahía un lápiz y lo sacaba y me acordaba de lo que había leído en la revista. Y las ponía a veces que le sobraban letras, a veces le faltaban. Pero era parecido.

For example, you have a box of cigarettes. . . . You see the letters and you say, well, this one is this one, and this one, like that, right, and you put them together, then later you begin to practice it yourself, and the day comes when you know all the letters, you put them together. Then later I began to write by myself, to write. And when I was talking to my friends, "Look, I can write," and "This is written this way, or that way." And then I continued practicing and practicing. . .

Some of my older friends there had magazines, stories, yes, comic book magazines, and they would lend them to me. And since I liked reading those magazines, I believe they were the basis of my learning more, because when you read a magazine and finish it, you have read almost all the words. So, my reading skills improved. When it came to writing it was more difficult for me; it was more complicated. But, if I found a cigarette package thrown away, I would finish by leaving it all scribbled on. I had a pencil and I would take it out and I would remember what I had just read in the magazine. And I would write with excess letters or with missing letters. But it was more or less the same.

These accounts reveal much about literacy learning stripped of formal institutional structures: a "bare bones" approach taken by highly motivated men. One man's account, and that of his *compadre* included below, provide details underlying their own views of this learning process and of written language itself. In the discussion that follows I address three aspects of these accounts: first, what they disclose about the process by which these men describe learning to read and write; second, what they disclose about the social nature of such learning and, for *mexicanos* especially, the important role *confianza* (trust) plays in this process; and third, what they tell us about significant features of the setting that provides the "motivation" to learn to write and read.

The process of literacy learning. The man quoted above, like the spiritual autobiographers from 17th-century England (Spufford, 1981), describes his acquisition of literacy as first learning the letters of the alphabet, then learning to put them together. Both accounts refer to learning to read first, then learning to write, and they both refer to writing as being more difficult than reading. Another man from the Guanajuato *rancho*, however, describes his process as the reverse: He learned to write (so that he could write letters home from the United States) but claims he still reads "only a little," including part of the *anuncios* (announcements) in church and a small part of the newspaper. He writes multipage letters about every two weeks, and he does so very laboriously, forming rather large letters. He does not read regularly in his daily life; he may, of course, read signs and other environmental print, but for him, apparently, this does not count as "reading." The following is how this man describes how he first learned to write, then later to read a little:

> *Bueno, yo empecé a escribir cuando salía de mi tierra, cuando empezé a escribir para mi casa. Entonces había un señor que me decía, "mira así, así se hacen las letras," me las apuntaba. Entonces yo empecé a pensar y a hacerle la lucha a escribir y yo escribía. Ya me empezaban a contestar y yo me sentía contento porque, sí me daba gusto lo que decía, ¿no? Ya, ya, ya la estoy, ya la estoy haciendo . . .*

> *Yo me ponía a escribir para mi casa. . . me acuerdo que la primer' carta que mandé me dure como dos dias, bueno, después del trabajo. . . Y entonces yo escribía mal hechito como podía, y me llegaba la carta. . . pero no podía yo leerlas. Yo la daba a leer porque no podía. Hasta, después ya con el tiempo ya fui a, poco a poquito a poderlas ir leyendo.*

Well, I began to write when I went out of my country, when I began to write home. There was a man who would tell me, "Look, this is how letters are made," and he would write them for me. So I began to think and try to write and I would write. Then they began to answer me, and I was happy because of what their letters said. (And I would think) now, yeah, now I am doing it. . .

I would write to my house. . . I remember the first letter I sent took me two days to write, well, after work I would work on it. . . And so, I would write badly, any way I could, and then I would get a letter. . . but I could not read it. I gave it to someone to read because I couldn't. Not until later, with time, little by little was I able to read them.

These differing accounts tell us that neither learning reading first nor writing first is more "natural." Both, however, can be acquired without schooling as a spontaneous part of daily life, when people perceive a need for these skills. These accounts also reveal how literacy is perceived by those coming to it on their own. Both of these men, for example, recognize that writing, especially in English, is not an exact reflection of speech. In their own words:

> *El inglés que yo escribía. . . no era exactamente como lo escriben en la escuela, o ni muchos menos siendo que yo lo escribía a manera que se pronuncia; o sea más bien, lo escribía yo en español. Sería decirlo así, verdad, yo lo escribía en español. . . por ejemplo. . . me decían eso se llama "coffee cup," yo le ponía, verdad, como se pronuncia.*

The English that I wrote . . . wasn't exactly the way they write it in school, much less so since I wrote it the way it was pronounced; in other words, I wrote it in Spanish, that's how I would describe it. I wrote it in Spanish . . . for example . . . they would say that is called "coffee cup," I would put it how it was pronounced.

Pero ya que yo escriba, yo sé que no las voy a escribir como debe de ser. Ahora, puntos, acentos, ¿Dónde los lleva? Quién sabe, no tengo idea. . . a lo mejor pensándolo digo, "a caray, pos sí, a lo mejor lleva el acento aquí," pero eso de que punto, coma y eso, eso sí no sé nada. Nomas las letras.

But once I begin writing, I know I am not going to write properly. Now, periods, accents, where do they go? Who knows, I have no idea . . . maybe when thinking about it I say, "oh wow, yes, maybe the accent goes here," but about periods, commas and that, I know nothing. Only letters.

Porque los que aprendemos a leer y a escribir acá lírico, qué vamos a saber de ortografía, qué vamos a saber dónde va un acento, qué vamos a saber que dónde está un punto se tiene uno que detener cuando está leyendo, ¿qué sabe uno de eso? Uno le sigue derecho. ¿Sí o no? Yo no me fijo en eso, que, está un punto debe de haberse parado un ratito. No, pos yo ese punto ni lo ví. Estaba muy chiquito yo sigo para adelante. ¿Me entiendes? Y la gente que está educada, que ha tenido su escuela, pos oye, ve un punto y se para. O ve unas rayitas allí que les dicen signos. . . le dan su sonido a la lectura. Yo no, yo, parejo. Nada de bajadas y subidas, no, no, no, no, ¿qué es eso?

Because those of us that learn how to read and write over here, lyrically, what are we going to know about spelling, how are we going to know where an accent goes, that when there is a period you pause when you are reading, what does one know about that? One goes on straight ahead. Yes or no? I pay no attention to that, and were one to tell me there is a period you should have paused a bit, well, I just did not see that period. It was too small for me to see so I kept going. Do you understand me? And people who are educated, that have had schooling, well, they see a period and they pause. Or they see a bunch of small lines there, and they are signs for them to give a special sound to their reading. Not me, I am even. None of those ups and downs, no, no, no, no, what is that?

These men, then, know that the writing system that they have learned to use includes not only the letters of the Spanish alphabet, but also accent and punctuation marks. The letters alone, however, are basically sufficient for their purposes: writing for themselves (at work and elsewhere) and writing to family and friends in Mexico. They view the accent and punctuation marks as signposts for reading, and although one of the men says that he reads "evenly" (no "ups" and "downs"), without heeding the accent and punctuation marks, he in fact reads aloud quite expressively and has done so in my presence.

One evening in his home, this man picked up some printed materials we had brought to them (a list of questions prepared by the Catholic Archdiocese to prepare people for the U.S. amnesty exam) and began reading it aloud, in English, as he walked around his living room. An acquaintance of his exclaimed in surprise, "What?! You can read?! But you always say you can't read in our class {at the local community organization}!" Everyone laughed uproariously at his cleverness. This anecdote serves two purposes here: First, it proved that, in spite of his statement about reading less "expressively" than he would if he had learned how to use accents, periods, and commas, he in fact read quite accurately and appropriately. His comment may reflect a belief that, if one doesn't learn to read "officially" in school, what one does when decoding print isn't "really" reading. That is, true reading is sanctioned by school learning. Second, this anecdote clearly indicates that what people say in one context (or in response to survey questionnaires or formal interviews conducted by strangers) is not necessarily what they do in other contexts. In this case, this man has literacy abilities quite beyond what would be predicted, especially based on his negligible experience with formal schooling, and he has literacy abilities that surpass even his own assessment of them. In a formal test of English literacy levels[7] this man achieved an extremely high score, the highest in his social network (Guerra, 1992).

Learning literacy *lírico*, then, is remarkably effective. Although formal schooling is the route to literacy for many people, schooling is clearly not essential. These personal accounts of this process provide other counterintuitive findings as well. First, some people learn to read first, then write, whereas others reverse this order and learn to write first, then read. Second, the writing system, that is, the alphabet, is seen as a way to represent speech, primarily through the use of the letters, but additionally through the use of punctuation and accent marks. The latter are seen as learned primarily through schooling, whereas the letters themselves can be "picked up" lyrically.

To learn *lírico*, then, is to learn informally, without books, and purely with spoken language. Things learned *líricamente* ("lyrically")— traditionally the guitar or even, according to another network member, English—are "picked up" without formal instruction. Thus, one network member in Mexico said she was learning to play the guitar *lírico* with a group of people at the church there; although there was a "leader" in this "class" who was more experienced in playing the guitar,

[7]We thank Aline Grognet and the Center for Applied Linguistics in Washington, DC for providing us with a pre-publication version of the English literacy materials prepared for use in amnesty classes.

learning proceeded informally, without explicit instruction or books—indeed without an actual "teacher." It is worth noting that although much of the practice in such "lyrical" learning goes on without a teacher, even when there is a teacher, the learning situation is informal, and in the case of the men who learned literacy *lírico*, something that happens between friends. The importance of this aspect of the process is discussed in the next section.

The social nature of literacy learning. I already have discussed how the men described here (like the 17th-century spiritual autobiographers) initially acquired some literacy from friends who had had some schooling while they themselves were working during childhood. Thus, minimal literacy skills had been acquired one on one from friends during childhood, along with much practice using any materials available, such as cigarette packaging and magazines. When these men began working in Chicago (at about age 17), they felt a renewed and increased desire for literacy skills in order to write letters to family and friends back home. Stressing its importance, one man refers to this as a "personal obligation" and says that many people have learned to write for this reason. Because of *compadrazgo*, it would be especially important for Mexicans to maintain close relationships with kin and compadres even while far away. Literacy is, of course, an available technology to serve this function, as is the more expensive telephone. Some of the families now regularly use the telephone to talk to relatives in Mexico; others, however, still rely on writing. Writing, however, is not only important in maintaining personal relationships, it also is acquired as a part of such relationships. These men describe themselves as fortunate in being able to learn writing from trusted friends.

> *Él era del estado de México siendo que yo lo conocí aquí en Chicago, y éramos muy amigos aquí en Chicago. Entonces, pues, muy sencillo. . . muchas de las veces tú encuentras algún amigo que en verdad es amigo, ¿verdad? Y cuando eso sucede el amigo sí se preocupa por tí. Sin, pos yo digo sin ventajas, o son amigos, que decimos acá nosotros, un amigo derecho, que te estima. Entonces esa es una de las razones que yo creo que él me ayudó porque viéndolo por el otro lado, qué le podría importar yo a él. Te imaginas, no somos ni siquiera vecinos, ni parientes, ni mucho menos. Entonces este hombre, creo que hizo mucho, mucho por mí.*

> He was from the state of Mexico and I met him here in Chicago and we were very good friends here. So, it's very simple...sometimes you find a friend who is a true friend, right. And when that happens the friend really does worry about you. Without, well I think that they do so without taking advantage, or they are friends, as we say over here, a straight up friend, one who really cares about you. So that was one of the reasons that I believe he helped me, because seeing it from a

different perspective, why should I have mattered to him? Can you imagine, we are not even neighbors or relatives or even much less. So this man, I think he did a lot, a lot for me.

Another way in which learning literacy is revealed as an intensely social process is found in the learning process itself. Both men describe the emotional support of the friends who taught them to write and comment on the trust (*confianza*) that had to exist between them during this process. These friends were selfless and generous in their efforts to teach literacy, but also they were very supportive. As one of the men explains it:

> *Bueno, yo ya sabía más o menos, pero yo creo que de allí para acá me empecé yo a, cómo te dijera, aprender más de lo que creí que podía aprender. Porque, en primer lugar, fíjate, que te voy a decir una cosa: cuando tú quieres aprender algo y hay alguien que te ayuda, te apoya sí se puede aprender. Pero si en cambio tú tienes un amigo que en vez de que te apoye se empiece a reir de tí, que "¡Ah, mira que eres un tarado, no se te pega nada!" en fin, te desanimas en completo.*

Well, I already knew how to [read and write] somewhat, but I think that from there I began to, how would I say it, learn more than I thought I could learn. Because, in the first place, listen, I am going to tell you something: when you want to learn something and you have someone to help you and really support your efforts, you can learn. But if you have a friend who instead of helping you laughs at you and says, "Oh, look you're so stupid, you can't grasp anything!" finally you become totally discouraged.

Thus, literacy is a social phenomenon in several aspects. First, it is a system, or tool, created by human beings and passed on from one human being to another. Often this is accomplished through formal schooling, but it is also achieved *lírico*, informally, as a natural part of (nonschool) life. Second, especially for those far from home, literacy is essential in maintaining human relationships, that is, for living up to one's personal obligations. Finally, supportive human relationships are crucial in the learning process itself; a degree of trust and commitment provide the human base from which learning and teaching are carried out. In the next section I discuss the setting that generates the motivation to pursue such learning.

The setting of literacy learning. Szwed (1981) defines motivation as "the nexus at which reader, or writer, context, function and text join" (p. 15) and adds that reading and writing skills will vary according to differing degrees of motivation. Clearly, the men being discussed here were highly motivated to learn literacy skills. What was the basis of this motivation? Using Szwed's definition, we can trace several aspects of the setting toward the nexus that yields motivation. First, the readers and writers in this case were men with virtually no formal schooling who were working in a foreign country without much competence (initially) in the dominant language and who had left an extended network of very close relatives and friends "back home."

In this context (Szwed's second aspect), these men felt, as one of them said, a "personal obligation" to maintain these social connections, hence they turned to an available cultural tool or technology—literacy— for long-distance communication. The problem, then, was how to learn to use this technology, a problem that, as has been explained, was solved socially with help from others.

The third aspect which forms the nexus for motivation, according to Szwed, is function. Here the function of literacy was to communicate over a long distance with loved ones and to maintain or extend important human relationships. One man describes the context in which he felt motivated to learn and improve his literacy skills:

> *Entonces ya después me vine para acá. . . le puse más interés a aprender. O sea yo creo que aprendí más bien aquí. . . cuando uno está lejos de su tierra, las circunstancias lo obligan a uno a aprender porque, eh, te imaginas que yo me hubiera ocupado una persona que me hiciera una carta, por ejemplo a la novia, ¿verdad? Primero se da cuenta el que está haciendo la carta que yo. . . Pondrá lo que le dices o le pondrá de más. A lo mejor en vez de decir saludos le manda decir "óyeme vete para el catre," pero con más malas palabras. ¡Te imaginas! Entonces, yo creo que esa es una de las razones las que la mayoría de nosotros nos hemos enseñado a leer y escribir.*

> So then afterwards when I came over here. . . I became more interested in learning. In other words I think I learned better here. . . when one is away from his country, the circumstances require that one learn because, well, can you imagine, if I had hired someone to write a letter, for example to my girlfriend, well, the person writing the letter would know before I. . . Perhaps he will put what you say or perhaps he will add something. Maybe instead of saying hello he tells her to go to hell, only in worse language. Can you imagine! So I think that this is one of the reasons so many of us have taught ourselves to read and write.

What is important here is the combination of factors that yields motivation. Motivation may be something an individual feels, but it clearly is not a quality that a particular person either has or does not have across various settings. Instead, it emerges out of the setting, out of the mixture of participants (reader and or writer, teacher and learner), function, and (potential or created) text. Therefore, these men were motivated to learn to write because of a combination of factors: first, those with whom they wanted to communicate were in another country; second, they felt a personal obligation to maintain these relationships and to maintain them *personally*; third, a cultural tool, writing, was available for this purpose; and fourth, others were able and willing to share their knowledge of this cultural tool.

People, then, cannot be said to be either with or without the quality of motivation, except in specific settings, and whether or not they are motivated to learn or to use literacy depends on specific aspects of those settings. I next describe how various members of this social network used literacy in their daily lives, across multiple settings.

LITERACY PRACTICES IN PUBLIC AND PRIVATE DOMAINS

The members of this social network are literate. Especially as a network, they deal more than adequately with the literacy demands in their lives, and various members use literacy to differing extents to achieve an assortment of personal goals. Although it is not often foregrounded as an end in itself, literacy is part of the texture of their daily lives. Literacy materials (e.g., hardback and paperback religious books, magazines, and books and pencils for the catechism class held in one family's home) are stored out of sight until they are to be used. When occasions for literacy arise, materials are retrieved and used; also, knowledge of literacy is among the resources that are shared across members within the network. Those who are more knowledgeable about literacy, either in terms of reading and writing skills or background knowledge relevant to written texts (i.e., either in terms of literacy skills or literate behaviors), are routinely called on by less knowledgeable individuals when the need arises. For example, those who have more advanced levels of schooling are called on to read official letters (in English) received by those whose formal schooling is less extensive. Thus, literacy is among the network's pool of shared resources, as are other kinds of knowledge, including information about potential jobs, health care, automobile repair, and so forth. As Velez-Ibañez and Greenberg (1989) have shown, this kind of sharing of "funds of knowledge" is especially characteristic of Mexican-origin social networks.

In analyzing the literacy practices of these families, I chose to emphasize domains in which literacy is used, rather than the functions of each literacy activity, as have other researchers (Heath, 1983; Taylor & Dorsey-Gaines, 1988). Many literacy activities serve multiple functions (for example, reading an official letter can serve both interactional and instrumental functions); moreover, domains allow a more social, rather than individual, perspective, inasmuch as they allow one to situate the literacy practice in the social relationships that exist within domains, as well as to situate the literacy practices more concretely within the larger view of daily life. I have adapted a framework of domains provided by

Goody (1986) that encompasses the four traditional "subsystems of society": religion, economy, politics (the state), and law. Goody provides an analysis and synthesis of the role of writing, historically and cross-culturally, within these four broad societal domains.

During the period in which I collected data for this analysis, adult family members were undergoing, with our assistance, the amnesty process established by the U.S. government with the Immigration Reform and Control Act of 1986. As a result, the families' literacy practices within two domains, politics (the state) and the law, coalesced; hence, for the purposes of this analysis, I also collapsed these two domains into one. In addition, I added two domains that involve the private realm of the families' lives (Goody's domains are all within the public, societal realm): the family/home domain and the education domain. The former is entirely within the private realm, and the latter involves both the public and the private realms because formal schooling for either adults or children is "public," and informal educational processes (e.g., learning literacy "lyrically" with a friend, or studying English or for the GED at home) are "private."

The following descriptions of literacy practices among these families are described within four of these five domains: religion, commerce, the state/law, and education. The fifth domain, that of family/home, has been treated in detail elsewhere (Farr, 1994).

The Religious Domain

Literacy practices are an integral part of the religious activities of these families, whether the activities take place within the church proper or within the homes of its members. Almost all of this literacy, moreover, is in Spanish, and much of it involves the reading, and sometimes writing, of relatively long texts. One older female member of the network is particularly known for her religious faith (although a number of the other women frequently read religious materials as well), and this woman regularly loans books to others that are intended to promote values and understandings encouraged by the church. The Catholic church itself plays an extremely important role in the lives of family members, although it plays a more direct role in the lives of the women and children who participate in church services and other activities at least weekly (and, for some members of the network, almost daily). In addition to services on Sunday, some members attend a prayer meeting on Tuesday (and some other) nights, and each Saturday morning *doctrina* (catechism) classes are held for the children in various church members' homes. During the period of data collection, the second-grade *doctrina* class was held in the center family's home, and it is this class that I attended regularly one autumn.

Many other religious activities cluster around holidays (e.g., Christmas), and special events are held in members' homes to celebrate the holidays. These phenomena are not only religious events, but literacy events as well, as they are occasions in which a piece of writing is integral to the nature of the participants' interactions and their interpretive processes (Heath, 1982). For example, one post-Christmas occasion, *el levantamiento del niño jesús,* or "the putting away of the baby Jesus," is organized partially by a Novena booklet that is in Spanish and was printed in Mexico: *Novena para las Posadas.*

In what follows I describe in somewhat more detail the literacy practices in two religious literacy events—*doctrina* and the *levantamiento*—in order to illustrate the nature of these activities and how literacy is part of the texture of these events.

The *doctrina* class was held from 10:00 a.m. until about 11:30 a.m. on Saturday mornings in the living room of the center family. About 10 children participated, all of whom were in second grade, as was the youngest child of the center family. The furniture was arranged in a rectangle on one side of the living room so that the children sat on sofas and chairs along three sides of the rectangle and the teacher(s) sat or stood along the fourth side, against the wall. *Doctrina* books and pencils from the church were retrieved from the compartment within the coffee table for use during class. The book used, *Creciendo con Jesus* (*Growing with Jesus*), was a large paperback volume that was printed in both Spanish and English. Lessons each week were structured around the lessons in the book. Classes were very schoollike, with the female teachers (junior and senior high school students who volunteer to do this) clearly assuming authority over the children and the children matter-of-factly accepting this authority. The children were eager participants, frequently asking to read aloud from the book, and shyly but proudly showing their written work to the rest of the class when the teachers brought them up to the front of the class to do so.

Throughout the class, reading and writing occurred continuously, and oral discussion of the written texts (those in the book and those generated by the children) was interwoven with the literacy activities themselves. Discussion centered around interpretation of the written texts. Singing also was an important part of the class, and this usually occurred toward the end of class, in part to keep the increasingly restless children occupied until parents arrived to take them home. Prayers, of course, also were an important part of the class; sometimes they were read from the books, and sometimes they were recited without the books, as there was an emphasis on memorization of such texts to make them a part of oneself.

All language use by the teachers during *doctrina,* whether oral or written, seemed to be geared toward teaching ethical values associated with Catholicism. For example, before Christmas, one *doctrina* class focused on "doing good" during Advent; the children were required as homework for the class to write two lists in an Advent Book (*Libro de Adviento*), which the teachers had made and passed out to each child. One list was for all the good deeds they intended to do during Advent, and the other list was for the good deeds they actually did. The message emphasized by the teachers in this lesson, and the next one in which these lists were reviewed and discussed, was that no one is perfect but everyone is forgivable: We all try to do our best, but we all make mistakes; God always forgives us when we are *really* sorry for what we did (and God will know whether or not we are really sorry in our hearts for our mistakes).

Doctrina class during Advent provides part of the structured celebration of Christmas, both at church and at home. A number of activities take place within homes during this season, including *posadas* (9-day celebrations in which people enact the holy family looking for an inn), the *acostamiento* (rocking and putting the infant Jesus to sleep), and the *levantamiento* (taking him up and putting him away for another year) ceremonies. At home, on Christmas eve, network members participate in a ceremony in which a doll representing the infant Jesus is put to sleep in a manger scene created on one side of the living room. About a month later, they enact the ceremony in which the infant Jesus is taken up from his crib in the manger and put away for another year. I describe here one particular *levantamiento* ceremony.

Immediately prior to the *levantamiento* ceremony in the center family's home, the mother retrieved from storage and passed out well-used xeroxed copies of a *Novena* booklet which she herself used during the ceremony. Songs (lyrics only) and prayers to be used during Christmas events, including this one, are printed in the booklet. As in the *doctrina* class, in this religious literacy event the activities were structured in part by print, which was used for praying and singing by the participants. Some prayers were read (recited from memory by some) together, and others were performed by the mother of the home. For some prayers, the mother "read" them verbatim (although it was not an unfamiliar text for her, thus the print seemed to serve to refresh her memory), for others she moved away from the printed text, expanding the prayer with her own formulaic additions. For the songs as well, all the participants clearly knew the parts and used the text to refresh their memories and to include less familiar verses. Other parts of this event, of course, were structured not by the printed booklet, but by custom. For example, at the end, everyone lined up to go up to the baby Jesus doll, which was held by an adult female whose birthday it was, kissed the doll (which was carefully wiped with a cloth after each kiss), and received a little bag of candy, cookies, and peanuts.

In both of these descriptions of religious literacy events, the literacy practices were so integrated into the events as to be almost invisible. Yet, they were a very important part of the events. They were simply taken for granted as a natural part of the ceremony; no special attention was given them. The same can be said for other religious literacy practices, for example, the occasional reading of religious magazines (*El Centinela, Maryknoll* magazine) that I observed in the homes. This "invisibility," in fact, is descriptive of most of the literacy practices in these families, whether in the religious or other domains. Literacy in the religious domain, however, is unique in two ways: first, the print read or written is almost always in Spanish; and second, it involves the reading and writing of extended texts, for example, books, magazine articles, prayers, and songs. In the other domains either English predominates or both English and Spanish are used, and the written language often consists of short sentences, for example, those used on bureaucratic or commercial forms.

The Commercial Domain

In the commercial domain there are four primary areas in which family members use literacy: on the job (for some of them, not others), in entrepreneurial business activities (e.g., the selling of items from catalogues and the rental of apartments or rooms within family-owned property), while shopping, and when paying bills. Job literacy is usually in English; entrepreneurial activities utilize both Spanish and English (e.g., the Jafra cosmetics order form is in Spanish, but the bag for sold products is printed in English); shopping involves print in both languages; and bills are usually in English. Biliteracy, then, is generally the norm within the commercial domain.

Literacy demands on the job vary greatly among network members. One person struggles to write reports in English as part of a quality control process in the factory in which she works. A number of the women use no literacy at all as they debone chicken breasts in a poultry factory. Some of the men report working from "punch lists" on their jobs; these lists are given to them by supervisors and indicate what work needs to be done—in one case by a team of painters, and in another case by railroad construction workers. The men describe "decoding" the lists using literacy skills, knowledge of English, and on-the-job content knowledge. If they cannot decode the entire list, they ask co-workers for help. Another group of the women in the network work at a warehouse that ships out catalogue orders; they report having to read orders and write, with large markers, on the boxes in which they gather the items that are ordered. In all these cases only one person described the literacy demands at work as being difficult for her (the quality control report writer); all the others seem to be managing well, regardless of the level of schooling they achieved in Mexico, which varies from no schooling (or a few months), up to graduation from *secundaria*. Most of the older adult network members have fewer than six years of elementary schooling. Nevertheless, virtually all of them are coping quite well with the literacy demands on their jobs, which, in some cases, are relatively minimal.

Many of the men and women maintain small businesses in addition to their jobs. The husband in the center family, for example, rents out apartments on the property that they bought; they live in the first floor apartment and rent out three small apartments in a separate building in the back of their property and two apartments on the second floor. They also provide living space (for rent) to other members of the network who spend some time each year working in Chicago. Some people divide each year between Chicago (working for pay) and their village in Michoacán; others spend several years at a time working in Chicago. All, however, return to Mexico whenever they are able to financially and can spare the time from their jobs. Some of the families, of course, live and work continuously in Chicago (and own property there), only visiting Mexico when they are able to take the time off from work. These families provide the base from which other kin and *compadres* can live and work when they come to Chicago. Maintaining records for such complicated arrangements requires some effort as well as both literacy and mathematics skills; the father in the center family is assisted in this by his eldest daughter, who attends a Chicago public high school.

Many of the women in the network maintain small businesses as authorized representatives of catalogue companies, for example, Tupperware, Stanley home products, and Jafra cosmetics. They sell items from these catalogues to other network members, friends at work, and other acquaintances. Their businesses entail recordkeeping, filling out orders, and exchanging monies as payment for items. Thus, both literacy and mathematics skills are required to maintain these businesses. One woman (the most active in such businesses), when asked whether she used a calculator to do the math, replied that she did not, because, although she had a calculator, one of her daughters always had it when she needed it, leaving her no option but to do the math by hand.

Shopping is another area in the commercial domain in which literacy practices occur. Before going out to shop, network members sometimes read advertising circulars which have been delivered to the house and/or ads in various newspapers (the *Sun Times* which is in English and *La Raza* or other local newspapers which are in Spanish). In stores they read labels, sometimes thoroughly, as happened one time in an herbal shop where we had stopped to buy tea for health purposes (e.g., to calm nerves, to alleviate constipation).

Finally, literacy practices in the commercial domain include the paying of bills. Some bills arrive in the mail; others, such as those from a hospital, are given upon discharge. In the latter case, more than the bill was given upon discharge; papers that indicated what the patient should or should not do for several weeks, as well as the treatment (including drugs and injections) the patient received while in the hospital, were also given to the patient. Literacy, as well as mathematical skills, are needed for dealing with all such papers.

To conclude, network members quite adequately respond to the demands for literacy in the commercial domain, whether this involves their jobs, their own entrepreneurial activities, shopping, or bill paying. In spite of the fact that most members have rather limited schooling (in U.S. terms), they are quite functionally literate in the commercial domain of their own lives.

The State/Law Domain

Two primary state institutions have consistently made literacy demands, primarily in English, in the lives of these Mexican immigrants: the Immigration and Naturalization Service (INS) and the Internal Revenue Service (IRS). The recent U.S. government's amnesty policy for undocumented workers provided a process by which network members without "green cards" could obtain legal status within the United States. Having worked in the United States for up to 17 years, virtually all such members had the required written evidence to prove they were eligible for amnesty. Because this policy took effect near the beginning of our research, we offered to assist members in the amnesty process in exchange for their cooperation in our research. Specifically, we provided a weekly class in the center family's home; this class, led by Juan Guerra and taught as well by Lucía Elías-Olivares and myself, covered the U.S. civic content material to be tested by the INS. We used a list of 100 civic content questions developed by Catholic Charities in Chicago (e.g., What do the stars on the U.S. flag mean? Who was the first president of the United States? Who are the senators of your state?) to cover the civic content material, and Juan Guerra developed a practice dialogue of an interview in English that was intended to approximate the ultimate INS interview of applicants in order to help network members prepare for the interview.[8]

---

[8]We used the materials developed by the Center for Applied Linguistics (see footnote 6) to determine levels of literacy skills.

Prior to the beginning of our in-home class, network members had been attending English classes at a nearby local community organization, and they had planned to attend amnesty classes there as well. Evidence of 40 hours of work in such classes was sufficient to obtain an INS interview and, it was hoped, legal status. Many family members chose to study in our classes, however, and take the optional written exam (passing it was considered equivalent to the 40-hour certificate) prior to the final interview. All network members who participated in our class passed both the written exam and the interview, thereby attaining legal status.

Occasionally, during the course of the amnesty process, various network members would receive correspondence from the INS regarding their own or a family member's status in the process. This correspondence, like other similar correspondence, often was deciphered fairly well by the recipient, even though most recipients had a limited knowledge of English and only basic literacy skills. Frequently, sometimes to decipher the message, but more often to check on their own understanding of the correspondence, recipients would ask other members of the network with more advanced knowledge of English and literacy to read and interpret the correspondence for them. Usually this meant a teenage member of the network who was attending high school in Chicago (or, in one family, a daughter who was attending college). After our research team became a part of the network (classes rather quickly became social as well as educational events and led to friendship), members asked us to assist in difficult literacy tasks. For example, the print on the INS forms which amnesty applicants had to fill out was extremely tiny and unclear, and even we, supposed experts in literacy, found it difficult to read and respond to the questions.

On other occasions, various network members would receive correspondence from the IRS. In one case in which I was asked to assist, this involved the questioning of a past claim by one of the network members. Again, even a college professor of English found the message confusing, and complying with the demands in the letter necessitated several telephone calls on my part to the agency in question. Thus, both oral language, in English, and literacy, also in English, were required to respond adequately to the demands of this bureaucracy.

To conclude, in this domain as in the commercial domain, network members coped quite well with literacy demands. It could be argued, of course, that they did so with the assistance of university researchers. Yet, there is no doubt that had we not been part of their lives, these families would have coped anyway, using the considerable literacy and English-speaking resources of their social network. The children of the adults who had migrated from Mexico up to 20 years previously were both bilingual and more literate (more schooled) than their parents and quite capable of handling most institutional literacy demands from the state. If demands arose that they were unable to handle, the social practices of this group would have led members to ask other acquaintances (e.g., at the community organization, or at work) for explanation and assistance. The overall picture, then, is of a social network of families exchanging resources with one another, as well as with others outside the group, in order to survive. And because of this active resourcefulness, they not only survive, but assert control over their own lives.

The Educational Domain

I include in the educational domain all education-related literacy activities, both those that are part of public institutions, for example, the school and the library, and those that are more personal and informal and that take place in the home. For the most part, these activities utilize English print, although on occasion (e.g., homework for bilingual education in grades K-3) they utilize Spanish print. First, the formal, public aspects of education are described and then the informal practices of various individuals.

Perceptions of education as a public institution have both ideal and real dimensions. The ideal of education is highly valued by these families; this is evident in their respect for educated individuals, their insistence that their children learn, and their seriousness about their own opportunities for learning. Their real experiences with formal education, in contrast, often are disappointing. For example, one summer a fifth grader in one family began summer school; her teacher had recommended her for a program that would strengthen her English and other skills. The expected teacher for the program, however, whom the child liked very much, decided to go to Mexico for the summer. The replacement summer school teacher, in the child's words, "yelled at them, told them they were already in fifth grade and didn't know how to act, and told them they were dumb." Her mother's comment was, "what's the use of going to school if it makes you so nervous you can't do anything?" She withdrew her daughter from the summer school program and enrolled her, along with four cousins and a younger brother, in the nearby public library summer program, where, the daughter told me, "you read books and then they ask you about them." Unfortunately, she was not very interested in these books, which she said were at the "sixth-grade level" and beyond her understanding.

In spite of such disappointing experiences with formal educational institutions (not all of their experiences are so negative), the ideal of advancing in formal education remains important. A particularly explicit example of this high regard for formal education occurred during dinner in one family's home; one of the mother's six daughters (the third born) was attending college out of town and majoring in psychology. The mother was explaining with manifest approval and admiration how her daughter had, as part of her coursework, counseled a potential suicide victim. She had, in fact, talked a woman out of committing suicide. Some time later, the police called the daughter and asked her to speak again to the woman, who once more was on the verge of committing suicide and who had asked for the daughter. Once again she soothed the suicidal woman with her words and calmed her down. Her mother and a friend who lives with the family were both extremely impressed with and proud about this event. The friend went on to remark how people with education (those who *estudian mucho* or "study a lot") have more ways of treating other people than those, like himself, who are not so educated. "We," he said, "tend simply to dismiss other people sometimes," and he used a gesture indicating such dismissal—an "eh!" and a turned head with a backward wave made with the back of the hand, as if to brush someone away. The mother then added that another of her daughters was also like that; the other daughter she mentioned was, at that time, the only other one with plans for postsecondary education. Thus, formal education is clearly seen as leading to enhanced abilities and not just academic ones. It is seen as enhancing one's abilities to deal more effectively with people and to handle life's problems.

Another indication of the approbation of formal education is seen in activities focusing on children's homework. Children are regularly and authoritatively directed to do their homework, and they do so even in the midst of parties (e.g., baby showers with dozens of relatives and friends in the home). At times I have assisted with this homework, often because the children have had difficulty with it and the parents have perceived my visit as an educational opportunity not to be missed. Frequently the problem has been that the child in question did not understand the tasks at hand. Once this involved a worksheet that required her (a) to add suffixes to words to change their part of speech, and (b) to read and comprehend relations of cause and effect. My assistance involved figuring out what was required and explaining and demonstrating the tasks. Once the child (then in fourth grade) understood the tasks, she quickly and readily accomplished them. Had she not completed these tasks, of course, her teacher might have concluded either that she was irresponsible or lazy, or that she was not intelligent enough to do so. In fact, however, the problem was that she did not understand what she was supposed to do. It is possible that the teacher simply passed out the worksheets without explaining how to complete them; it is also possible that she provided an explanation that the child (and probably other children as well) did not understand.

A similar problem occurred some months later in another family's home. This time the homework in question was math. It became clear to me while helping two children (one in third and one in fifth grade at the time) that their problems stemmed from not understanding the underlying concepts involved. One of the girls, the fifth grader, evidently had been learning multiplication tables by memorizing columns of figures; she had not understood that by adding the number in question to each answer one could anticipate the next answer. For example, 8 x 5 = 40, and 8 x 6 = 48. Adding another 8 to the 40 would result in 48, the same answer as 8 x 6. Conceptually, multiplication tables "work" by adding the number in question to each answer progressively. Again, once I explained this, she caught on quickly. And again, I wondered whether her teacher had explained it this way, or simply had told them to memorize the tables. It is, of course, possible that the teacher did explain it conceptually, but in language (whether Spanish or English) that the child did not understand. In this example, as in the previous one, the children had difficulty doing their homework because they did not understand until the conceptual basis for the work was explained to them at home. Parents, of course, expect such conceptual bases to be provided by teachers at school; to the extent that these cases represent a more regularly occurring phenomenon, there is a serious gap between parental expectations and the realities of school. This point is taken up more directly in the conclusion of this chapter.

So far I have described the formal, public aspects of literacy practices within the educational domain. Now I turn to more personal, informal practices which various adult members carry on in their homes. These practices fall into two primary categories: those activities in which adults involve children directly and those activities which adults carry on themselves, that, it could be argued, impart implicit messages to children about the importance of literacy and learning.

Two scenes in particular illustrate adult-child literacy activities; in both cases, children were practicing writing. In the first case, a 4-year-old boy was sitting on his mother's lap learning to write the letters of the alphabet. His hand held the pencil with which he was writing, and his mother's hand held his hand, guiding it in making the letters. Line by line (on white, lined paper) they wrote each letter of the alphabet many times. In the second scene, a father was supervising two young boys (then in kindergarten) who sat on the floor at his feet, using the coffee table to practice writing their names. These two boys are cousins and share the same first names; the father joked to me that they were practicing each other's name. This father, interestingly, learned writing *lírico*, outside of school; his achievement in this regard is described earlier in this chapter. What is striking to me in both of these scenes is the importance attached to writing, such that it requires parental action and direction outside of the children's formal schooling.

Another scene underscores the importance with which writing is regarded. Early in my fieldwork, I asked, during a living room conversation with the father in the example above, whether he ever used writing or reading at work. He responded enthusiastically and at length, vehemently explaining that, yes, he did indeed. He summoned his eldest daughter to retrieve some papers from a bedroom and displayed them to me. They appeared to be directions for tasks at the railroad construction company where he works. Some of the papers were incomprehensible to me, as I did not recognize many of the listed items, although they were written by his boss in English. Each item was simply a few words; none were a complete sentence (nor did they need to be). He interpreted them, however, with on-the-job knowledge; he understood that the listing of a certain item (e.g., a railroad tie in a particular place—so many feet north of a certain location) meant it needed to be repaired or replaced. The father illustrated how he "decoded" the writing on the list (he sounded out a word letter by letter) to understand the referent, then added his on-the-job knowledge to carry out the work. He pointed out that I did not understand the writing on the papers because I did not work there. When we had finished looking over the papers, the father rather ceremoniously returned them to his daughter with instructions to store them again. This way of treating pieces of writing, although not involving parents and children together directly with print, nonetheless sends yet another implicit message to children about the high regard for writing held by their parents.

In addition to the informal literacy activities which children observe (and implicitly learn from), a number of the adults in these families from time to time pursue personal literacy activities which advance their own learning. On various occasions I have been shown books that individuals study on their own for a variety of purposes: to learn English, to pass the GED (high school equivalency) exam, or to pass the citizenship test. These books are primarily in English and are of a variety of types: one household of adult men (whose wives, mothers, and children remained in their village in Mexico, while they worked in Chicago and sent money home) used a rather old U.S. science textbook (entirely in English) for learning English; a *compadre* of the center family who lives in Waukegan, IL (about 1 hour north of Chicago) is admired by many in the network for having taught himself English with an English textbook after he migrated to the United States; a single young woman of 24 uses an excellent, recent edition textbook for Spanish speakers learning English; and a young married woman who attended some elementary school in Chicago (although she finished her schooling at the *secundaria* level in Mexico) has used two books for personal study, one (in Spanish and English) for the U.S. citizenship test (so that her Mexican husband could become a documented resident), and another (in English) for the GED exam.

Thus, in formal and informal ways, both the adults and the children in these families participate in literacy activities that further their educations. The children pursue these activities on a daily basis during the school year and usually in the summer as well, as part of summer school or other institutional programs. The adults direct the children in homework and other literacy practice, and they pursue their own learning as time permits, either after work or during periods when they are not working (e.g., one young mother studied a citizenship book when she was home from work for a few months following the birth of her daughter). As in the other domains, literacy activities in the educational domain are interwoven throughout their daily lives.

CONCLUSION

The primary goal of this chapter has been to provide a description of literacy within one social network of Mexican immigrant families in Chicago. This description focused, first, on how literacy was learned by network members, either through formal schooling or "lyrically" outside of school. To learn literacy or other skills *lírico* is to learn informally, without books, that is, purely with spoken language. This process is at heart a social one because the skill that is taught and learned is passed on from one person to another. The fact that these men learned literacy primarily after migrating to Chicago because of "personal obligations" to write to their families and friends back in Mexico indicates that the motivation to learn is a product of contextual factors, not an intrinsic quality which an individual either does or does not possess.

The second aspect of the literacy description provided in this chapter involves the actual literacy practices of network members within four broad domains. Domains treated in this chapter include those of religion, commerce, the state/law, and education. The first three domains are entirely public; the last domain has both public and private aspects. A fifth domain, that of the family/home which is entirely private, is described elsewhere (Farr, 1994). A primary finding from this description is that literacy practices are abundantly part of the stream of daily life within these families. This literacy is "functional" in the sense that with it, network members cope quite adequately with a variety of institutional demands and pursue personal, economic, and social goals to meet their own needs. Whereas some of these individuals do not regularly spend extensive amounts of time reading or writing entire "extended" texts such as novels or other books, as has been described for some mainstream (Heath, 1983; Taylor, 1983) as well as nonmainstream (Taylor & Dorsey-Gaines, 1988) groups, many of the women in the oldest generation (between 35 and 55 years old) regularly read religious materials, including magazines, books, and the Bible. All network members are, however, literate, in that reading and writing, in both Spanish and English, are a regular part of their daily lives. As a network especially, these families are literate; that is, literacy, like other kinds of knowledge, is shared as a resource among the members of the network.

This description is a synchronic one: It focuses on the current lives and the current literacy skills/behaviors of a particular group of people. Such descriptions are important as they provide fuller understandings of what literacy "is" in modern societies and especially because they contribute the perspectives of nonmainstream groups to a broader definition of literacy, as called for by Heath (1982).

What implications do these findings have for educational policy? Implications can be discussed for two kinds of educational institutions—those for children (from elementary to high school) and those for adults. The two examples provided in this chapter of children having difficulty with homework raise some serious questions. The children in these families are normal and well socialized, with an eagerness to learn. Their parents are strictly supportive of formal education and very much "on-the-job" as nurturing, supervising parents. Yet, the children are not learning at their full capacities. It is clear (Goodlad, 1984) that much current instruction, especially in inner-city schools, focuses on rote learning rather than on "higher level" thinking processes. Was the problem demonstrated in these examples caused by higher level thinking not being taught? Both the worksheets and the multiplication assignment required conceptual thinking for completion, but neither of the children understood how to proceed. One explanation is that their teachers did not teach them the underlying concepts they needed to learn in these cases. Another explanation is that the teachers did so, but the communication was not successful, (e.g., these children were able to speak English, but they acquired most of their command of English during the late elementary school years, and fourth grade in particular is difficult because it is the transition year from bilingual education, which extends in this case from kindergarten through third grade, to English-only instruction).

Although I did not observe the two classrooms in question and so cannot judge their "quality" or effectiveness, some tentative conclusions nevertheless can be drawn from these examples. First, when children are being taught "basic skills" such as language structure (the suffix example), reading (the cause and effect example), and mathematics (the multiplication tables example), they should be taught the relevant underlying concepts, both to learn the current material and to progress to more difficult material. Consequently, more instruction, in the language children know best, should focus on concepts, not just on memorization and rote learning. Goldenberg's (1991) appeal to utilize insights from two oppositional traditions of educational research—skills-based and holistic—might be fruitfully applied here.

Second, facilitating the learning of children such as these warrants improvement *within schools* rather than within homes. Recent calls for "parent involvement" often appear to be attempts to locate the source of learning problems within families rather than within classrooms and schools. No doubt there are some instances in which such an assumption may be accurate, in both inner-city and middle-class neighborhoods. Too often, however, all inner-city families are presumed to be dysfunctional, or to operate with deficits of some sort, and parents increasingly are expected to "become involved," that is, to institute literacy practices in their homes that resemble those of the school (and those of white middle-class families). For the children whose families I have come to know, this is an unfair burden. If the schools were able to achieve at the level of these parents' expectations and trust in formal education, many frequently cited problems in the education of inner-city populations would be well on their way to solution.

The findings reported here have implications for educational institutions serving adults as well. Many of the adults in this social network, especially the younger adults (those in their 20s) have indicated an interest in continuing their educations. They are constrained in doing so by the demands of blue collar work and of their extended households. Such realities often make it difficult for them to attend classes at night on a regular basis; the women, moreover, are reluctant to venture too far from their homes because of dangerous neighborhoods, especially after dark. Nevertheless, many would like to be able to obtain high school equivalency degrees, primarily in the hope that they could then obtain better paying and less physically tiring employment.

Programs that could serve such a population would have several important features, among them an emphasis on (a) developing Spanish-English bilingualism, and (b) practice in reading and writing texts that are relevant to their lives (Farr, 1994; Moll & Diaz, 1987). It is important to note that developing fluency in English would best not be carried out at the expense of Spanish. The bilingual individuals in this network have been able to take advantage of more opportunities than those monolingual in Spanish, and it is their bilingualism, not just their knowledge of English, that has been important in these opportunities.

This finding is corroborated by other research on Mexican-origin populations (Macías, 1985) which indicates that bilingualism has a more positive effect on income than does either Spanish or English monolingualism. Yet other research (discussed in Duran, 1987) clearly suggests, depending on age and other factors, the pedagogical value of beginning literacy practice in the native language of the learner and later moving to literacy in the second language.

Finally, programs that could be truly useful to populations such as the families discussed in this chapter would seriously take into account their culturally defined attitudes and perceptions, as well as the everyday realities of their lives. That is, programs should be both culturally and socially sensitive. For example, these adults would not respond positively to a program that placed a high value on promoting individuals at the expense of relationships within the family and the social network. One man described in this chapter refused to read aloud in class at a local community organization. He claimed he could not read, although I observed him reading both silently and aloud later in his home. Also, when publicly asked in the class what he did for a living, he represented himself as a dishwasher when in fact he was the foreman of a railroad construction crew.

A socially sensitive program would take into account the difficulties adults such as those discussed here would have in attending classes at night, particularly if they are located far from home. Whereas some men are reluctant to attend classes in public schools because they view them as being for children, some women are reluctant to attend classes in community organizations, especially if they are not accompanied by husbands or other family members. Many of these women, however, do go on a regular basis to the local Catholic church at night during the week. A literacy program located within the church, especially if it provided not only instruction for adults, but also assistance for children doing their homework, would appeal greatly to the adults in these families.

In sum, then, the findings from this research can be used to develop or improve literacy programs for similar populations. These programs should be (a) aware of and respectful toward the literacy skills and literate behaviors already used by such adults in the various domains of their lives, (b) supportive of Spanish-English bilingualism and biliteracy, (c) sensitive to the cultural values characteristic of Mexican immigrant populations, (d) sensitive to the social realities of working class jobs and specific neighborhoods, and (e) based on the reading and writing of texts that appeal to learners and are directly relevant to their lives.

REFERENCES

Acosta-Belén, E., & Sjostrom, B.R. (Eds.) (1988). *The Hispanic experience in the United States.* New York: Praeger.

Al filo/At the Cutting Edge. (1986). Chicago: Latino Institute.

Barragán López, E. (1990). *Más allá de los caminos.* Zamora, Michoacán, Mexico: El Colegio de Michoacán.

Chicago Fact Book Consortium (Eds.) (1984). *Local community fact book: Chicago metropolitan area, based on the 1970 and 1980 censuses.* Chicago: Chicago Review Press.

Coulmas, F. (1989). *The writing systems of the world.* Cambridge, MA: Basil Blackwell.

Damien de Surgy, J., Martínez, R.K., & Linck, R.M. (1988). *El auge del aguacate: ¿Hacia que tipo de desarrollo?* In H. Cochet, E. Léonard, & J. Damien de Surgy (Eds.), *Paisajes agrarios de Michoacán.* Zamora: El Colegio de Michoácan.

Delgado-Gaitan, C. (1987). Mexican adult literacy: New directions for immigrants. In S. Goldman & H. Trueba (Eds.), *Becoming literate in English as a second language.* Norwood, NJ: Ablex.

Duran, R. (1987). Factors affecting development of second language literacy. In S. Goldman & H. Trueba (Eds.), *Becoming literate in English as a second language.* Norwood, NJ: Ablex.

Elías-Olivares, L. (1990, August). *Hablar con sinceridad: Variedad discursiva del Español Mexico-Americano.* Paper presented at the XI International Conference of ALFAL, State University of Campinas, Campinas, Brazil.

Elías-Olivares, L., & Farr, M. (1991). *Sociolinguistic analysis of Mexican-American patterns of non-Response to census questionnaires.* Final report to the U.S. Census Bureau. Chicago: University of Illinois at Chicago.

Farr, M. (1989, November). *Learning literacy lírico: Informal education among mexicanos in Chicago.* Paper presented at the annual meeting of the American Anthropological Association, Washington, DC.

Farr, M. (1990). *Oral folk texts and literacy practices among Mexican immigrants in Chicago.* Proposal to the Spencer Foundation. Chicago: University of Illinois at Chicago.

Farr, M. (1993). Essayist literacy and other verbal performances. *Written Communication, 10*(1), 4-38.

Farr, M. (1994). Biliteracy in the home: Practices among mexicano families in Chicago. In D. Spener (Ed.), *Biliteracy in the United States.* McHenry, IL and Washington, DC: Delta Systems and the Center for Applied Linguistics.

Finnegan, R. (1988). *Literacy and orality.* New York: Basil Blackwell.

Gee, J. (1989). *What is literacy?* (Tech. Rep. No. 2). Cambridge, MA: Education Development Center, The Literacies Institute.

Gibson, C. (1966). *Spain in America.* New York: Harper and Row.

Goldenberg, C. (1991, July). *Two views of learning and their implications for literacy education.* Paper presented at the Language Minority Literacy Roundtable, University of California, Santa Barbara.

Goodlad, J. (1984). *A place called school: Prospects for the future.* New York: McGraw-Hill.

Goody, J. (1977). *The domestication of the savage mind.* Cambridge: Cambridge University Press.

Goody, J. (1986). *The logic of writing and the organization of society.* Cambridge: Cambridge University Press.

Goody, J. (1987). *The interface of the written and the oral.* Cambridge: Cambridge University Press.

Goody, J., & Watt, I. (1963). The consequences of literacy. *Comparative Studies in Society and History, 5*(3), 304-345.

Graff, H.J. (Ed.). (1981). *Literacy and social development in the west.* Cambridge: Cambridge University Press.

Guerra, J. (1992). *The literacy practices of an extended Mexican immigrant family.* Unpublished doctoral dissertation, University of Illinois at Chicago.

Hannerz, U. (1980). *Exploring the city: Inquiries toward an urban anthropology.* New York: Columbia University Press.

Heath, S.B. (1982). Protean shapes in literacy events: Ever-shifting oral and literate traditions. In D. Tannen (Ed.), *Spoken and written language: Exploring orality and literacy.* Norwood, NJ: Ablex.

Heath, S.B. (1983). *Ways with words: Language, life and work in communities and classrooms.* Cambridge: Cambridge University Press.

Heath, S.B. (1987). Foreword. In H. Graff, *Labyrinths of literacy.* London: Falmer Press.

Horowitz, D. (1985). Conflict and accommodation: Mexican-Americans in the cosmopolis. In W. Connor (Ed.), *Mexican-Americans in comparative perspective.* Washington, DC: Urban Institute Press.

Horowitz, R. (1983). *Honor and the American dream: Culture and identity in a Chicano community.* New Brunswick, NJ: Rutgers University Press.

Hymes, D. (1974a). *Foundations in sociolinguistics.* Philadelphia: University of Pennsylvania Press.

Hymes, D. (1974b). Ways of speaking. In R. Bauman & J. Sherzer (Eds.), *Explorations in the ethnography of speaking.* Cambridge: Cambridge University Press.

Hymes, D. (1980). *Language in education: Ethnolinguistic essays.* Language and Ethnography Series. Washington, DC: Center for Applied Linguistics.

Juárez-Robles, J. (1990). Hispanics say Edgar unfair to undocumented aliens. *The Chicago Reporter, 19,* 9.

Kerr, L.A.N. (1977). Mexican Chicago: Chicano assimilation aborted, 1939-1954. In M.A. Holli & P. d'A. Jones (Eds.), *Ethnic Chicago.* Grand Rapids, MI: Eerdmans Publishing Co.

Kozol, J. (1985). *Illiterate America.* New York: Doubleday.

Kyle, C.L., Lane, J., Sween, J.A., & Triana, A. (1986). *We have a choice: Students at risk of leaving Chicago Public Schools.* A report to the Chicago Board of Education and Illinois Attorney General. Chicago: DePaul University Chicago Area Studies Center, Center for Research on Hispanics.

Lomnitz, L.A. (1977). *Networks and marginality.* Trans. by Cinna Lomnitz. New York: Academic Press.

Macías, R. (1985). National language profile of the Mexican-origin population in the United States. In W. Connor (Ed.), *Mexican-Americans in comparative perspective.* Washington, DC: Urban Institute Press.

Miller, G. (1988). The challenge of universal literacy. *Science, 241,* pp. 1293-1299.

Milroy, L. (1980). *Language and social networks.* New York: Basil Blackwell.

Mintz, S.W., & Wolf, E.R. (1950). An analysis of ritual co-parenthood. *Southwestern Journal of Anthropology, 6,* 341-365.

Moll, L. & Diaz, S. (1987). Teaching writing as communication: The use of ethnographic findings in classroom practice. In D. Bloome (Ed.), *Literacy, language, and schooling.* Norwood, NJ: Ablex.

National Assessment of Educational Progress. (1986). *Literacy: Profiles of America's young adults.* Princeton, NJ: Educational Testing Service.

National Assessment of Educational Progress. (1989a). *The Reading Report Card, 1971-1988.* Princeton, NJ: Educational Testing Service.

National Assessment of Educational Progress. (1989b). *The Writing Report Card, 1984-1988.* Princeton, NJ: Educational Testing Service.

Ogbu, J. (1987). Opportunity structure, cultural boundaries, and literacy. In J. Langer (Ed.), *Language, literacy and culture.* Norwood, NJ: Ablex.

Olson, D. (1977). From utterance to text: The bias of language in speech and writing. *Harvard Educational Review, 41,* 257-281.

Ong, W.J. (1982). *Orality and literacy.* New York: Methuen.

Philips, S.U. (1983). *The invisible culture: Communication in classroom and community on the warm springs Indian Reservation.* New York: Longman.

La Raza. (1991, February). El doble de hispanos en Chicago. (p. 4).

Sampson, G. (1985). *Writing systems: A linguistic introduction.* Stanford, CA: Stanford University Press.

Saville-Troike, M. (1989). *The ethnography of communication: An introduction.* New York: Basil Blackwell.

Scollon, R., & Scollon, S. B. (1981). *Narrative, literacy and face in interethnic communication.* Norwood, NJ: Ablex.

Scribner, S., & Cole, M. (1981). *The psychology of literacy.* Cambridge, MA: Harvard University Press.

Spufford, M. (1981). First steps in literacy: The reading and writing experiences of the humblest spiritual autobiographers. In H. Graff (Ed.), *Literacy and social development in the West: A reader.* New York: Cambridge University Press.

Street, B. (1984). *Literacy in theory and practice.* Cambridge: Cambridge University Press.

Szwed, J. (1981). The ethnography of literacy. In M. Farr Whiteman (Ed.), *Variation in writing: Functional and linguistic-cultural differences.* Hillsdale, NJ: Erlbaum.

Taylor, D. (1983). *Family literacy: Young children learning to read and write.* Portsmouth, NH: Heinemann.

Taylor, D., & Dorsey-Gaines, C. (1988). *Growing up literate: Learning from inner-city families.* Portsmouth, NH: Heinemann.

Vasquez, O. (1989). *Connecting oral language strategies to literacy: Ethnographic study among four Mexican immigrant families.* Unpublished doctoral dissertation, Stanford University, Stanford, CA.

Velez-Ibañez, C., & Greenberg, J. (1989, November). *Formation and transformation of funds of knowledge among U.S. Mexican households in the context of the borderlands.* Paper presented at the American Anthropological Association Annual Meeting, Washington, DC.

Warren, R., & Passel, J. (1987). A count of the uncountable: Estimates of undocumented aliens counted in the 1980 U.S. Census. *Demography, 24,* 3.

2

From Mountaintops to City Streets: Literacy in Philadelphia's Hmong Community*

Gail Weinstein-Shr
San Francisco State University

INTRODUCTION

"A designer in Paris named Louis Reardon first presented the bikini at a fashion show in 1946." This is the first of 40 sentences that I saw when I first peered over my friend's shoulder as he sat to do his homework. His task was to change the active to the passive for each sentence. Chou's wife Sai kept the children away as he sat by the light of the window, plowing through the exercise. His early years of schooling served him well; he finished the task within two hours. Next he looked at the pile of bills and letters, but chose instead to work on translating his pastor's sermon into Hmong for the new arrivals.

Chou Chang is one of 70,000 Hmong refugees from the mountains of Laos who have been resettled in the United States (Office of Refuge Resettlement, 1983). Before Chou became a soldier at the age of 12, he had four years of study with missionaries, during which time

---

*Some of the material in this chapter appears in "Literacy and Social Process: A Community in Transition," B. Street (Ed.), *Cross-Cultural Approaches to Literacy*, 1993, Cambridge University Press, NY. Reprinted by permission.

he was able to acquire rudimentary literacy in Lao. In contrast, many of his compatriots had little experience with print before their exodus. As subsistence farmers in Laos, the Hmong had little use for literacy or formal schooling. Thus, in his urban neighborhood, Chou finds himself nearly alone with his English literacy skills, a fact that has important consequences for his life in the community.

Why should we bother to examine the ways in which Chou Chang uses literacy? What do the consequences of literacy for this young man reveal about the nature of literacy and social process?

For the last couple of decades, there has been great interest in the ways in which the introduction of literacy transforms individuals (e.g., Olson, 1977; Ong, 1982) and societies (e.g., Goody & Watt, 1968). More recently, scholars have documented a plurality of literacies (e.g., Gee, 1990; Street, 1984) or "literacy practices" (Street 1991) that exist in any literate setting. This permits a shift in emphasis from what literacy does to societies and individuals to what individuals and groups do with literacy to make it their own and make it serve their own purposes. It also makes it possible to see literacy practices as a communicative means through which relationships are negotiated.

With a shift in focus, new questions become appropriate. How does life in a literate environment affect or change social relationships? How do social relationships influence the way that literacy is acquired and used? The Hmong from Laos who have come to the United States provide an exciting opportunity to look into the relationship of literacy and social process. Because literacy is a relatively recent innovation for the Hmong, it is possible to observe rapid changes as literacy is introduced into their repertoire of communicative resources. The experience of the Hmong as they adapt to their new environment provides an opportunity for gaining insight into the interaction of communicative technology and social organization.

In this chapter, I begin by providing a general picture of the Hmong community, the circumstances that led them to Philadelphia, and the kinship and literacy resources that they brought with them. In the second section, I provide a "portrait" of three individuals, examining how both kinship and literacy operate in their lives. In the third section, I return to the community, placing these individuals in the context of a larger picture that, I suggest, becomes more interesting in light of the individual stories.

By examining the functions and uses of literacy for specific individuals in specific communities, it is possible to learn a great deal about the nature of those communities. Furthermore, by examining real communities, I argue that we can in turn learn about the range of literacy practices, their scope and their possibilities.

PORTRAIT OF A COMMUNITY: FIRST GLANCE

The Hmong of Philadelphia

The Hmong are a hill tribe who trace their origins to China. Many of Philadelphia's adults can trace a direct link through grandparents or great grandparents to the China Mainland. For the last 150 years, the Hmong have been on the move, beginning with migration from China into other Southeast Asian countries (Geddes, 1976). Accounts of the movements vary: Some say the migrations were caused by pressure from hostile neighbors; others say this was part of a semi-nomadic lifestyle associated with the search for farmland and livestock.

Known for their strongly developed clan organization and fierce resistance to rule (Dunnigan, 1982), many Hmong in Laos were hired by the U.S. government in the 1970s to fight under the leadership of General Vang Pao against the Pathet Lao Communist movement. When the Pathet Lao gained power in 1975, those Hmong who had been hired by the United States had to flee the country. The lucky ones made it across the Mekong River into Thailand, where they found refuge in camps before their resettlement in the United States.

Hmong refugees began arriving in Philadelphia in 1979. Over the next six years I had the opportunity to observe at close range the strategies and struggles of my new neighbors as they brought their enormous resources to bear in their transition from the mountaintops of Laos to the streets of Philadelphia. During this time I surveyed each household in the city to discover the kinds of social resources available for adapting to life in the United States. In addition, I developed several in-depth "portraits" of Hmong adults in the city to document language and literacy use in daily life, as well as patterns of interaction with kin and non-kin, both within and across ethnic boundaries (for more on the study, see Weinstein-Shr, 1986).

My first discovery was that contrary to the images of helpless peasants painted in the media[1], the Hmong in Philadelphia had sophisticated strategies for managing life in the United States. Ironically, the same clan organization that served them as fighters in Southeast Asia also operated to assist with adjustment to life in a western urban setting. The second discovery was that to describe the Hmong community in America as "illiterate" is to oversimplify a community that is complex, with complex resources for solving literacy-related problems. I now turn to these two resources—kinship and literacy.

---

[1]Stereotypes of helplessness and primitiveness are perpetuated by headlines in the *Philadelphia Inquirer* such as "At the Mercy of America" (10-21-84); "Shock and Confusion when Worlds Collide" (3-20-85); and "The Primitive Paradise of the Hmong" (6-9-85).

Traditional Resources: Kinship

In the Hmong community, kinship relations are the primary features of a person's identity in the social order. The patrilineal clan system dominates Hmong social organization, as well as serves as a primary integrating factor in Hmong culture as a whole (Barney, 1981). Altogether there are 20 clans known as *xeem*, each of which traces its origin to a common mythological ancestor. Hmong kinship has been characterized as "segmentary" because of the ways that agnatic descent groups are divided and subdivided. First, the *caj ces* (lineage), literally "root branch," is a subdivision of the clan. If two members of a clan who speak the same dialect meet for the first time, they will compare genealogies to see if they *yog ib caj ces* "are of one lineage," that is, if they can trace their connection back to any common ancestor. Members of one lineage are likely to conduct rituals in the same fashion and can depend on one another for more extensive help than clanmates from a distantly related lineage (Dunnigan, 1982).

Second, *pawg neeg* "sublineage" is the primary unit whose members traditionally have lived in one village or a cluster of proximate villages. Ties to this lineage group are the most durable and dependable relationships that a Hmong individual has over his or her life (Reder, 1985).

Finally, the smallest unit of social organization is the *tsev neeg* "family" or "house people." This has been referred to in the literature as "household," a misnomer which can cause confusion because *tsev neeg* is a unit including all persons under the authority of a "householder," whether they live in the same house or not. This can include a man and his wife (or in Laos his wives), his unmarried daughters, and his sons and their wives and children. So one *tsev neeg* often consists of three generations. If a married son builds a new house near his father's house, it is not considered a new *tsev neeg*. It is only at the point when the son moves to another village that his home will be considered a separate household.

When a Hmong child is born, he or she automatically becomes a member of his or her father's clan. The child receives the father's clan name in addition to a given name, signaling membership. Strangers who share a clan name are considered to be siblings and signal this relationship with the form of address *kuv ti/kuv tyo*—literally meaning elder/younger sibling. A man can depend on his clan members for hospitality when traveling, or a woman may have to depend on clan ties to defend her rights in a marital dispute if she has no close relatives nearby. Clans are exogamous: Members must marry outside of the clan.

When a young woman marries, she usually moves to the household of her husband (or her husband's father). Because of the exogamy taboo, she may marry into any clan except that bearing her own clan name. Marriage is not an individual matter, but rather is the formation of an alliance between clans. Traditionally, marriages were arranged by household heads for their children with bride price an integral part of marriage negotiations. *Neej tsa* (in-laws) then become members of a network of marriage alliances (affinal ties) that strengthen their kin resources as networks are broadened.

Hmong people in Laos do not have a "first" or "last" name. As mentioned above, they automatically receive the clan name of their father, signaling their membership in that clan, as well as a name given to them by their family. The order of these names is not significant. For legal purposes in the United States, most Hmong have adopted their clan name as their "last name" and use their given name as their first name (except for leaders, who seem to distinguish themselves by using their clan names first).

It is impossible to talk about Hmong families in Philadelphia without referring to the clans to which they belong. Among the 20 Hmong clans that exist, 11 are represented in Philadelphia by male household heads. These include Chang, Hang, Kue, Lee, Lo(r), Moua, Thao, Vang, Vue, Xiong, and Yang. Attempts to take a census of Hmong families in Philadelphia confronts the researcher with the contradictions in Hmong and American ways of reckoning family units. As described above, the term "household" for the Hmong, need not refer only to those who live in one house, but rather includes any persons under the authority of the householder.

The U.S. social welfare system, in contrast, is organized around the notion of nuclear families. A list compiled by the Hmong Association, in its role as liaison to the U.S. bureaucracy, lists "families" that are headed by any married man or by women who are divorced or widowed. This is to facilitate the distribution of welfare and social security benefits. In 1985, the list included, for example, nine Kue families. Any Kue who was asked for the number of Kue families in Philadelphia, however, would have replied three. In fact, these nine "families" were under the authority of three household heads.

The Hmong list officially divides the Hmong in Philadelphia as living in two nonadjacent neighborhoods—Weston and Norton (not the real neighborhood names). In a survey of September 1985, I found that Philadelphia's Hmong community consisted of 58 nuclear families comprising approximately 28 households. Families tend to live in clusters, sometimes with entire households occupying the same building. Especially noteworthy is the division of clans by geographical area. Families belonging to the largest clans in Philadelphia—Lo and Kue—all lived in Norton, as did members of the Hang clan. The Xiongs and five of six Moua families all lived in Weston. The few exceptions to the rule of virilocal residence include widows or divorcees who seem to be less predictable in their residence choices, as well as two men who are the sole representatives of their own clans in Philadelphia. Without any kin of their own, they live near the kin of their wives. Clearly, geographical cohesiveness is the general rule for clans in Philadelphia. (The division between Norton and Weston, reflected by residence patterns, is characterized by other features which are discussed later.)

Life in Laos was characterized by the comfort of knowing that the mountains were webbed with a haven of kin, known and unknown. If a man made a long journey, he could be sure that in any village, as long as he found a clansman, he would be housed and fed along the way. Similarly, this web of kin connections still operates for some Hmong in urban America. Hang Chou, the president of the Hmong Association, describes his experience attending a conference in San Francisco. Upon arriving at the airport, he simply opened the phone book to the "H"s, calling the first Hang listed. He was then picked up, housed, and fed for the duration of the conference by a family he had never before met.

Resettlement efforts that recognize the continuing operation of traditional kinship structures such as the lineage, sublineage and household have a better chance of success. Doctors, for example, who need permission for certain medical procedures are more likely to get cooperation (i.e., the necessary signatures) if members of the appropriate subgroup are included as information is given and decisions are made (Dunnigan 1982). Health clinics in Minneapolis, among other cities, have found substantial improvements in patient cooperation when treatment took into account the operation of kinship networks and the ways in which these affect decision making and action (Dunnigan, 1982).

Whereas categories of kinship may have remained the same, ways of reckoning the members of those categories have gained enormous flexibility in the face of the drastic changes entailed by resettlement. Although *pawg neeg* translates technically as "sublineage," for some it has come to mean "helping group" in a much broader sense. War orphan Ying Lo now counts among members of his *pawg neeg* members of the Hmong student club at the local community college (who study together and plan special events), as well as other orphan bachelors who collectively lend money in turn to one another for the bride price as they get married. Even the *tsev neeg* or "family" (literally house people) has become fluid enough to begin healing gaps left by the terrible losses of war. Although Ying reports living with his "blood brother," neither of the men can identify the point of connection on their respective genealogical charts.

These flexible ways of reckoning kin have made it possible for some Hmong people in Philadelphia to continue relying on traditional kinds of relationships for support while adapting to the realities of the social decimation caused by death and diaspora in the wake of a decade of war and flight.

New Resources: Literacy and Schooling

Although the Hmong have a history of well-developed clan organization, they have a very short history of experience with formal schooling. Because of their isolation in Laos, virtually no Hmong in the mountains had any formal education before World War II. The first village school in the high mountain region was set up in 1939 (Barney, 1967). Even after the number of village schools grew, children had to go to larger towns if they were to study beyond the third year. Although schools became more accessible after World War II, there was a high dropout rate as Hmong children became older, had to travel further to secondary schools in larger towns, and took on more responsibility for family farm activities. In addition, classes were taught exclusively in Lao, creating yet a greater obstacle to success for Hmong children (Yang, 1975) for whom this was a foreign language.

The Hmong in Philadelphia have brought with them educational resources consistent with this history. I found that of the 167 adults in Philadelphia, only 16% reported having more than 3 years of schooling in Laos. It is interesting to note the distribution of education by clan. Among the nine clans in Philadelphia with members who have more than 6 years of education in Laos, all of the larger Philadelphia clans are represented (2 Hangs, 3 Kues, 2 Los, 2 Mouas, 1 Vang, 1 Xiong, and 1 Yang).

Table 2.1 shows the number and percentage of Hmong in Philadelphia over the age of 14 who received some formal schooling in Laos.

Table 2.1. Number of Hmong by Age Group Who Received Some Education in Laos*

Age	Male		Female		Overall	
	#/Total	%	#/T	%	#/T	%
14-19	4/28	14	0/16	0	4/44	9
20-24	15/22	68	1/9	11	16/31	52
25-29	3/8	37	1/9	11	4/17	24
30-34	7/12	58	1/8	13	8/20	40
35-39	5/7	71	2/8	25	7/15	47
40-44	2/4	50	1/5	20	3/9	33
45-49	0/6	0	0/2	0	0/8	0
50 +	2/14	14	0/9	0	2/23	9
Total	38/101	37	6/66	9	44/167	26

*Note: These figures have been compiled from Community Profile interviews.

This table suggests that schooling was not the domain of any particular clan. Rather, it was a rare commodity for which lineage groups had to pool their resources to invest in the eldest or brightest boy. The low percentage of women is consistent with this explanation.

Traditional Hmong society might be characterized as "nonliterate." Smalley (1976) describes such a culture as one in which:

> a child can be born and grow up, an adult can live and die, without a strong need to read and write. He can live a normal existence within his own community without a feeling that he is in any way culturally deprived by lack of ability to communicate through marks made on paper. Life as he knows it does not include reading and writing as a major component. (p. 2)

Indeed, until the early 1950s, the Hmong of Laos did not have a system for writing their spoken language. Smalley is one of the missionaries who developed the Romanized Popular Alphabet (RPA) at that time, for purposes of religious teaching. The RPA was easy to learn; Hmong in Philadelphia report learning it informally from friends or relatives or by studying a primer on their own. They report mastering the system in time periods ranging from one afternoon to four weeks.

Within 10 years, use of the RPA began to spread for purposes such as newsletters, the recording of history, and oral literature (Reder, 1985). In the late 1960s, missionaries created another Hmong writing system based on the Lao script to accommodate the Lao government and with their concern for unity in Laos and control over ethnic minorities. For those who became literate, the choice of script was a political one, signaling alliance (or lack thereof) with the government.

In Philadelphia, the number of Hmong who report being literate in Lao corresponds exactly with those who report having received formal schooling in Laos. Thus, Lao literacy and formal schooling are inextricably bound. In contrast, many who never had experience with formal schooling have at least some literacy skills in Hmong. Most learned to use RPA informally after their flight from Laos, either in Thai refugee camps, or in the United States. Table 2.2 reports the numbers and percentages of Hmong who report some literacy in their native language.

Self-reports of household heads for themselves and their families indicate that 60% of those between 20 and 45 years old are now able to read and write Hmong, despite the very low rate of formal schooling in Laos. Because literacy has become a resource that is spread by non-institutional means that does not require setting aside lineage resources, women have caught up to men in their acquisition. The mode of transmission has changed the possibilities for acquisition and for use.

How do old and new resources affect one another? Does coming

Table 2.2. Self-Reported Hmong Literacy by Age Group

Age	Male		Female		Overall	
	#/Total	%	#/T	%	#/T	%
14-19	8/28	28	5/16	31	13/44	29
20-24	15/22	68	5/ 9	55	20/31	64
25-29	5/ 8	62	4/ 9	49	9/17	52
30-34	8/12	67	3/ 8	38	11/20	55
35-39	3/ 7	43	6/ 8	75	9/15	60
40-44	2/ 4	50	4/ 5	80	6/9	67
45-49	0/ 6	0	0/ 2	0	0/8	0
50+	2/14	14	0/ 9	0	2/23	9
Total	43/101	43	27/66	41	70/167	42

to a literate environment change who depends on whom? Do kinship relationships have any affect on who learns to read and write and for what purposes? Both educators and social scientists can profit from understanding the interaction of these two social resources. In the next section, this interaction is examined in the lives of three individuals and in their communities.

THREE LIVES IN FOCUS

In order to see at close range the ways that kinship connections and literacy figure in real people's everyday lives, it is useful to focus on individuals and their families. What kinds of problems do people have to solve? How do they go about solving them? More specifically, how do people use literacy and solve literacy-related problems? How are kinship ties used in the context of radically changed circumstances? What other kinds of social resources are being developed in the process of adapting to a new setting? This section examines the lives of three individuals who have selected very different strategies for adapting to life in the United States, including the functions and uses of literacy in each person's life and in terms of kinship relationships.

The first portrait describes Chou Chang,[2] was a young man of 25 when I met him. During the time of the research he successfully completed his high school equivilancy diploma. I watched with awe as Chou and his wife grappled with an impossible bureaucracy that had

---

[2]All names have been changed to protect privacy.

immediate power over their survival and sustenance. I suggest that for Chou Chang, literacy can be seen as an addition to as well as an agent of change in the communicative economy, producing profound effects on his relationships with others.

The second portrait describes Pao Joua Lo, when I saw him as a failing student when I first met him in my community college classroom. He never spoke, never completed an assignment, and never passed an exam. I had no idea at the time that this mysterious older man had experience with education and literacy that most of his Hmong contemporaries did not have. He learned Lao literacy in military camp and taught himself to read and write in Hmong. It was not until several years after he flunked out of school that I would learn about his power in the community and his considerable resources for solving problems.

The third portrait is of Bao Xiong, another "perpetual beginner" at the community college, who eventually dropped out. This energetic woman is not literate in any language, although she can effectively communicate verbally in three. Over the years my perspectives about her were also to change radically as I came to know her outside of the English language classroom.[3]

As I learned more about each individual, the things I knew about the others became more interesting. The contrasts were striking in these individuals' ways of using literacy, their other kinds of resources, their desires, and their ways of making meaning in their new lives in the United States. The contrast between them illuminates revealing contrasts in Philadelphia's wider Hmong community.

Chou Chang: Literacy and Changing Relationships

I first met Chou at a Lutheran church service. In his role as assistant he sat patiently beside the pastor until it was time to give a Bible reading in Hmong to the mixed Hmong and American congregation. After the service, I was introduced to Chou as an English teacher who was interested in the neighborhood refugees. Characteristic of his interest in Americans, Chou invited me to his home without hesitation.

When I arrived at the fire-gutted row in Weston, I was welcomed into the end house, the only one intact. The second-floor apartment was clean and uncluttered with two babies sleeping in a heap of blankets and a table full of Thai herbs growing in plastic pots by the window. Chou invited me to stay for dinner. Having heard that Americans prefer bread to rice, Chou had his wife, Sai, place half a loaf

---

[3]My relationship to these individuals and their families and my role in the community over the six years of the research include that of language teacher, language learner, community activist, and ethnographic researcher. For more on these roles and the inherent conflicts among them, see Weinstein-Shr (1990).

of Wonderbread on my dinner bowl. They were anxious to please, in contrast to what I would later experience in Pao Youa Lo's house, where my presence was tolerated with unhostile indifference.

In order to learn the Hmong language and to observe the functions and uses of literacy for one family, I arranged to move in with Chou and Sai for four weeks in the winter of 1981. During these weeks, I came to see Chou Chang as a literacy and culture broker who used his language skills for surviving urban bureaucracy as well as for creating new roles and relationships for himself in his new setting. The data presented here are drawn primarily from that homestay.

Adult literacy teachers are often sensitized to the extent to which managing life in urban America entails dealing with literacy. Students often bring in their baffling documents, important-looking letters, insurmountable forms, and questions about what they see around them. Life in the Chang household provided a sampling of some of the problems to be solved that required literacy skills.

One Tuesday afternoon, Chou received a letter from his caseworker instructing him to report to her office Friday morning, or his "case" would be "closed." He was to bring four documents with him, including one that had to be stamped by an agency several miles away (and not easily accessible by public transportation), and others that required picking up various forms with signatures from different places. That evening, Chou spent his homework time fixing his bicycle because he knew it would be impossible to complete the tasks on foot in one day. He called his English teacher to tell her he would be absent.

On Friday, Chou reported to his caseworker with all of the forms that he had gathered. Both his signature and Sai's were required, and both had to be made in the presence of the caseworker. So when Chou got home at about midday, he took over the childcare so that Sai could repeat the ritual. She did not yet know how to use the subway, how to distinguish the north- from the southbound platform, nor how to read the sign for the Springgarden stop. Because Chou was unsure whether I would be able to accompany her, he memorized the location of the correct platform and counted the stops to report to Sai for her journey.

Chou was generally satisfied with his caseworker because "she help us everything." Not all found her so helpful. An older Hmong woman living one floor below Chou who did not know how to decipher forms, letters, or bills found the preparation of the required documents to be an insurmountable task. In exchange for Chou's help in procuring gas money through the caseworker, the woman allowed Chou to use her oven to save on his own gas bills.

When the old woman was unable to solve a literacy-related problem, she sometimes brought it to Chou. When Chou was stymied

by bills or difficult homework, for example, he turned to me or to
another American in his church. Sometimes favors were returned in
kind, as illustrated above with the story of the gas money. Other
requests for help caused conflict.

Chou had been complaining for a couple of days about a man
who wanted him to write a fraudulent letter to the welfare department.
The man, who lived six blocks away, had asked Chou to claim that he
lived with him so that he could pick up a welfare check at Chou's
address. Chou complained: "He want me to cheat for him . . . he not my
relative, he never help me anything. He just make trouble for me." Chou
felt that the request was inappropriate and that it jeopardized his own
standing with welfare. The visitor was neither a neighbor nor a clan
member. He called on Chou for this favor because Chou was among the
few literate household heads who would be able to perform the task.

Chou later received a call from a Hmong social worker, asking
him to sign the fraudulent letter. As in many other cities, social service
agencies hired the earlier Hmong arrivals who became bilingual to work
in the resettlement process. These people have become the prime
mediators between U.S. caseworkers and the Hmong population in the
area. Not coincidentally, Chou reports, the members of some clans seem
to fare best in matters that require attention from the social service
system. In Laos, this leader would appropriately be expected to aid
members of his own clan. As a caseworker in Philadelphia, however, he
is perceived by Americans as a representative of "the Hmong" and is
asked to be an advocate for members of many clans. The old and new
expectations do not always harmonize.

The social worker, then, called Chou asking him to write the
letter to welfare. As the phone continued to ring, and Chou's homework
lay neglected, he shouted in exasperation, "Too many calls! Too many
questions!" With that, he pulled the phone wires out of the wall and sat
down to do his homework, complaining, "Everybody want something
from me!"

In these examples, decoding and composing documents play an
important role in economic survival. For Chou Chang, the ability to
decode bureaucratic messages in a timely way meant the difference
between keeping and losing government support. Relatives and
neighbors also turned to Chou (with or without success) to help them
negotiate the maze of literacy-based channels to gain access to resources.
Those who have literacy skills must use them to gain and maintain
benefits, and those who do not must often rely on those who do. The
homestay with Chou Chang made it evident that who may rely on
whom has become problematic. Whereas dependence relationships once
resided wholly with families and clans, new categories such as

caseworker/client, co-tenant, or urban neighbor pose new possibilities and pressures for different kinds of interaction in this new setting.

Members of Chou's church grappled with how to effectively accommodate the large new population of refugees. Incorporating the Hmong into religious life was a priority. On any given Sunday, one or more Hmong couples were baptized, thereby becoming full members of the "church family," a term used by one of the Sunday school teachers. Chou used to spend several hours each Saturday studying the Bible with the pastor. Thus prepared, he led Sunday school Bible lessons in Hmong for new arrivals and others who could not understand English. When Chou did his short Bible reading in Hmong for the whole congregation, on the other hand, he introduced some Hmong culture to Americans. His seat next to the pastor during the service and his name printed in the service program legitimized both the task and Chou himself as mediator in the exchange.

Chou's role as mediator extended past the boundaries of the church. During the homestay, a social worker from a neighboring church who had heard of Chou's writing skills called and asked him to translate a sign from English to Hmong for a clothing room. That evening he put aside his homework to write and rewrite the message until he was satisfied that it was well done and then invited the woman to call on his help at any time. Thus, Chou also conveyed information to Hmong people outside of his church, and in so doing, became a mediator for the wider neighborhood.

Chou spends time deliberately cultivating relationships with Americans. Before I moved in with his family, Chou would often call me on the phone to chat. One afternoon during my 4-week stay, when I returned to his apartment Chou was going systematically through his memo-pad phone directory calling each American on his list, one by one. The content of each conversation was more or less the same, as he asked each person what was "up" and told his own news. It seemed clear that Chou made efforts to connect with American friends, teachers, and church members. The decision he and Sai made to let me live with them for a month was another daring move to allow an American into their world.

For Chou Chang, literacy skills are resources that enable him to take the role of culture broker. Hmong compatriots including those in his church relied on Chou to bring them information and access to enable them to participate in American institutions. The pastor and the social worker cited above are among many Americans who called on Chou to effectively reach members of the Hmong community. Chou actively sought to incorporate Americans into his network, and he cultivated his role in linking these two cultural worlds. What are the rewards for this role? Why did Chou Chang devote so much energy to this difficult task?

Chou once commented to me, "I don't have family here—I have my church. People help me, give me a desk, dresser, chair . . ." Indeed, the church has been a source of furniture and clothing for Chou and Sai. During my short stay at their home, individual congregation members lent a space heater when the heat was broken and moved to investigate the delay in bringing Chou's brother over from Thailand, among other acts. They provided those things for which, in the past, Chou could only turn to "family" or clan.

The new ties could not provide enough support, however, to see the Chang household through a turbulent summer. In the hottest months of 1981, some Hmong in Weston were the targets of senseless violent attacks. Neither Chou nor any of his family members were victimized. However, he told me that he had no kin to help in the event that anything did happen to him. Because of his feelings of vulnerability, he packed his family in his car and headed for the midwest on the day that his Philadelphia car insurance ran out.

In sum, for Chou and Sai, literacy was a critical tool for navigating through educational and social service bureaucracies. It enabled Chou to complete homework exercises that were useful for little other than "getting through school." It was also a tool that enabled him to mediate between culture groups. As this new mode of communication has entered the social fabric, for people like Chou Chang, the use of literacy has accompanied important changes in their relationships with others. Without strong kinship connections, cultivating new relationships and becoming a literacy broker provided a strategy for managing life in a difficult new setting. It did not protect him, however, from a sense of vulnerability that would ultimately lead to his flight.

Pao Joua Lo: New Technologies, Old Ties

I now direct the reader's attention to a man with entirely different circumstances and strategies for getting along in urban Philadelphia. Two years after the homestay in the Chang household, when I expressed interest in getting to know another Hmong family, my Hmong teacher offered to introduce me to his (clan) brother, a man 51 years old. Having heard that this man had declined the nomination for President of the Hmong Association because of his poor English skills, I was prepared to offer English lessons in order to have a chance to observe life in another household. The man was none other than Pao Youa Lo, the hopeless student from my community college classroom several years earlier. Oddly, I felt embarrassed, as if I had been the one who had failed. He showed no such discomfort. Pao Youa was not interested in the tutoring sessions I offered. His wife and daughters, however, were delighted by the prospect and agreed to have me come to see them twice a week.

Entering Pao Youa's Norton row house, I was immediately struck by the portraits framed and hung on each wall of the front room. On the first wall is an austere photograph of a balding man staring resolutely ahead, with a heavy silver necklace prominent on his chest indicating he was a man of means. Pao Youa explains that this is his uncle, a brave and respected fighter who died in Laos. On the same wall is a photo of Pao Youa himself in combat fatigues, standing with General Vang Pao, under whose leadership the Hmong fought and fled to the United States. On an opposite wall hangs a family photograph of all the Lo men, with occasional children filling fathers' laps. Each photograph has a slip of paper taped at the bottom with an explanation typed in Hmong, as well as the date of the photograph. Although the enjoyment of family photographs is typical among the Hmong, the carefully typed embellishments are not. Centered over the false fireplace was a certificate with Lao writing, declaring Pao Youa's courage and his contribution as a soldier to the war.

What was going on here? How could it be that my most pathetic and helpless student was pictured beside the Hmong community's greatest leader? Who was this man and how did he manage? Over the next year, I was to learn about resources that are simply not visible to a community college English teacher.

On any given day, when Pao Youa is home, he usually sits by the large window, where he has arranged a u-shaped cluster of tables stacked with pads and notebooks, his chair nestled inside. There is rarely a morning or afternoon that goes by without a visit—usually from a clan brother. On a typical afternoon Pao Youa may chat with several of these brothers about topics such as fishing, prospects for income during the new blueberry picking season, their own travels, or the impressions their sons had gotten of life in other states.

It is at gatherings such as these that the need for help is voiced and cooperative strategies are agreed on. Cheng Mao Lo had just moved into his new home. The purchase was made possible by pooling money for the down payment. When the mortgage payments were under control, Cheng Mao would return the funds to be made available for the next cooperative approach to individual problems.

Gatherings of kin are not always small or informal. Pao Youa's house is arranged, like many other Hmong people's rowhouses, with furniture that is easy to push aside. Pao Youa hosted several parties over the period of my regular visits. He was often invited to the parties of others in both Philadelphia and in other states as well. I rarely attended a party in Norton in which Pao Youa was not present. Part of Pao Youa's position in Philadelphia is created and supported by the alliances his family has made with other Philadelphia families. Pao Youa's eldest daughter married the son of Hmong Association President Hang Chou in 1984. The wedding was an event that created a bond between two of Philadelphia's more powerful families. Such a bond strengthens and perpetuates existing alliances.

Pao Youa's popularity is not limited to Philadelphia, however. During the New Year season, Pao Youa traveled to Boston and Rhode Island among other cities to attend New Year festivities, which indicates that his support network is wide and strong. Pao Youa's eldest daughter married a clan "nephew" of the number one Hmong leader in the United States, General Vang Pao. This continues the alliance formed when Pao Youa himself married Lee Vang.

The invitation to run for the presidency of the Hmong Association in 1983 was a clear signal of Pao Youa's high regard in Philadelphia's Hmong community. His absence on the official slate, evidently, did not interfere with his leadership role. Nine household heads, including the elected president of the Hmong Association, reported they went to him for help with family and other problems. Pao Youa's role as leader raises a host of interesting questions about the nature of leadership. Even though his younger affinal kinsman was elected as spokesperson of the Hmong community, elders are, in some cases, maintaining traditional roles of authority. Although certain kinds of problems, such as negotiating with English-speaking institutions, require new solutions, other age-old conflicts such as marital discord persist, requiring the intervention of traditional experts with traditional solutions. Old and new forms of authority coexist as different sorts of problems require the wisdom of different kinds of experts.

Pao Youa does not have a job. Because of a leg wound suffered in the 1970s he cannot be long on his feet. Nevertheless, he was rarely idle. In his window niche I often found him reading, browsing, jotting notes, or cutting and pasting. Behind him stood a tall cabinet filled with books and albums that he himself created.

The first thing an observer notes when Pao Youa has a book or magazine in his hand is that he leafs through with an obvious goal. It becomes clear that he is drawn to photographs of powerful leaders. If a picture of Reagan or Thatcher appears on the page, for example, he studies the picture. If the caption is brief, he follows it with his finger, trying to read each word. "Reagan very good man," he smiles, "very strong against Communism." Pao Youa showed me a scrapbook made from a 1979 desk diary. Each page was covered with pictures of world leaders and accompanying text or with pictures alone. His fascination with powerful leaders is in keeping with his own stature as a soldier and a military strategist.

Pao Youa has also used his literacy skills in the creation of elaborate personal chronicles. In a typical document, the reader opens the first page to find a photograph of Pao Youa in combat fatigues with several other men. At the top of the page is a neatly typed slip of paper that reads (in Hmong): "The first person here is Pao Youa Lo. The second person is. . . ." The next page translates: "This is Mrs. Pao Youa's book 9/28/85." The reader meanders through images of family members and friends, some posing solemnly in traditional Hmong clothing, some gathered in ragged groups at the Thai refugee camps, and others smiling from behind their sunglasses near their American inner city apartments.

Other chronicles include Pao Youa's life story, with a detailed account of his days as a soldier in Laos, particularly during the war. Britannica Yearbooks for 1971, 1972, and 1974 are highlighted in yellow marker in the sections that provide the historical context for the story. One steno pad is filled with Pao Youa's version, in careful Lao lists, of the history of French and U.S. intervention in Laos. Fue explains that his father is the history "expert" and that people come to him with any questions they have about history.

With albums, scrapbooks, reference materials, and personal journals, Pao Youa has created a rich and varied chronicle. He is satisfied to think that his efforts will help his children to understand the country from which they came and the events leading to their flight and relocation in their new home. They will surely also come to gain some understanding of their father's role in the historic saga.

Pao Youa's interests are not confined to the distant past, nor are his efforts solely a family affair. His interest in current news events has become integral to his role in the community as an expert on world events, both past and present. During a party in Pao Youa's home, as is the custom, the children and women scattered after the meal, and the adult men gathered around the freshly cleaned table for beer and talk. Pao Youa passed three letters written in Lao around the table, and the literate men read them aloud to their kin who were unable to read. From a California-based organization, these letters discussed plans for guerrilla warfare against the government of Laos. Fue explained an article about the MIAs and military activity in Laos from that morning's U.S. newspaper to the whole group.

Each day, Pao Youa monitors the media for news of the United States, of the world powers, of individual heroes, and of leaders. His findings are often the topic of discussion when kin come to call. Pao Youa is also the focal point for information about Laos. Members of the community depend on him for information and at times for analysis. A great deal of Pao Youa's time and creative energy is given to activities that support his role as newskeeper and newssharer.

One of the ironies of dislocation is that new technologies make possible the maintenance of old ties in novel ways. This is illustrated by some of Pao Youa's activities. Pao Youa keeps a notebook in which he is carefully compiling (in Lao) a list of every Lo family in Philadelphia with members' names, sexes, birth dates, and relations to the householder. He is collecting these, he explains, to contribute to the effort of identifying the Lo families worldwide. The information is forwarded to an elder Lo at "Lo headquarters" in Omaha, NE, a site chosen for its centrality to Los on both coasts and between in the United States. Every year, members of the clan gather from all over the United States to discuss topics of mutual interest, including how to support the education of the children.

It is ironic that literacy has provided Pao Youa and his family with a tool for studying Hmong oral tradition. During the last years of the research, I heard complaints from elders that the young people do not know the love songs anymore. They don't know the appropriate courtship, marriage, and funeral songs. In 1985, under new leadership, the Hmong Association created "Culture Classes." Every Saturday, for three hours, four mej koob (marriage go-betweens) were paid out of a grant raised by the Association to teach the old customs and appropriate songs to younger men. The old men complained that they were getting too old to travel so often and to drink so much (as is required in the negotiation of marriages), and they were relieved that younger men were learning how to take over their role.

The students, including Pao Youa, were predominantly Los. The younger students took turns spending Friday nights with the teacher for that particular week, helping to prepare notes and written aids. They then assisted in the actual class as well. Fue says that he sometimes took notes in Hmong when the exact words were required, but that for general information it was faster to write Lao. With the help of young mediators, then, the old men taught oral traditions in a classroom format, which became the most efficient and comfortable setting. It would not be surprising, if, in a few years, when a traditional marriage is desired, one of the Lo men would be called on to negotiate the terms and aid in preparation for the wedding. In their newly learned traditional roles, these young men will use literacy tools, for better or worse, that were not available to their mentors.

In sum, Pao Youa is a professional soldier who has created for himself the roles of history- and newskeeper. Members of the community see him as an expert and depend on him for information about the past and the current state of affairs in the world. In these pages literacy is presented as a way of celebrating powerful people and a means through which to tell the story of what is happening. In addition, for Pao Youa, literacy provides a way of keeping himself and his community informed and connected with one another, with their traditions, and with their past and present.

Bao Xiong: Culture Broker and Entrepreneur

> I am born in Xiang Khoang, in the small town Ba Hong [Laos]. Then when I a little girl, I live with my mother and father. My mother have 8 children, then we have 8 brother and sister together. My father he had 5 wife. My mother she is second wife . . . but now my brother and sister all dead. Now we have two brother and sister live together. The second, he's a what do you say? He go to the water to fish [he drowned?] Yes, and he die. He's a boy only 22 years old. He is very handsome. He die. Third, he's die too, but he only 8 years old. I think he's malaria. He go to the mountain to get some food. And he die. Then, I'm the third, yeah, the third.
>
> When I about 5 years old, I have learn my sewing. My mother she teach me. Then we have sing Hmong song flute, like that. When I had my age just only seven, my mother she's die. She out new baby. When she out new baby she has some fever . . . then my father have a new wife and we live with new mother.
>
> When my mother die I very sorry little girl, I must take care of my brother and sister together. Three they die. . . . Another wife, they have many children too, they not interested in me, too busy.
>
> Then I little girl I learn play [dya], Hmong flute. I count my song, I have 700 song. I sing song about people die, then the song about people get married, then the song about ... we say their soul out to with God. And some song about my mother died and song about we have no mother. . . How do you say? Yes, I sing a song about orphan children then I got some money from some people.[4]

So begins the story, as Bao tells it, of her life in Laos. From her tales of her life in Laos, her marriage to a Thai soldier, and her flight through Asia, it is clear that Bao Xiong is a survivor who knows how to meet adversity head on with unfathomable resourcefulness. Her situation in Philadelphia is consistent with her remarkable history.

I first met Bao Xiong in 1979 at the community college. Although my contact with her was brief, the impression was strong and lasting. Very few Hmong women were at the college at all—and those who did come were often shy and quiet. Bao sat among her mostly male classmates, working at the English language with humor, energy, and in

---

[4]As told to by Bao Xiong to GWS, recorded in 1982.

the areas of reading and writing, with futility. What struck me most was her friendliness toward the instructors in the Learning Lab. Few of her compatriots, male or female, were as outgoing or talkative.

In late August of that year, I arranged for community college Hmong students to visit an agricultural community in Pennsylvania. By the end of the visit, Bao had befriended our hostess and had promised to come back to give a workshop/performance of Hmong traditional dancing for the community members. As I was to learn, it was entirely typical for Bao to make contact with Americans wherever she went, to learn about their interests, and to arrange performances, sales, exhibits, or a variety of colorful events.

In this section I describe Bao's life in Philadelphia during the last years of the research. The incidents described illustrate how Bao has become adept at "packaging culture" to her advantage. I then discuss the role of literacy in Bao's entrepreneurial activities. Although she began to develop a notion of literacy and its uses in Laos, Bao was never to become a skilled technician. However, it is clear that she has a very sophisticated notion of what the tool can accomplish. It is also evident that Bao has been very successful in mobilizing others to help her with literacy-related tasks to accomplish her specific purposes. Finally, this section closes with reflections about Bao's use of the old and the new and of her selection of resources from the cultures she has at hand as she and her family grow and prosper.

On any given weekend, Bao is hard to reach. She has become known to many Americans as the "Hmong Craft Lady." Summer weekends find her in Headhouse Square among the artisans with a table of embroideries. In winter she may be giving demonstrations at department stores, schools, or fairs. For a commission, she markets the work of other women who, bound by the constraints of their culture and/or personality, are unable to interact cheerfully and assertively with the American public.

> You like this one? This one tell story about Hmong culture. This show old custom, you see? Hmong lady cut rice like that. Yeah, this one show Hmong people live in Laos. . . . How long? This take long time. Everything I do by my hand. So maybe take three weeks, [if I] work all day every day. But I not time, so maybe take four weeks, five weeks, like that.[5]

When Americans ask Bao about the crafts she is displaying, she knows what they are looking for. She knows that when they ask about time, they value the hours that have gone into the handiwork. She also

---

[5]From a conversation between Bao and an American, recorded at a craft sale held in my apartment in 1983.

understands that Americans (at least the ones who come to Hmong craft sales) like to hear about "quaint" customs. When Bao is selling her things, she brings traditional Hmong dress to wear. If other women are working with her, she has them wear the turban, skirts, and sashes as well. She knows that Americans are drawn to her when she is exotically (to them) dressed. If the setting permits, she also brings a Hmong dish resembling spring rolls with a spicy peanut sauce. "This one is Hmong food!" she tells them, knowing that this particular Asian food is always a hit with Americans.

Every year, at the Hmong New Year, Bao climbs on stage with her sons, nieces, and nephews clad in colorful traditional dress from different "color" tribes.[6] For the benefit of the Americans in the audience, she gives a talk in English about each costume as her nephews and nieces model and pose in turn. A Hmong man once commented to me that she had given a few pieces of misinformation. She had not lived in Laos for nearly two decades as she had been in Thailand for 10 years before coming to the United States. He mused that when she was unsure of something she simply made it up. But accuracy was not the issue— rather her accessibility to Americans and her successful packaging of her "knowledge" have been far more important.

Bao is eager to develop her role as "culture teacher." She happily participated in a "Folklore in the Schools" program and brought her father to the school auditorium stage, where he told stories that she translated. Yer Kao, with his multicolor hat and cherubic face, and Bao with her brilliant sashes, never disappoint their audiences, whether these are composed of children or members of the university community.

It is evident that Bao relishes her role as "culture teacher," a lucrative position from which she promises Americans a link to a mysterious and colorful culture. However, the packaging of culture does not only go one way. At a soccer game for the Hmong Bao's husband caused quite a stir as he pulled up in a brand new two-tone Cutlass LS Sedan. Some envious admirers told me how much money the family had put down and how much was yet to be paid. I was stunned for a moment when Bao stepped from her new car with her hair cascading about her shoulders in unprecedented curls. At the next party she held, two of her nieces showed up with short hair, the first I had ever seen among Hmong women. Whether it is curls or cropping, the change from long straight black hair typically twisted and clipped to the top of the head is a striking one.

It seems that among her own compatriots, Bao is an innovator who selects and introduces new forms. Thus, the culture teaching goes

---

[6]Hmong dialects and subgroups are so named after their traditional clothing, that is, Philadelphia has both White Hmong and Blue Hmong. Black, Green, and Flower groups, for example, still exist in Southeast Asia.

both ways. Part of her expertise has included her understanding of American habits and tastes, which makes it possible for her to guide the women who sew with her in terms of the kinds of items Americans will buy and in which color combinations they will be interested.[7] Although most women who sew find it difficult to think beyond the decorative square, Bao has demonstrated her creative imagination:

> I know how to make Hmong sewing, about flower, about dress, when you make a dress then you put some sewing in the front, then sometimes you make a skirt, sometimes you put a belt, sometimes you put a pocket for sewing. I know how to make tablecloth, about sewing or wallhanging, or for Christmas tree, like that.

Bao's skill in recognizing and selecting features from each culture has contributed to an enormously successful craft business, to be discussed in the next section.

As Bao tells in her story, she did have a chance to study reading and writing (in Lao), both from the wife of a missionary, as well as from her brother. However, she did not have the luxury of refining the skill, especially in light of the years of flight and her subsequent resettlement in Thailand. At community college, although Bao was unable to keep up in her English assignments, she was the star pupil in terms of befriending her teachers and gaining their interest and admiration. As a matter of course she gave each of her teachers a bookmark with a traditional pattern of hand cross-stitching with the word "Hmong" embroidered across the top so that they might remember her. Indeed, even after she dropped out of school because it became too difficult for her, Bao kept in touch with several of her teachers.

From among English teachers and social scientists (such as folklorists and myself), Bao has nurtured a corps of willing literacy helpers for a variety of business-related tasks. Now when Bao sets up a table at a craft fair, she displays a large sign announcing the work of "Hmong Women from Laos." Here, literacy provides a method, in her business, for helping to package and explain the origin of the art work.

To find customers for particular sales, Bao adopted a method from craft sales I used to conduct. With the help of one of several American friends, Bao designs flyers bordered in ink with a typical Hmong embroidery pattern that includes information about the sale nestled inside. She has these printed at a xerox shop and distributes them in part by batches through her American network.

---

[7]Although Americans are drawn to the quality of Hmong handiwork, only folklorists, artists, or other specialists are interested in the sewing in its traditional forms. The bulk of Hmong handicrafts that sell successfully in the United States, although produced with traditional sewing techniques, have been adapted to American uses and color schemes. For more on this subject, see Peterson (1982).

During the last two years of the research, Bao adopted more sophisticated marketing techniques. With the help of an American friend, Bao designed a business card that identifies her with both her own and her husband's surnames (an accommodation to American custom), a subtitle "Hmong handicrafts," and her home phone number. She attaches one to each piece she sells and has them with her at all times. Her home has been turned into a veritable craft shop, with every wall covered by murals and symmetrical pieces, and every couch and chair crowded with embroidered pillows. At one sale I found her house literally jammed with browsers. On a table in the front room she had an enormous "Guest Book." It was full to the middle, where it lay open. Bao has developed a mailing list with the help of her sons that includes hundreds of names from her guest book, attendance sheets from sewing workshops, and other records of contacts she has made. Bao's social abilities combined with new recordkeeping systems give her the ability to fill a room with buyers at any time she pleases.

In 1984, Bao and her family moved to a three-story home in a quiet (mostly Greek) community in the suburbs of Philadelphia. Indeed, Bao's craft business has helped to make possible for her, her husband, and six sons a lifestyle enjoyed by few other Hmong in America.

I asked Bao Xiong about her prospects for the future. She replied:

> I like Philadelphia, easy to find job. My six sons, they all speak very good English. They know how to play soccer, and then they know how to play drum, they know how to sing song, American song, and then some Hmong song, some Thai song, then they know how to dance. Hmong custom dance, Thai custom dance, then American dance. Then I know how to play Hmong music, Hmong flute, we say Hmong dya, then my husband know how to play Thai song. And I know how to make Hmong sewing. . . Then I think maybe everybody in Philadelphia we have a very happy about be here.

PORTRAIT OF TWO COMMUNITIES: A SECOND LOOK

It is possible to better understand the nature of literacy in these individuals' lives when they are seen in social context. The differences between Chou Chang and Pao Youa Lo are characteristic of two subcommunities with distinct features. Bao Xiong manages with one foot in each community. The contrasts explored below highlight the relationship of literacy skills and problem-solving needs on the one hand, with kinship as opposed to other social relationships on the other.

Norton and Weston: Two Separate Communities

In the summer of 1984 I drove out to Wisconsin to see Chou and Sai. Before the journey, Pao Youa Lo held a large supper. To protect me on my journey, several of the men tied strings around my wrist, saying prayers for my safety. The strings were to keep the evil spirits from luring my soul away from my body. When I arrived in Wisconsin, after the children climbed down and the excitement of the greetings calmed, Chou and Sai noticed the strings. They were noticeably displeased. "Where did you get these?" Chou asked. I told them, guessing that they might be jealous that I was becoming involved with other Hmong families in their absence. It was not until a year later that I would learn what was really bothering them.

In the spring of 1985 it began to seem that money would become available from a local foundation for indigenous refugee education projects. I spoke with Pao Youa and his sons about ways to use the money. They spoke of their interest in creating culture classes. Specifically, they wanted to learn:

- *txiv xaiv*—funeral songs; songs of death
- *fiv sou*—message to mother of bride from hopeful suitor
- *kav xwm*—correct way to bring messages between clans
- *tus mej koob*—how to be a middleman and correctly negotiate weddings on behalf of particular family or clan

When I asked about where these classes could be held in order to accommodate both Weston and Norton Hmong, they laughed. Weston Hmong are not interested in old customs, they said. No need to worry about accommodating them. I asked Bao Xiong, who elaborated:

> Hmong people we have Weston way and Norton way. Not the same. Some things the same, like language, like some custom. But Norton Hmong people they still have *ua neng* [shaman], play *qeej* [talking reeds], want to learn old song, keep old custom. Weston culture not the same. Weston Hmong very want to be Christian, not dance or sing. They think that bad. They want to forget old way, maybe they afraid the hell. They think the new way, that's better. (Fieldnotes 1/5/86)

Chou and Sai are indeed devout Christians who had lived in Weston. The day they welcomed me into their new Wisconsin home, they were recoiling at my indulgence in "superstition," then evident on my wrist. Some of the differences between "Norton way" and "Weston way" were to become more evident, with certain features characterizing each group.

In this section Chou and Pao Joua are portrayed in the context of their own communities. Their ways of getting along demonstrate that types of kin networks and new nonkin relationships go hand in hand with the ways people solve problems, the immediate need for literacy skills, and the kinds of uses to which literacy, as a tool, is put.

According to Bao's characterization, a chart of Norton versus Weston "culture" is depicted in Table 2.3.

Pao Youa fits Bao Xiong's characterization of Norton. He owns a *qeeg*, which he is teaching Fue to play. He can often be found repairing and maintaining it so that it can be passed on. His clan brother and neighbor is a shaman. Many families in Norton bring their children to him when they are sick. Members of the Lo family are interested in the old songs, the formulas for traditional negotiation of marriages. They spend long hours both learning in a class arranged by the Hmong Association and studying at home.

Chou's decisions are in keeping with the characteristics Bao paints for residents of Weston. He relies exclusively (albeit with reluctance and suspicion) on the American medical establishment. Chou and Sai do not like to talk about shamanism—they seem to be embarrassed by the idea. Unlike young people in Norton, Chou and Sai have no tapes of Hmong music—either the young people's rock and roll nor more traditional ballads and love songs. The only songs they sing or listen to are from hymnals that have been developed by missionaries.

As for Bao herself, she is hedging her bets. At her son's wedding, Bao showed yet again her ability to integrate old and new. New Christian forms and traditional gift giving, clan negotiation, and Western prayer were reconciled and carried off in a way that made sense to the traditionalists and satisfied the new Christians. I asked Bao which "culture" she was in. "If people tie string, I can tie string," she said. "I can do the old culture, the old customs. I can do new way too. I can be Christian. I can with everybody, [Norton] or [Weston], it not matter." It seems fitting that Bao lives in the suburbs, slightly apart from either community.

Table 2.3. Norton vs. Weston according to Bao Xiong

NORTON	WESTON
use *ua neeg* (shamans)	only use doctors
play *qeeg* (talking reeds)	no traditional music
use old songs	no music or dancing
old spiritual beliefs	follow Christianity

Neighbors, Networks, and Solving Problems

The differences between Chou and Pao Joua demonstrate that to understand the process of adaptation of "the Hmong," it is necessary to recognize changes in relationships and differences between individuals in their ways of coping. A focus on the networks of each provides a way of looking at individuals as actors making choices as they selectively develop or draw on the social resources available to them.

It became evident that Chou and Sai were willing to incorporate me into their lives to the degree that I dared ask. They took me in, housed and fed me, and allowed their children to grow to love me. They told me their troubles and asked my help often. Sai and I developed a relationship in which we could talk about our worries, our marriages, and our lives. She began to call me elder sister. Their intimacy with me, however, was not out of character. It reflects an openness to allow Americans into the fabric of their lives. During my homestay, there were many occasions in which Americans were invited into the house. Church members came by to bring furniture and warm clothes. Neighborhood workers seeking help in establishing contact with the community were welcomed. Even Jehovah's witnesses who came to the door were invited in and given courteous audience, despite Chou and Sai's lack of interest in their message. My own invitation to the first visit was characteristic of Chou and Sai's interest in welcoming Americans into their home and in cultivating American friends.

As Chou and Sai try to integrate Americans into their lives, confusion sometimes ensues. In 1986, Chou and Sai anticipated a visit from me by planning a party for their baby son to coincide with a welcome party for me. About half of the guests were Americans. They included church members, two neighbors, past and present English teachers, and the landlord. When Chou gathered everyone for a long Hmong prayer, the Americans did not know whether they were expected to go into the room where the prayers were being said or not, and Chou did not know whether or not to invite them. They were also confused by the rules for eating because they were invited to eat first, to be followed by the Hmong men and then the Hmong women. Some guests were obviously distressed that the seating did not permit the hosts and hostesses to eat at the same time. Chou tried to assure them not to worry, that they would eat afterwards, but he was obviously uneasy as he sensed his guests' distress.

In contrast, such confusion rarely exists at Pao Youa's house. Notes from six months of intensive fieldwork contain no record of any American (besides myself) ever being present in the house. The English lessons I offered the women were gladly accepted—and food was generously shared. However, the Los never asked my help in solving a problem. During the fieldwork period, I was never asked to leave, but I was never asked to come! If I overheard news of a party, or if I learned of the telltale trip for a pig, I was welcome to be there. Efforts were rarely made, however, to inform or invite me. I have no record of ever seeing another American at a Lo party.

Pao Youa rarely expresses concern about getting along. He is surrounded by kin who can help him deal with most bureaucratic problems (Table 2.4). At most parties he attends, he is likely to drink with Chai Mao Lo, a clan brother and job placement worker as well as with Hmong Association President Hang Chou, the father of his daughter's husband. At the Hmong Association Office, Hang and other Association workers act as intermediaries for welfare distribution. Pao Youa typically fishes with his clan brothers Chai Koua and Chou Lao Lo, whose children attend college and have become experienced in dealing with American institutions.

Chou Chang, on the other hand, although he lived in Philadelphia, complained that he was without relatives. The economic survival of the Chang family depended on the whim of American caseworkers to whom Chou reported directly. He enlisted the aid of teachers, the pastor, the social worker, and any contact provided by the new institutions that had come to play a role in his life. Although there was some overlap, particularly in the church community, the people in the other institutions had no contact at all with one another (Table 2.5). Their roles in Chou Chang's life were singular and institutional.

The differences between the Lo and Chang households are characteristic of their neighbors. It is entirely typical for families in Weston to seek the help and friendship of Americans, whereas those in Norton tend to solve problems, socialize, and interact rather exclusively within Hmong networks. As a natural consequence, the degree to which problem solving is done through informal versus institutional means is different for the two groups.

Table 2.4. Network Chart of Pao Youa Lo

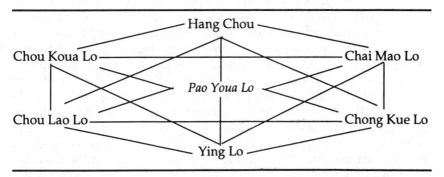

Table 2.5. Network Chart of Chou Chang

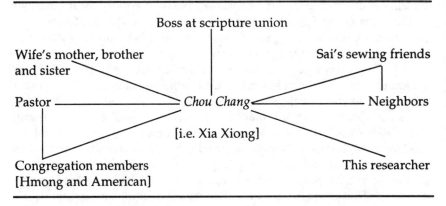

When asked about the greatest problems of the Hmong in Philadelphia, residents of Norton and Weston did not differ in their answers. Language barriers and educational problems were most commonly reported. Low English language skills were blamed for isolation of the elderly as well as for limited job options and thus low pay and bad job security for the young. Fear of street crime was mentioned frequently and was, unfortunately, well founded in experience. Finally, several people interviewed were concerned about home ownership and unethical landlords.

Although the problems cited were similar, the mechanisms for coping differed between residents of Norton and Weston. Weston residents reported turning to Americans for help, whereas Norton residents did not. One Weston household head reported that most of his relatives had left Philadelphia, but that he had decided to stay because of his job and because of Americans who were helpful to him in solving problems.

In addition, the closure of the interviews themselves revealed differences between Weston and Norton Hmong. At each interview I offered to repay the favor of the interview by providing help in any way desired by the interviewee. Household heads in Norton, although polite and cooperative, remained rather formal and invited no further interaction. In contrast, interviews conducted in Weston had rather different outcomes. In response to my offer one man immediately enlisted help in dealing with a car swindle. A second man's son asked for my office number at community college where he is a student for help in English should the need arise. The desire for exchange of resources did not only go one way. A third man placed his 4-day-old baby in my arms, offered me beer, and invited me to the celebration of the birth. Two families prepared meals for me. One man had added my name to the phone list on the wall at the time I called to set up the interview. Most asked when I could return to visit again.

Indeed, Pao Youa and Chou Chang are not unique in their dispositions toward me. They are typical of their subcommunities and act in ways consistent with the degree to which their networks are open to the integration of Americans and the ways in which their networks permit the solving of problems (Table 2.6).

Pao Youa and Chou behave in ways consistent with their subcommunities; Bao's network is more enigmatic (Table 2.7). With her father and brothers close by, she is comfortably surrounded by kin. One brother is a social worker who can help solve bureaucratic problems. Bao has organized the wives of her brothers among other women to put together an impressive craft collection. This part of her network is dense

Table 2.6. Problem-Solving and Networks: Norton vs. Weston

NORTON	WESTON
interact with real and fictive kin	report isolation from kin
solve problems within household or clan	seek help from Americans in solving problems
networks: 　mostly Hmong 　highly dense 　multiplex 　informal	networks: 　include Americans 　little overlap 　single roles 　institutional

Table 2.7. Network Chart of Bao Xiong

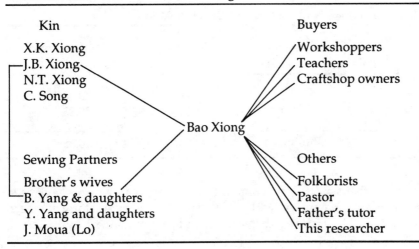

and multiplex, stretching from her own family in Weston to women in Norton. On the other hand, Bao has cultivated an army of American contacts, including teachers, culture students (folklorists and me), craft enthusiasts, and buyers who are, for the most part, unacquainted with one another.

Her networks are largely separate—at a craft show put together by Bao, only the few Hmong women needed to help with sales are present. At her son's wedding, only Hmong (except me) were present. Among the Hmong, Bao has blood kin support for daily living, as well as nonkin cooperation for her business venture. Her impressive corps of American contacts, mostly connected by their interest in her craft, rarely have any connection with one another or with other Hmong in her network.

The Hmong side of the network closely resembles Pao Youa's network in its features, including multiplexity and informality. On the other hand, the American side of the picture resembles the network of Chou Chang in its structure. Bao seems to be able to maintain two almost discrete networks, just as she operates fluidly between many cultural worlds, drawing on the resources of each.

The differences between Chou and Pao Youa discussed here include differences in residence choice, religious preference, and interest in tradition, as well as structure and content of networks. The clues that these differences provide about divisions in the community are further reflected in the choice of names for children.

Of the children born to Hmong in Philadelphia during the six years of the research (and thus, most likely, born in America), 58 children of 101 (57%) have been given Hmong "first names." However, the distribution of Hmong and American names were significantly different for Norton and Weston (Table 2.8).

Table 2.8. Given Names: Norton versus Weston

	Hmong names	American names	Total # children	% Hmong names given
Norton	53	22	75	70.66
Weston	5	19	24	20.83
Total	58	41	99	58.58

Whereas 71% of the children under age 7 in Norton have been given Hmong names, only 21% of their agemates in Weston have been so named. The striking difference might be explained by differing exposures to American names, by differing desires for integration into the host culture, or by differing pressures from kin networks.[8] In any case, it is clear that child-naming practices are consistent with the data on the makeup of networks of Norton versus Weston Hmong.

The Social Context of Literacy

This section has focused on two communities and the place of three individuals within those communities. Pao Joua Lo, Chou Chang, and Bao Xiong use literacy skills for very different ends with different consequences. Just as literacy plays a different role in the lives of each, so too does each individual play a distinct role in the life of the community.

Table 2.9 summarizes observations made concerning the uses and functions of literacy in the lives of Pao Youa Lo, Chou Chang, and Bao Xiong. It also highlights aspects of their roles in their own communities.

The literacy activities delineated in these portraits, summarized by Table 2.9, are characterized by striking differences. Pao Youa's literacy activities are directed inward to his family and clan, reinforcing his connection with his tradition and with his history. The documentation in which he engages affirms old ties and keeps old connections vital to kin, to the past, and to Laos. Chou, on the other hand, uses literacy to reach outward, connecting with new kinds of resources and creating new relationships in a social world of Americans that Chou takes risks to explore.

The conditions under which Pao Youa and Chou interact with print are vastly different. When Chou comes home, he and Sai open mail. They both read out loud as they slowly process the correspondence. A letter can mean the difference between continuing or losing their welfare benefits. One afternoon I watched first Sai, then Chou, read aloud through a long computerized luggage advertisement before deciding, in the end, that it did not interest them. They did not have the mechanisms yet for quickly screening important documents from "junk" mail.

Pao Youa need not concern himself when screening mail. His son can perform a second screening, and Hang Chou, his affinal kin, can tackle the more difficult problems. Pao Youa is free from the responsibilities of solving bureaucratic problems or of coping with enigmatic English language documents.

These two men differ in the degree to which they must solve problems themselves. Pao Youa's strong kin network permits a division of labor that enables him to delegate literacy tasks to others (while he

---

[8]One Norton man reported he wanted to give his child an American name, but his wishes were overridden by his father-in-law. This practice is in keeping with tradition in Laos, in which household heads (who are often grandparents) ordinarily name children.

retains prestige and responsibility for a wide range of problem solving). Chou must perform most of his own literacy-related tasks himself or turn to an American with whom he has an institutional relationship. This is often a last resort because there is little way of reciprocating the favor to Americans who have little use for Chou's resources. The men also differ in the ends for which they use literacy. These uses are obviously constrained and affected by the kinds of problems which they must solve.

Bao Xiong does not control the technology of literacy. However, with kin networks characteristic of Norton, and access to literacy skills like those found in Weston, Bao uses literacy with great success for very instrumental purposes—the success of a craft business. She has been able to see the possibilities for what literacy can do for her and has mobilized a team of Hmong and American helpers to accomplish her purposes.

The data from the in-depth studies are corroborated by data

Table 2.9. Functions and Uses of Literacy for Three Individuals

USE	FUNCTION	ROLE
Pao Youa Lo		
scrapbooks	celebrate leaders	professional soldier
chronicles	document past	history expert
news articles	keep informed on	news expert on world news
correspondence	keep connected w/Laos	authority on Laos
notes-culture	learn about tradition classes	authority on family matters
Chou Chang		
translations of & Bible lessons	mediate between culture groups	mediator and culture bridge
forms to negotiate with new institutions	secure economic benefits	self-helper
forms to help non-literates with literacy-related tasks	change role in social order	literacy broker
Bao Xiong		
business cards	increase sales	culture packager
flyers	and	and broker
guest book	expand business	saleswoman

collected in the larger community. Although there are some individual deviations, in general, Norton and Weston are characterized by different clusters of features including different religious preferences, social networks, and literacy needs and practices. The relation among these is not incidental. The most obvious relationship is that between religious conviction and literacy in which the explicit motivation for learning to read, and the prime literacy activity thereafter, is reading the Bible. The relationship between literacy activity and the nature of social network is less obvious but equally compelling.

A person whose social network is comprised of kin is likely to have a rich pool of resources that will be at his or her disposal. When many kin are involved, the relationships are multiplex, assuring a variety of means of reciprocity. In the case of Norton Hmong, dense and multiplex networks permit a division of labor in which specialists can be relied on for negotiation with institutions or for solving other literacy-related problems. Services can be repaid with cooking at special occasions, with contributions toward bride price, or in any number of ways that kin support one another.

A person who has a network that is less dense, with relationships that are singular, has to work harder to get a particular problem solved. Problems cannot be casually brought up while fishing, but rather must be addressed in a telephone call specifically for that purpose. Such a person has less means at his or her disposal with which to reciprocate and therefore must turn to institutional relationships to get things done. The costs can be considerable for depending on people with whom one does not have a trusting or long-term relationship. In situations in which networks are less dense and multiplex, relationships may be less stable. It is not surprising that the troubled summer of 1981 resulted in the exodus and dispersion of most of Weston, whereas Norton remained intact.

As a result of the instability of helping groups, literacy becomes a commodity that is needed by each family that is faced with solving its own problems. Without specialists in advocacy positions, literacy is a critical tool for survival in a dangerous world of bureaucracy.

SUMMARY AND CONCLUSIONS

In this study, the uses of literacy of Hmong in Philadelphia were examined in the context of other modes of communication, and their kinship ties were looked at along with other kinds of helping relationships. Both of these were viewed as social resources that were drawn on to solve various problems in adapting to life in the United States. I compared the social networks of three people as well as the differences in how literacy is used in their lives. Pao Youa uses literacy to connect to the past and to Hmong tradition, Chou uses literacy to make new relationships, and Bao uses it for her entrepreneurial ventures. These individuals were then placed in the context of the larger community. There are really two subcommunities of Hmong in Philadelphia in which the members engage in very different kinds of meaning-making activities involving different kinds of literacy events. Differences in literacy use both reflect and create differences in social relationships. For the three individuals described, uses of literacy both reflected their aspirations while also creating new roles for them in their respective communities.

When I first met Pao Youa and Bao in the classroom, I could only see them as failing students with poor prospects for success. Chou Chang, on the other hand, plodded through, allocated the time and resources necessary to complete enigmatic grammar exercises, learned the rules of classroom behavior, and came out with his high school equivilency degree. A teacher who met these three in the language classroom alone could not have imagined the kinds of resources available at the command of the older students, nor could she have imagined the difficulties of the star pupil, who would eventually leave Philadelphia in despair of his social isolation.

If education is the hope of America's future, then classrooms must become places where students' resources can be recognized and nurtured. I believe that scholars of literacy have much to contribute by discovering and providing insights into the ways in which human beings make meaning in their lives and by providing information that can help educators to see the range of possibilities in general and to understand the purposes of those they serve in particular.

REFERENCES

Barney, G.L. (1967). The Meo of Xieng Khoung Province, Laos. In L. Kundstadter (Ed.), *Southeast Asian tribes, minorities and nations* (Vol. II). Princeton, NJ: Princeton University Press.

Barney, G.L. (1981). *Hmong of Northern Laos. In Glimpses of Hmong history and culture.* Washington, DC: Center for Applied Linguistics.

Dunnigan, T. (1982). Segmentary kinship in an urban society: The Hmong of St. Paul-Minneapolis. *Anthropological Quarterly, 55*(3), 126-135.

Geddes, W. R. (1976). *Migrants of the mountains.* Oxford: Clarendon Press.

Gee, J. (1990). *Social linguistics and literacies.* New York: Falmer Press.

Goody, J., & Watt, I. (1968). The consequences of literacy. In J. Goody (Ed.), *Literacy in Traditional Societies.* Cambridge: Cambridge

University Press.

Office of Refugee Resettlement (1983). *Report to Congress: Refugee resettlement.* Washington, DC: Department of Health and Human Services.

Olson, D. (1977). From utterance to text: The bias of language in speech and writing. *Harvard Educational Reviews,* No. 47.

Ong, W. (1982). *Orality and literacy.* New York: Methuen.

Peterson, S. (1982). *The art of pa ndao: Symmetry, skill and survival in the Hmong community.* Unpublished manuscript, Philadelphia: University of Pennsylvania.

Reder, S. [Project Director]. (1985). *The Hmong Resettlement Study* (Vol. 1, Final Report). Prepared by Literacy and Language Program, Northwest Regional Laboratory, for Office of Refugee Resettlement, Portland, OR.

Smalley, W.A. (Ed.). (1976). *Phonemes and orthography: Language planning in ten minority languages of Thailand* (Pacific Linguistics Series, #43). Canberra, Australia: Linguistic Circle of Canberra.

Street, B. (1984). *Literacy in theory and practice.* Cambridge: Cambridge University Press.

Street, B. (1991). *Cross-cultural perspectives on literacy.* Paper presented at Conference on Attaining Functional Literacy, University of Tilburg, UK.

Street, B. (Ed.). (1992). *Cross-cultural approaches to literacy.* Cambridge: Cambridge University Press.

Weinstein-Shr, G. (1986). *From mountaintops to city streets: An ethnographic investigation of literacy and social process among the Hmong of Philadelphia.* Unpublished doctoral dissertation, University of Pennsylvania.

Weinstein-Shr, G. (1990). People, process and paradox: Qualitative research as journey. *Qualitative Studies in Education, 3/4,* 345-354.

Yang, D. (1975). *Les Hmong du Laos au face du development.* Vientiane, Laos: Siaosavath Publishers.

Toward a Dialogical Understanding of Literacy: The Case of Navajo Print

Daniel McLaughlin
Kayenta Unified School District

NAVAJO IS FOR THE NAVAJOS

From the Benally's camp, with ranch-style and traditional hooghan structures, can be seen the local community school's twin water towers some five miles away.[1] Red rocks and long vistas frame deep stillness. I have come here to interview the Benally's third-grade daughter about Navajo literacy. I have known the family for five years, taught two of the six children at the community school, and employed the oldest son, now an undergraduate at a prestigious west coast university, as my translator, guide, and research assistant. I am a white man, an outsider, but nonetheless a known entity. Still, the parents navigate new ground when they greet me, tape recorder and questions in hand. Foregoing the usual small talk, I am ushered directly to Bernice. We go into a back room. After explaining again my research purposes, albeit simply, that I want to describe how people use Navajo literacy and what they think about it, I ask, "What are the most important things you learn in school?" Without hesitation, she replies:

---

[1] All place names and references to individuals in this chapter are pseudonyms.

We learn reading and how to write Navajo in school, and the most important is Navajo reading and writing. We're Navajo, and we have to learn our own language and how to do things in Navajo. I read workbooks in Navajo, and you have to choose the right word.

We write stories, too. One time, I wrote about my whole family. Other kids read it, and the teacher put it out in the hall. We write stories like that. The teacher grades them, and if it's parent-teacher conference, the parents see them, too. They see how we do our work and how we write.

"Do you read and write Navajo outside of school?"

Sometimes I write Navajo when I'm not at school. I write letters in Navajo to my relatives. I also write Navajo when I play "teacher" with my brothers and sisters at home. I teach them how to do it. It's a lot of fun.

"Do you think it is more important to learn English or Navajo?"

I think kids should learn Navajo the most and English the next because we are Navajos. You have to speak your own language and act like Indians. English is good for talking to Anglos, and that's why we should keep teaching both languages. But Navajo is first. Navajo is for the Navajos.

That Bernice's answers to my questions are unremarkable, insofar as the sociolinguistics of her school and community are concerned, is significant. For elsewhere across the Navajo Reservation, a large geographical area of some 50 small, isolated communities that span three southwestern states, oral communication happens in Navajo (increasingly in English, too), but nearly all reading and writing occurs only in English. Not that Navajo writing systems have not been in existence; they have been present for almost 100 years. The earliest efforts in support of Navajo print were those of Catholic and Protestant missionaries at the turn of the century. In the 1920s, Edward Sapir, a prominent anthropologist, developed a writing system that indicated tone. In the 1930s and 1940s, following a standard orthography developed by Robert Young and William Morgan, the Bureau of Indian Affairs (BIA) published teaching materials in written Navajo. In the 1960s and 1970s, on the wave of civil rights and self-determination protests, a dozen community controlled schools promoted Navajo language, culture, and literacy instruction. However, despite all of these efforts, Navajo literacy has never caught on. It has never been used for purposes beyond the church and school. Moreover, despite tribal educational policies in support of Navajo language and culture instruction, at present nearly all support for Navajo literacy, in or out of schools, has fallen by the wayside.

Mesa Valley, where the Benallys reside, is an exception to this rule; from outward appearances, however, the area is indistinguishable from other reservation communities.[2] A K-12 school, mission church, trading post, and chapter house—site of local tribal government—comprise a small village proper. Widely separated camps of matrilineally related families stretch out from the village into a surrounding landscape of limited rainfall and work possibilities. Opportunity is restricted, and unemployment is high. Similar to many other communities across the reservation, families tend to survive on weaving, subsistence livestock raising, seasonal forest-fire fighting, and welfare.

All the same, in important ways Mesa Valley is unique. For the past 25 years, the local community-controlled school has gained an international reputation for its bilingual program. Children who enter school with few or no English skills learn initially to read, write, and count in Navajo. English literacy is introduced in the second grade and maintained along with oral and written Navajo throughout the elementary and secondary levels. The program has been effective. Mesa Valley students have consistently scored higher than other reservation children on standardized tests of reading, language, and math in English. In addition to Navajo programs at the school, for more than three decades the local church has developed Navajo reading materials to spread the word of Christianity. Community members have organized Navajo literacy classes for nonliterates, translated portions of the New Testament, and conducted weekly meetings that focus on the meanings of Biblical texts in Navajo.

As a result, Mesa Valley community members read and write Navajo in significant numbers for purposes unrelated to the church and school. As I have described elsewhere (McLaughlin, 1989a, 1992) and as Bernice alluded to above, in addition to Biblical and pedagogical texts, people read and write letters, lists, journals, and songbooks in significant numbers for a variety of purposes and audiences, all of which is noteworthy in light of previous descriptions of the nonacceptance of Navajo script.[3]

Again, as I have previously analyzed, reasons for the spread of Navajo literacy into indigenous domains at Mesa Valley are principally threefold. First, both the church and the school, over a period of three decades, painstakingly incorporated Navajo language into the content and process of governance, daily activity, and literacy instruction.

[2]The section that follows on the sociolinguistic description and uniqueness of Mesa Valley can be found in revised versions in McLaughlin (1989a, 1989b).

[3]See Spolsky and Irvine (1982) for a sociolinguistic analysis of the Navajo Reservation as a kind of diglossia; the unmarked language or oral communication remains Navajo, whereas the unmarked language for reading and writing remains English. For historical descriptions of efforts at promoting Navajo literacy, see Holm (1971), Young (1977) and Spolsky and Boomer (1979).

Second, community people took an active role in governing and performing all activities in the two institutions. Third, in both church and school instances, activities were advocacy oriented. Rather than legitimize instructional counseling procedures that blamed the individual for academic or personal failings, the activities functioned to celebrate the cultural and linguistic resources of the community and to help people broaden understandings of themselves and of the world. In so doing, they fundamentally altered how the church and the school served the community and how community people perceived uses for Navajo print.

The local pastor, who took over the congregation in the mid-1960s and remained in the community until 1990, explained the development of the three processes at the church. He began preaching with an interpreter in 1965, but quickly realized that, with an intermediary, there were too many possibilities for misunderstandings:

> Right from the beginning after my first couple of years, my wife and I encouraged Navajo participation, as such as we could and as fast as the stages of development would allow. Very soon on, the first Navajo evangelists, Navajo lay preachers, began to preach. Now, our service is unlike any other in the denomination. I sit in the pew ninety percent of the service. We have about thirty members each week who perform all sorts of services. They will either preach, lead the singing, read the scriptures, or sweep the church. . . . The long-term, ultimate goal, obvious to us, is that we must be entirely Navajo-controlled, Navajo-managed, and Navajo-operated. This has been obvious.

The same political processes underpinned governance, daily activity, and instruction at the community-controlled school. Over a period that parallels closely the pastor's tenure at the mission, the director of the school, Alan Glass, used Navajo language and literacy for the content and process of instruction, promoted the active collaboration of local people, and designed K-12 instruction to celebrate the cultural and linguistic resources of the children.[4] When he and his wife first came to Mesa Valley in 1960, the school had the lowest test scores on the Navajo reservation. At first, their goals were basic. They wanted the students to do better and for the parents to get more involved. In time, the director studied ways for improving English language and reading instruction. Mesa Valley was one of the first Navajo schools to develop an ESL program. Soon thereafter, the local School Board contracted with

---

[4]The director of Mesa Valley School to whom I refer here was, at the time of this study, in fact, an assistant director. He stepped aside from the director's position in 1980 to allow a community person to assume leadership duties at the school. Moreover, by the time of this writing, he and his wife had moved from the school and the community. For clarity's sake, however, I have refrained from including this background information in the narrative of the chapter.

the Bureau of Indian Affairs to wrest decision-making powers from the federal authorities. At the same time, as the director's wife related, the school embarked on a comprehensive program of bilingual instruction:[5]

> Starting the bilingual program was difficult because these were all totally new notions. . . . We had to create materials overnight, especially for the Navajo teachers to use. The fact was that there were no teaching materials in Navajo. This is how we really got started with Navajo literacy. At the time, Alan felt that teaching initial reading in the native language would work better than trying to teach English. We went with this idea of reading-readiness in Navajo and simply added onto it.

Prestige, equality, and training were all problematic at first. Navajo teachers did not accept themselves as equals to the English teachers. Nor did many believe in what they were doing. The main benefit was that the teachers had jobs. "But things changed," as the director's wife explained:

> Part of our aim was to train local people. So, we started college classes to try to get people degrees. We were totally committed. We didn't want trained teachers looking at the Navajo teachers as mere aides. You know, "Go ditto these papers for me," this kind of thing. We had to give equal pay. We lowered administrative pay and upped the Navajo teachers' scale. We worked hard at equalization first to get people to believe in what they were doing, and that wasn't easy.

Within several years, the director started other programs. He brought uneducated, non-English-speaking parents into the classrooms to teach Navajo clanship. Others started livestock instruction and a Navajo song and dance festival. At first the programs were an embarrassment. Parents who taught clanship and others who taught livestock and Navajo singing were apologetic. But in time, tolerance grew, and with it, more pride in what local parents thought about themselves and about Navajo language and literacy:

> People used to put their heads down when they had to talk Navajo, but after a while, it got so that speaking Navajo was normal—which is what it should be. . . .

> All along, we learned that the bilingual program by itself doesn't work. You have to make bilingual education possible for it to succeed. And to do that, you have to make the necessary social changes. . . .

---

[5]Historical analyses of Indian education in general, and of the development of Indian community-controlled "contract" schools that came into existence with the passage of P.L. 93-638, can be found in Leap (1993), Reyhner and Eder (1989), Szasz (1974), and Thompson (1975).

Those conditions have to be created. To do that, you have to do all the things that we did. You have to get people believing that what they're doing is going to be successful. It's not just a "mickey-mouse" game for having a job. Even with this situation, though, the only time Navajo reading and writing really works in schools is when the administrators are really involved. If they aren't, the program will die out. Nobody will keep promoting it. Somebody has to be very strong to make that possible.

At Mesa Valley's church and school, then, institutional activities and ideologies structured uses for Navajo literacy. At both places, vernacular language served as a vehicle for, and an object of, pedagogical activity. Upon assuming the leadership of the mission congregation, the pastor soon realized that "if any message was to get through to the people, it would have to come [in Navajo] from one of them," and that Navajo literacy was a powerful way to promote Christian conversion. In similar fashion, Alan Glass and his wife understood native language instruction to be one and the same as community control. At both institutions, community participation was highly collaborative. Navajos performed most church services in the Navajo language using Navajo texts. The performance of the services and processes of decision making behind the scenes involved local people. The same situation developed at the community school. Local people became classroom teachers, created curriculum, supervised academic programs, instructed Navajo clanship, and, as administrators and School Board members, oversaw all aspects of program development and implementation. The overall posture of church and school activities, moreover, was advocacy oriented. The aim was "to build people up," as the pastor urged at a weekly prayer session, and "to strive to help the students learn about, accept, and affirm their people and themselves," as Alan Glass exhorted at a graduation exercise. One important result of these institutional activities and ideologies is for individuals to read and write Navajo for indigenous purposes in home settings. Thus, for Mesa Valley residents it makes sense, as Bernice Benally described, to write letters in Navajo, play "teacher" in Navajo, and understand native language and literacy as "for the Navajos."

ON A DIALOGICAL UNDERSTANDING OF LITERACY: THE PRIMACY OF VOICE

The analysis of Navajo reading and writing in one isolated corner of the Navajo reservation, although far removed from mainstream concerns, provides a window to understandings of literacy in theory and practice. My aim in making connections here between the specific configurations of Navajo language usage to a broad theoretical framework is less to pose an alternate way of understanding written Navajo than it is to validate a critical model of literacy.[6] In so doing I recognize literacy as a set of concepts and practices that operate within a cultural context. Rather than view culture a politically, as a series of sociocultural functions or mentalist beliefs, the need is to see culture in terms of individuals' interactions with dominant truths and power relations in society. The need is to examine communicative functions in relation to institutions and literacy-related beliefs in relation to ideology. In sum, the meanings of literacy derive from individuals' *struggle for voice* within institutional and ideological contexts in which forms of oral and written communication are embedded.

I argue here for a dialogical understanding of literacy. Central to such an understanding is a politicized notion of *voice*. By voice, paraphrasing Giroux and McLaren, I refer to the discourses available to us for making ourselves understood and listened to, and for defining ourselves as active participants in the world (1986, p. 235). The assumption is that what people believe, say, and do are both constrained and enabled by social institutions that produce, distribute, and reify particular beliefs, forms of knowledge, and social relations. Put simply, voices do not become manifest in a sociopolitical vacuum; on the contrary, they occur within a general politics of truth that affirm certain, and only certain, beliefs and forms of knowledge and make them function as true.[7]

In the section that follows we turn directly to Mesa Valley's "general politics of truth." We will hear the voices of a cross-section of Mesa Valley people. Focusing on print, we listen to 12 conversations that locate the individual's voice within a finite set of discourses that Mesa Valley people have available for understanding literacy. The choices are few and can be seen either as a function of ideologies of the local church and the school, which promote self-understanding and empowerment, or as a function of mainstream ideological beliefs that equate access to power and social mobility with reading, writing, and speaking only English. My aim in portraying what people say about Navajo literacy is to make clear the connection between uses for and beliefs about print on the one hand and individuals' voices on the other.

---

[6]See Apple (1982, 1987, 1990), Aronowitz and Giroux (1985), Cook-Gumpertz (1986), Cummins (1986), Freire and Macedo (1987), Heath (1983), McDermott (1987), McLaren (1988), McLaughlin (1991, 1992), Ogbu (1987), Scribner and Cole (1981), and Street (1984) for detailed descriptions of social structure and cultural boundaries as they dialectically shape, and are shaped by, forms and functions for print.

[7]That "truth is a thing of this world," produced by multiple forms of constraint evident in what people voice as true, is analyzed in depth by Foucault (1980, pp. 109-133).

The idea of opposite organizes the presentation of the interviews. We listen first to the former Mesa Valley School Board president who was instrumental in creating the bilingual program at the community school and in assuming decision-making powers from the BIA; then we hear from his theoretical opposite, the daughter of another School Board member who was opposed to local control and Navajo language instruction.[8] Next, we listen to a local politician, an elderly monolingual Navajo who has struggled over the course of his professional life with an inability to speak English and read and write forms in mainstream print; then we hear from his theoretical opposite, a chapter official one generation younger to whom many individuals in the community turn for literacy-related help. The other eight interviews are organized in similar fashion. We hear from one individual, then from his or her theoretical opposite.

Attributes that constitute opposite, as they are described in the introduction to each interview, shape how power becomes manifest in the Mesa Valley community. As the community members speak of these dimensions in their everyday forms, we see how power takes shape; how it constrains and enables what people think, say, and do; how they map onto themselves; how they evolve; and where literacy fits in. These attributes include gender, religious affiliation (adherence to traditional Navajo beliefs, to different strands of Native American church beliefs, or conversion to Christianity), political affiliation, position of nominal status within one or more community institutions, and abilities to use and beliefs in support of English and Navajo print.

VOICES

Elmer Nakai

Elmer Nakai was president of the Mesa Valley School Board when members of the Board traveled to Washington in 1971 to petition government officials for the right to govern the school locally, and he presided over most of the social engineering efforts of the Glasses. He speaks English, but with considerable difficulty. Here he describes the effort to gain decision-making powers from the Bureau of Indian Affairs and his feelings about the utility of Navajo literacy, both of which allow for, in his words, "our own children [to] teach in and run the school." The interview transpired with the aide of an interpreter in Navajo but is rendered below in English.

---

[8]The idea of organizing interviews according to "theoretical opposites" comes from Agar (1980, pp. 119-136).

"How did the bilingual program at Mesa Valley begin?" I asked.

We were told to teach in both languages by Washington. Richard Nixon was then president. He said, "Walls are caving in on me. I am trying to stand up with all the weight of your problems on me. I have an idea. How about you deciding things for yourselves, you Native Americans. Maybe, you can accomplish things. If you do, it will be good. Then, you can run things and plan things yourselves." This is what he said.

We told ourselves, "Hey, let's try it. Maybe we can do it. We have minds. We can plan. We can speak for what we believe in." There were six of us on the School Board, and we all agreed on this idea.

We got ready and set aside some money, and we left for Washington with the president's idea in mind. We decided that bilingual education would be good for the children. Our language is something we couldn't give up. In Washington, we submitted a request. We waited and waited. We finally received word that our proposal had been approved. People signed it, and we headed back for home.

When we returned, we had a meeting with all of our relatives whose children attend Mesa Valley School. We told them about the meeting in Washington, and we told them about our plans for the school. We wanted Navajo thinking, planning, teaching, and procedures. We wanted the kids to know who they were, what the Navajo way was all about, and what kind of land they have.

Way in the future when those kids grew up, we wanted them to enter college, travel to many lands, live among various cultures, but always remember who they were and remember their people, their culture, their language, and their land. We wanted them to say, "I come from Mesa Valley. Those are my people, and that is my land. Let me go back and help out whoever I can with my knowledge, wisdom, and experience. It was good that I went to school. It was good that my leaders said those things to me."

This is what we wanted them to say, and that's how we wanted them to return. This is why we worked so hard to have a bilingual-bicultural school. Maybe none of the children's fathers, mothers, and grandparents know how to speak and read and write English, but we know about traditional ways of life, and we value the land, livestock, and Navajo philosophies. We wanted our children to know and respect all these things. We wanted them to know so they could be proud.

To some degree, the goals that we set forth have already been achieved. Look at it now. Our own children teach in and run the school. They used to be the little ones when the school was just started. But now, along with a group of good-hearted Anglos, they are in charge. We like it, and we are very thankful that things have turned out this way.

"What are your feelings now about teaching the children to read and write Navajo?"

It's good that our children are learning their own language. It's good that they are learning to read and write Navajo. I know it is useful. Let me tell you why.

I have a son. He used to attend Mesa Valley but graduated from [a nearby BIA boarding school]. He continued with his education and later attended university. He was at Mesa Valley when the school first went contract. He learned to read and write Navajo. He didn't have any trouble. He used to come and show me what he had learned, and I saw what he could do.

One day, we planned a Five Night ceremony. We asked a medicine man to come, and he arrived. The medicine man told us that there were many plants and herbs necessary for the ceremony. He told us that we could find most of the plants in the mountains. There were many medicines that he needed.

I asked my son if he would make a list of the necessary items. The medicine man went over again all of the herbs and plants. My son listed them. It was a long list. He divided them into different groups, according to where they grew. Finally, when he had written the last item, my son and I left to gather the herbs.

When we got to the mountains, I asked my son which medicines we needed and where we would find them. From the list he made, my son knew what we needed, and we got those things easily. At the same time, he was marking off each item we gathered. We got everything and came home. The medicine man then checked everything and told us nothing was missing. From then on, I believed that Navajo writing and reading was good. It was useful and helpful in certain situations.

There is more of that these days. More kids can read and write Navajo. There are plants around here that have many names. The kids know them. I pick some of the plants for my wife who works down at the school. I tell her the names of things and how they are used. I tell her to tell anyone who asks anything about them. It's good that the children know. It's good that they know about the plants and about their own language and how to read and write it.

Jeannie Joe

Jeannie Joe is Elmer Nakai's opposite, the daughter of a man who served on the School Board with the former Board president when all of the officials petitioned Washington for local control of the school. Married, the mother of four children, she struggles with GED classes to finish high school. She does not believe in native literacy instruction, perhaps because of her own difficulties with mainstream literacy. For this reason, she removed her children from the Mesa Valley program and enrolled them at a nearby boarding school that stresses the early acquisition of English. Her reasoning is a familiar one and makes sense in light of pervasive reservation joblessness and the need to read and write English to find work off the reservation "in town."

Her house consists of one room, a rectangular area 12 x 15 feet large, in which we conducted the following interview in English. "We got a few books, mostly old textbooks that the mission gave away," she says. "They're all stored away in the trailer." Navajo radio plays in the background all day long.

My father worked with the president of the School Board when Mesa Valley went contract. I remember how hard it was on people back then. Even though the Board eventually contracted with the BIA, there were different people on the Board who were against contracting. My father, he was against it. He was against having the school run by Navajos. Even though he was Navajo, he didn't think contracting would work. It wasn't a good idea. "The Anglos can teach better than Navajos can," he was thinking. "That's why it's important that they teach us." He went along with the other Board members to Washington only after a lot of pleading. He really didn't believe in the idea of community control.

"What do you think about the idea?"

The school runs pretty good now, but I think they teach too much Navajo literacy. I took my kids out of Mesa Valley because of that. One was in second grade last year. The other was in kindergarten. They were just learning to read Navajo. They weren't reading books. I want them to read good, to learn to read books real good. That's why they are going to [a contract-boarding school nearby]. When my kids first started over there, they were getting Cs and Ds. But that was only for the first grading period. Now, they're doing OK. They're getting As and Bs.

"Do you read Navajo?"

I don't read or write Navajo. I don't need to. This one time, though, I had a hard time [laughter]. My kids left a note for me in Navajo. I had gone to the trading post to get something. They were herding sheep, and they came back here when I was out. They left a note saying, "T'iisgóó deejéé'. Dibé éí díwózhiitahdi naakai." Then they signed their names. I got back to the house, and nobody was home. I tried to read the note, but I just couldn't! The note said they'd gone down to the big cottonwood tree with the sheep.

When they got back, they just laughed and laughed. I had left them a note a long time before that in English. They couldn't read that English note, so I teased them about it. Now, the kids wanted to get even with me. They really got after me. "Mommy, you know how to speak Navajo, but you can't read your own language. It's easy!" They really gave me a hard time.

It's OK to read Navajo, but I want my kids to be good at English. Me, I have a hard time with English. Sometimes I don't know what letters mean. My husband and I keep getting all these letters from the IRS, saying we owe money on taxes from 1979. I never know what to do with them. Sometimes, I just throw them away. If I keep getting new ones, I'll call up the number that they give. I'll explain as good as I can, but I know it's better to put it in writing.

Emmis Largo

Emmis Largo is Mesa Valley's chapter president. Until the early 1980s, he was the community's tribal council delegate. But in 1982, a much younger, more ambitious candidate narrowly defeated him, most residents say, because he cannot speak, read, and write English.

In the interview, translated from Navajo below, Emmis equates Navajo reading and writing with knowledge of traditional culture, which he deems essential to personal strength. Even though he has worked in tribal government for five decades, in which all reading and writing is in English, and has experienced increasing difficulty getting by without mainstream language and literacy skills, he believes the key to personal success involves Navajo language and culture, and he sees great utility in vernacular literacy as a means of fostering Navajos' self-awareness. He cautions his children, "Don't be like me," knowing only the Navajo way. "With the Navajo way alongside the Anglo way," he says, "Navajos will be strong throughout their lives."

I never went to school. My mother had only one child, me, and she did not have anyone else to help with our livestock. Helping with the cows, sheep, and horses was the only job I had growing up. I asked and asked to go to school, but there were not many schools back then. The old stone building at Mesa Valley wasn't even built yet. I was around when people were building it, but I was never able to attend school over there.

Back then, only traditional ways were taught. That's how I grew up. I didn't grow up like a king, as many kids grow up today. I was poor and needy. Most people were like that. They were survivors of poverty.

When I was old enough to work, I went around to different places. Because of World War II, many jobs became available. At these different jobs, I met many white men. I didn't understand their language, but I could ask other Navajos, "What is that man saying?" This way, I gained a little English. That's the English I use. I just know a limited amount. It's the same way with reading. My knowledge is spotty. I only know this and that.

While I was working at different jobs, I learned different things. I learned to measure and to count. But I have found out, if I don't use what I know, I forget. Only the things I have been exposed to and use daily are the things that stay with me. Nowadays, many things are done differently. Sometimes, I ask people at the chapter house, "It used to be done this way. Is it still the same?" I am never sure.

"How have you been able to get by without knowing how to read and write English?"

I have learned through my involvement with politics. I first got into politics in 1968. Then, I joined [the tribe's Legal Aid office] as a local representative. [It] was just starting out. The people chose me to be on a committee. When I first started, the people I worked with explained everything to me: the bylaws and other complicated matters like that. I asked around, too. Gradually, I got familiar with what they were doing. That's how I learned things and got started. In addition to being a chapter officer, I am still a [Legal Aid] representative today.

I still don't speak English well. I'm still getting familiar with it. The words escape me. That happens when you don't use it. You forget certain parts, and you ask yourself, "What does that mean?" It puzzles you. That's what happens. When someone is talking to me in English, I can understand certain parts, but only like it's all cut up.

Because I didn't have an education, I tell my kids, "Me, I didn't get schooling. The work I do today and the work I have done before have been difficult for me because I didn't know about papers or about the Anglo language. I cannot tell an Anglo exactly what I feel and what I think. I cannot ask him whatever I want to. It's hard for me. With a Navajo, I can talk face to face. It's not hard. It's comfortable. I just wish I could talk with Anglos the same way."

"What kind of education do you want for your children and grandchildren? What do you tell them?"

"Why don't you educate yourselves?" This is what I tell my children. They must not go to school only for me. They must get an education for themselves. They must do it for their own benefit and so their children can learn from what their parents know.

I tell my kids, "Knowing English is good, and so is knowing the Navajo language, culture, and values. Knowing Navajo is useful at home. Knowing about traditional practices is the only way you will live in harmony. You will be strong that way. With the Navajo language alongside the Anglo way, you will be strong throughout your lives. Don't be like me. That is no good."

Today, the [tribal president] says, "The Navajo language will be known, and English will also be known—by all of our children." I think this is good. Around here, if the children do not know the Navajo language and culture, they are not strong. When they go out into the Anglo world and return, they do not know how we do things anymore. They do not know how to do things for themselves. When their jobs with the Anglos run out, they do not know what to do back here to survive. It is hard for them. They leave the reservation and go far away. Although for some it is OK, for many others, things go wrong.

Forgetting your language is like forgetting your mother. You leave your mother behind, she gets old, and you can no longer recognize her when you return. That is what it is like.

Knowing the Navajo language and knowing how to write it is great. If you know, you will be aware. "This is how it is," you will say.

It is also important to know the traditional Navajo prayers. We were put on this earth with those prayers. But today, the old stories are dwindling. The prayers and practices of the Anglos are the ones that are rising. I hope that education can steer this trend.

Roy Begaye

Working alongside Emmis Largo, Roy Begaye is Mesa Valley's chapter vice president. Because he is one generation younger than Emmis and adept in English and Navajo, he represents the ex-councilman's theoretical opposite. Before entering ninth grade, he left the reservation to live with a Mormon family and attend high school in Utah. "That's where I learned to read and write well, but I really had a hard time readjusting when I came back home. For a long time, I was lost." Driving back from Window Rock, recording our interview on the road, having spent the day "shuffling papers," he tells me in English about the need to put chapter house work in writing.

"What does your job involve?" I ask.

Mostly it involves paperwork, something most people really don't appreciate. There's just a whole lot of it. When I was secretary, right after the meeting when I go home, I get out my report. I usually try to finish my report that same evening if it isn't too late. Get all the basic, general things that's been discussed. The main things. You get these outlined, put it on paper. Then the next morning, the receptionist at the chapter house types it up. That takes all day. Next day, I work on resolutions that needs to be drafted. When everything's ready, I take it all down to Window Rock.

If we have proposals to do, that takes a long time. Sometimes it takes a month. Then, the chapter officers meet. The [chapter's council delegate] usually writes the thing up. If we don't understand something, if we get stuck somewhere, if it's really complicated, then we go back to the department in Window Rock. We get a representative to help us. Then, we take the whole thing back to the community. That's where we do translation. Sometimes, though, the community won't believe what we are telling them. They'll request the representative to explain things to them.

When those guys come, some people at the chapter meetings will ask a lot of questions. They'll talk and talk and talk. Maybe one guy'll ask a question, make a suggestion, but first he starts introducing himself. Then he has to greet us all, every people. Then he has to talk about his past, about how he didn't know about the meeting at first. He'll tell what he was doing all day, where he was before the meeting. Takes a lot of time. He might get to the point when everybody begins to sit back.

Talking like that is in the Navajo tradition, but I have my own way. I just start talking where it needs to be talked about. I just start talking about specific things right away. It's just like starting the engine, warming it up, putting it into first gear, second gear, third gear, fourth gear. Then when it goes smooth, you have to get out the problem. To me, it's like that.

"For chapter officers, then, it's important to be able to speak Navajo."

Yeah, but talking isn't as important as reading and writing. Nowadays, you got to have it in black and white. Have records and files. Talk by itself doesn't work. This one time, one of our chapter officials went to Window Rock. He doesn't speak English or read and write it. I told him we should have the trip on record. Have it on paper. But he just took off and went over there anyway. He tried to get something done verbal. He didn't get it. Then I ended up writing papers for him. That's how it goes.

I would rather have all the chapter officials have a good education, more of it, too. People are thinking that. People want somebody in there that's educated, who can do paperwork without problems. That's how [the current council delegate] got in there.

"Is that how you got in there, too?"

I don't know how I got in there [laughter]. I used to work over at the school. Used to be an [reading tutor]. That time, they were having a chapter meeting. I was at the store. This little guy came over, told me that the community wanted me over there. I was puzzled. I was wondering what they were up to.

I went over to the chapter house. I guess some of the community nominated me for secretary-treasurer. I got all confused. All these people were looking at me. I didn't say anything. Finally, I said if they want help, it's OK by me. Everybody started hollering, clapping. Yeah, I was embarrassed. So I been trying to do a good job.

This one time, a tribal official was observing me. He told me I did 80% of the chapter president's job. At that time, the guy who was president wasn't educated. He didn't know how to read and write. He couldn't speak English. I had to do lot of translating for him, responding to letters. I went all over translating for him. That guy observing me saw all this. That's what he meant by "80%." For the chapter vice president, it was the same way. For the council delegate then, the guy from the tribe said I done 50% of his job. The achievement award they gave me, I think it was for all the interpretation, the letter writing I did. Those other guys just didn't know how to do paperwork.

Lorena Tso

Lorena Tso works and worships at the Mesa Valley Church. Having converted to Christianity, as a user of Navajo literacy, and as a teacher at the mission's school, she represents the theoretical opposite of the chapter vice president. Until she reached the age of 17, she never attended school, nor did she leave the Mesa Valley area. She grew up speaking only Navajo. As a young adult, she spent two years studying at Intermountain in Utah. At present, she takes GED classes to earn her high school diploma and teaches Navajo literacy at the mission school.

I teach Navajo literacy at the mission, and I do a lot of translating. I prepare lessons for the kids. Mostly, what I teach has something to do with the Bible. I also translate long letters we get from different places. The letters come from all over. They're testimonies. Some come from white people; some come from Navajos. We get lot of them from Bible students in Colorado. They write in English, and I translate them into Navajo. Mrs. Davis and I do the correction. Then we send them into Farmington where the testimonies are printed into those religious pamphlets.

I used to teach the ladies in the church. I taught them how to read Navajo. Some got it right away, but others had a real hard time. A few never got it. For those few, we would tell them to pray really hard. For me, it's easier to write in English. It doesn't take too much time, and it doesn't take too much paper. But with Navajo, just one word can be very long. Sometimes, it's hard to know where one word stops and another begins.

But I think it is really important to teach Navajo literacy. I want my people to learn to read and write their own language. If you are Christian, you always want others to learn how to read the Navajo Bible. That's why we all want the kids to learn to read Navajo. That way, they can really understand.

Annie Jones

Similar to the mission's teacher of Navajo literacy, Annie Jones is an active member of the mission congregation. She was one of the first individuals to become Christian in the Mesa Valley area. She differs from the teacher of Navajo literacy, however, in her inability to read and write the script. Since her conversion from traditional beliefs to Christianity, as she explains in Navajo, she has tried and tried to learn how to read Navajo. "She has never given up," the pastor's wife has said, "but at the same time, she has never gotten the hang of it." That she has struggled to acquire Navajo reading abilities, never reached her goal, but never gave up trying, positions her as a theoretical opposite of Lorena Tso.

She lives in a two-room house several hundred yards off the main highway. In the kitchen is a Navajo inscription from the Book of Mark. In the bedroom is a Navajo Bible. Otherwise, the house is furnished sparingly, and there is no other literacy.

Annie's daughter and three grandchildren live in an adjacent trailer. The grandchildren attend the community school, read and write Navajo, and occasionally help Annie to read chorally from the Navajo Bible. For this reason she is grateful for the school's native language program. In the house, Annie lives alone. Our interview transpires in Navajo with the interpretative help of Annie's daughter.

> In the past, the missionaries tried their best to teach me how to read Navajo. They put letters of the alphabet on cards so that I would be able to learn to read, but I just got confused. They showed me different cards with the different vowels on them. They told me to pray for myself. I was told that, through prayer, I would be able to understand the material. I only learned a little bit after I started memorizing everything. Going to church and listening to sermons helped me, too. Still, I get confused when they try to teach me by writing things down on paper.

> When I first expressed faith in God, I thought that all one must do is "believe." But I found out that there is more than just believing. At times, you may not believe in some of the things that the Bible says. You may not understand the material well enough. When this happens, other Christians explain things to you until you understand. They may help you act to know yourself.

> The first stage of being a Christian is like being a child. You start from the beginning. Just as a child is reminded constantly to understand the Word of God. There is so much that the Word, the Bible, teaches: self-realization, forgiveness, and prayer. I realized that prayer is the most important thing in the Christian faith. Whatever you want, you must pray for it. Also, when you give of yourself totally, you are truly saved. I didn't know this at first.

I didn't understand other things, also. I didn't understand grace and love. I didn't know what they meant. But I learned. I learned that you have to have a "beautiful home." Although I stay home alone, I learned that God is with me always. I pray, and through prayer, I ask for the things I want. Although it takes time, the Lord answers. Before I became a Christian, I didn't know how to pray, but now I understand what prayer can achieve.

I like the way they teach Navajo at the school. When I have trouble reading Navajo words, I ask my grandchildren. They read well, and they help me a great deal.

I have been learning for 40 years. I have a great desire to be able to read the Navajo Bible easily. I pray that I will someday. Many people who became Christians before and after I did can read the Bible in Navajo now. They read better than me. I still haven't gotten the hang of it, but I will keep trying.

Joseph Nez

Although Joseph Nez occasionally attends Sunday school and church services, he does not consider himself Christian. "I still have these faults," he says. "I do a lot of bad things, lot of bad thinking. I'm not Christian yet. I'm still learning." To this extent, he is an outsider to much of what goes on at the mission church, and he represents a theoretical opposite to Annie Jones. Here he describes how he began to convert to Christianity and how he tried to read the Bible and acquire Navajo reading skills. In the final analysis we hear from him about the politics of religious conversion and of the multiple ways that print weaves through that process. He speaks a great deal about the role of interpreters of the Bible. "A couple of [the Navajo lay preachers] preach pretty good," he says. "They all had the same problems. . . . I can relate to them." And indirectly, although not accepting the Christian faith himself, he speaks about ways that Christianity make sense in terms of the problems that drive people to embrace it.

Christians? Well, they have services on Sundays and prayer meetings on Thursdays, and generally, I guess, they help people turn from the Navajo traditions to Christianity. That's the way I feel about it. I hear everybody say that Christianity is the white man's religion. But it's not like that.

Mostly, the missionaries here are real good. They try to help people. Most of them have been around for 20 years. Everybody that lives here has at least got help some way from them. But some are against them. They don't want to help. I don't think they consider the mission as part of the community. That's why those guys are all by themselves over there. Like one time, we had a chapter meeting and passed a resolution saying we can help the mission with their parking problems, water and drainage problems, stuff like that. But nothing came of it. People just voted and forgot about it.

The mission helps people. Like medical help. They don't even charge much for medicine. Also, when somebody dies, they arrange the funeral. They do that because some of these old people, the traditional ones, they shy away from a dead person. Missionaries arrange all those things because the Navajo people are scared. They also help people by giving them clothing and food.

Still, it's hard to change your old ways and become a Christian. It's a hard thing. You got to change your old traditions. If you do, I heard you become a new person. You're born again. But that's hard for me to say. To be born again, you got to start a whole new life. You were born this one way, but you got to make a 90-degree turn. Forget about your old ways, try to become a new person.

Me, I was away from this community for a long time, but my home has always been here since I can remember. In my earlier years I spent most of my time in boarding school. Then I was in the service. In 1968, I came back to the reservation. So, I'm saying that I been around a little bit. I'm not traditional in my religion. But I'm not Christian yet either because I still have these faults I do, these sins. I have guilt.

For Christians, you got to read the Bible. That's just like being in contact with the Lord, through reading, through the Bible. You converse with God when you read the book. You talk with God directly. The Bible, they claim, it's all these stories written by Almighty God. When you read it, I guess you got to read it, but sometimes it's hard to understand. Some people have different interpretation of it, and my reading of it doesn't always come out right with me.

I'm not good at reading Navajo, so I read the Bible in English, but to tell the truth, I don't do much Bible reading anymore. I used to do it in the morning. My wife and kids would just read it. They have Bible passage that they're supposed to read and a related story that goes from day to day. They got them from Sunday School. Different passage from the Bible would be for each day. But I didn't do it. My wife, she does it. She reads. But I just leave in the morning, don't come home until late in the evening. I just go and hang around the store [laughter].

I tried and tried to read. My wife got the whole family involved. We had it going for about a week one time, but it just didn't work out. I guess it's just me. I don't particularly pay any attention to what the Bible is saying. I'd rather watch TV than read the Bible. My wife wants to do that, and because I don't, things get hard on her. She reads the Bible and makes us take turns, and there's all kinds of confusion. I think it's better just to have one person read it.

I used to carry those small Bibles. I'd read it through, sometimes just one page, sometimes whole chapters. I was really gung-ho for awhile. We went to prayer meetings, Sunday School, men's Bible study, all that. But I didn't want to go. I didn't really want to do it.

I'm not doubting the Bible; it's me. I'm still hanging on to my old lifestyle. I'm not going back to church. I rather hang around just here and there. Only reason I still go to church every now and then is because I'm taking my children.

A couple of those guys preach good. You know, [one of the lay preachers], he's real good. I pay lot of attention when he's talking. He explains lot of things I don't know myself. Even though he's still young, seems to me like he's been a Christian for a long time. I can't remember all the things he says so I try to write it down. I'll write notes to myself when he's preaching—about what this verse means or what that saying is all about. I can't say right off why he's good except that he knows how it felt to be low. Everything he says, I agree with because his experiences and mine are about the same. All those lay preachers, they all had the same problems. They talk about how they used to be, how they used to drink, how they almost got killed, all this. I relate to that.

Most of the time, though, those Christians, they'll say the same old thing. They'll talk about how they became a Christian. They say that a lot of times. Seems like they're still down there. They're not growing.

You know, some talk to you good and some don't. The good ones you can understand what they're talking about, but the others, some of them use low tones and just get you confused. They don't put themselves across clearly.

Each person has a different interpretation of the Bible passage, whatever that Bible passage might be. Each person has his own interpretation, and each one says this is how it is, this is what the passage really means. This one verse of the Bible, here's what it's talking about. I'm telling you. But then another person comes along, he has a different version. So it's different every time you hear it. It's different each time you hear somebody explaining it to you. In the end, I don't know which version is true, which interpretation is correct. I guess you just have to read it yourself to see how it goes.

I heard [the pastor] say this one time, the only way God can hear you, you got to become a born again Christian. But I disagree. The Bible says God's a loving God. He loves everybody, sinners and all. That's my feeling about it. I kind of disagree with the pastor. If He hears at all, I think He hears everybody.

Howard Benally

Howard Benally is a Roadman, a traditional medicine man, with the Native American Church, and the principal of Mesa Valley's secondary school.[9] As someone who reads and writes Navajo and is an important insider at the community school, he is a theoretical opposite to the relative outsider at the mission church. He mastered the ability to read and write Navajo in the 1970s in order to get a part-time job creating Navajo curriculum materials while attending graduate school. At present he uses the script at school to teach Navajo history and government. He also uses it to record traditional knowledge for his own heuristic purposes. Here he explains why Navajo literacy is worthwhile and how it could play an important role in maintaining traditional beliefs in the face of rapid cultural change across the Navajo Reservation.

> Navajo literacy is good. It should be very valuable to the Navajos. But people don't use it much. They just use it in churches and schools, seems to me. Even the oral language is not used by Navajos nowadays. Even with the council meetings in Window Rock, a lot of the communication happens in English. There is more and more competition between English and Navajo. Now, I think English is taking over. More and more, that's what's happening.
>
> People say it's hard to learn to read and write Navajo. I studied it for a long time but actually learned it in one week. This one person I know, she learned it in one day. I didn't believe her. I was trying and trying to read and write Navajo. So I asked her, "How did you do it?" She told me, "All you do is forget about English." Which is what I did.
>
> The thing was, I'd never really tried. All I was doing was learning. I'd take a test and get an "A", but I'd never used the writing. I didn't even care much for it. But then I got this job writing Navajo materials for schools. I was offered the job while studying at college. Everything had to be written in Navajo. "Can you write in Navajo?" they asked me. I said no. They gave me a two-week deadline, then I met this one lady. She got me going, and I really hit it.
>
> The main problem when you learn Navajo literacy is in the sounds. My problem was that I was using English vowels and consonants when I should have been using Navajo ones. How the English language is written and structured was conflicting with the Navajo, too. So, one whole week I never read anything in English. I concentrated on written Navajo. After that, I had no problem. I could go back and forth.
>
> Most Navajos don't read and write Navajo, but there are different ways

---

[9]Aberle describes a Roadman as "a leader of peyote ritual" (1966, p. 408). See Appendix E of the same volume for a discussion of leadership within the Native American Church.

that different people are using the literacy. Me, I have used it for recording history. Mostly legends, mostly for myself. I don't know if you could call it diary writing or journal writing, but that's kind of what it is. I use Navajo to remember something. It gives me a record. It's just like a tape recorder. I record a certain person's philosophy. When I can't remember exactly what this person said, I look into my notes. Then, I use that philosophy or theory or whatever you want to call it to give my speech or perform whatever I want to do. Maybe I want to give a prayer. I write it down first. If somebody asks me to pray for him, I look into my notes and see, oh yeah, this is how it is said. Then, I remember, and I perform the prayer.

I also write documentary histories. I might ask a Navajo person about the history of the Navajos. It is pretty hard to translate his ideas into English and then retranslate it back into Navajo, so I record exactly the way the older person says it, just the way he tells me.

I listen. I have the patience not to challenge this individual. I listen and agree and try to follow what the individual is talking about. Until you really understand what he is talking about, you got to hold off with specific questions. When you listen, as you go along, you'll develop certain questions. Your questions start developing. Later, much later, you can ask, "What do you mean here? What did you mean there?" My learning with Navajos is like that. Listen. Don't ask questions. Have patience.

One of the things I always say is that I have all night to learn, all the rest of my life. It doesn't matter if it takes me a long, long time to follow this guy's speech. Until I thoroughly understand, I won't ask anything. If you do, if you immediately ask him a question, you chop him off. He'll turn and go away. If you want to learn from Navajo philosophers, you must have patience and listening skills. You have to develop trust. When you ask right away, you challenge that person. "OK," he'll say, "you win." And you'll learn nothing.

So I listen before I write. And I think carefully before I read and speak it back.

I use Navajo literacy to learn songs. I pay a medicine man to record them for me. Then, I transcribe the songs from the tape. With the songs written like that, I can memorize them pretty easy.

I got different songbooks for different ceremonies. One's for Windway ceremonies, another's for Squaw Dances, and there are others. And for each song, there are different prayers. The songs themselves are color-coded: black, blue, white, and yellow. These colors are the four holy colors and they indicate the colors and holy people that certain verses of the songs refer to.

     His Windway songbook is a leather-bound journal, half-filled with 21 pages of song and prayer transcriptions. A set of songs includes four basic units and a number of variations. He has organized the units so that specific elements line up beneath a basic pattern, in the same way that substitution items line up beneath a phrase in dialogue memorization exercises. He has indicated different songs with underlined headings. Everything is in Navajo.

> I write other things in Navajo, too. I write lesson plans in Navajo. I teach Navajo economics, and I write in Navajo for that. I write the tests in Navajo. I have some relatives that read and write in Navajo, and we write notes sometimes to each other. We don't do it all the time, just sometimes. One of the older guys learned to read during World War II. He was never a Christian. He just learned by practicing on his own.

> From the Anglo point of view, teaching Navajo literacy is a transition to English, but from a Navajo point of view, the most important thing Navajo reading and writing does is help keep the culture. The world does not only hold the English language. There's all kinds of languages. Each one is not just a language. It is part of the identity of a certain social group. For us, it's the same way. Navajo language is the basis of Navajo-ness. It plays a big part in a Navajo's feeling proud of himself.

> I know English is important, but if we forget about our language and only speak English and live in a dominant society, then we have melted into a melting pot. Culture and identity go together. They are both important to me. They are both things I will never give up.

> We have already given up a lot of things. We gave up many cultural practices, gave up some of the language, and some of the religion. But to me, there are some Navajos still strong, still holding on.

> My way of thinking, maybe 20 or 30 years down the road, hardly anyone will be able to speak Navajo. Everyone will be speaking English. By then, somebody will document the written language. Maybe people will begin to study it again. Literacy will then become a way of preserving the language. People will document the writing and study ways that people used to use it. Later still, Navajo literacy may be used as a history. People will use it to learn how Navajos used to live. One thing you can be sure of. You and me will never see it used like that. Reading and writing Navajo and studying history like that is a long ways off.

Ruth Begay

Ruth Begay is a senior at Mesa Valley School. In the secondary school's bilingual newspaper, she relates her views about Navajo literacy instruction. In contrast to her principal she finds written Navajo of no utility "because students need to develop good English skills for their careers," as the following describes.

Because our first language is Navajo, a few students have trouble writing in English. Because English skills are important to the students' careers, students should spend a lot of time studying English, not Navajo, in high school. Classes which require Navajo reading and writing should be a choice, not a required class, in high school.

The Navajo culture and the Navajo writing system reinforce the language spoken at home. The basics of reading and writing Navajo should be required from elementary through junior high because students learn about their heritage, which promotes pride in their cultural background.

On the other hand, Navajo literacy classes shouldn't be required in high school because students need to spend time developing good English skills for their careers. Students are more likely to get jobs off the reservation than on because there are more jobs off the reservation. Jobs off the reservation make very little use of Navajo literacy skills.

Many graduates will prepare for their careers at a college. To do well in college students must be able to read and write English well. A lot of jobs off the reservation will require English reading and writing skills; for example, if a student wants to be a business administrator the student should have good English writing skills. Business administrators do a lot of writing. They write reports for their bosses, memos to their employees, letters to other firms, and explanations of their department's budget. People need good English skills to be in positions such as this.

Only a few jobs on the reservation require Navajo literacy skills. Students who want to use their Navajo literacy skills in a job may want to be bilingual curriculum writers, bilingual teachers, or bilingual administrators. These jobs require more than the basics in Navajo literacy. Navajo literacy should be offered as an elective for those who are interested in developing their Navajo literacy skills. These students can get proficiency in the elective class. But otherwise, high school students should not be required to take Navajo literacy classes.

Jimmie Tsosie

Jimmie Tsosie is the translator for the community school's largely monolingual school board, and thus a key player when decisions are made at school board meetings. In terms of gender and status at the school, he is a theoretical opposite of the high school senior. What he describes is decision-making powers that accrue to individuals who can translate oral Navajo to written English. These abilities are key not only in communicating decisions that the school board makes, but also in shaping the decisions in multiple ways for multiple purposes that sometimes go beyond the school board's original intent. From written notes that Jimmie takes at school board meetings, the individual who runs them—often Alan Glass—produces a polished draft of meeting minutes, which a secretary types and disseminates in abstract form. The notes and the drafts of the abstracts are in English, although, he explains, "it would be good if they were in Navajo."

> School Board meetings, you know, they're supposed to start right at 10 o'clock, but people take their time and all that. We don't really get going until 10:30, sometimes close to 11. What's on the agenda is what the Board discusses. Some of the things go real fast, like internal requests. But other things take a long time, requests from outside the school. The longest thing is when there's an interview with a parent about a kid who's having problems. That takes up a whole day sometimes.
>
> I translate, right, but a lot of times I don't know why they need me. Three Board members went to school and speak English. They read and write. The other three don't read or write or speak English, but the guys who do could translate just as easy as me. I feel like telling them, "Look, you went to school. Why don't you just say in English what you think instead of me having to try to get it right. I might not say what you think. You do it. Tell it right."
>
> I translate all the written stuff, but sometimes I can't find the right word in Navajo to get across something in English. Words like "policy, regulation, bylaw." What are they in Navajo! Translating everything from English into Navajo takes a lot of time. When you look at the written agenda, seems like we should only take 30 minutes. But all that written paperwork has to get said. Board members talk and talk and talk about this and that, see. And if I'm translating what they say into English, I sit there, not writing down everything word for word, but listening, taking notes in English, waiting for them to come to the main point. I just wait for those few words to come out. Then I write them down.
>
> It gets frustrating, boring. When the older members start talking, the uneducated ones, they talk about old stuff. They don't get right to the point. Sometimes, they'll tell the whole dang history of Mesa Valley. You might be sitting there, wanting a job, getting interviewed. Normally in an interview, you know, they want to know where you're from, where you worked, all that stuff.
>
> But the Board members who don't speak English, they don't come right out and ask the usual questions. "This is our place," they say. "We been here. We got sheep, cattle, horses. I got a wagon that's so many years old. The weather is like this. We live way over there, away from nobody. It's about 16 miles from there to town." That kind of beating around and around and around. Meanwhile, you're just sitting there, and I got to translate everything. But why you got to hear it?

All that talk. It's just repeating yourself. Over and over and over. I guess it's just like that with older Navajos that didn't go to school, but it's different for those that are educated. They don't repeat themselves when they're talking. It's those who never went to school that repeat themselves before they get to what they want to say.

The Board members don't write because they don't need to. All they ever write is their names to sign the sheet saying that they are here. Then, they get paid. Otherwise, they just draw. You can walk around and see what they draw: designs, horses, things like that.

The ones that can't read and write, they'll pretend. Somebody'll bring in a newspaper. "Let me see that," one'll say. He'll look at it, but he don't know what it says. He'll be studying it real close, though. I'll look at it and say, "Oh, this is what happened." It's the same way for other things: interview papers, for instance, or applicant files. "What about this experience you got here," one of the members will ask, pointing to the guy's application. He can't read it, but he pretends like he does.

All kinds of written stuff comes to the Board. It's all in English. Internal requests come from inside the school. Then, there's contracts, grants, budgets, financial reports, and revisions. We also get a lot of letters from other schools, from people who say they want to visit us. More letters come from senators, congressman, and lawyers.

Almost all the reading and writing that happens in the meetings is in English, but there's been a couple of times that a request or a letter has been written in Navajo. One time, one of the Navajo elementary teachers submitted a request all written out in Navajo. It had something to do with a field trip to publish some kind of book. We had a hard time reading the request, but one of the Board members is a Christian and was able to understand. That person read it for all of us. It was pretty interesting. Everybody was looking at it—everybody, all the people who can read and all the ones who can't. That request drew everybody's attention, all right.

This other time, a teacher who'd been taking summer classes in Flagstaff wrote the Board a letter in Navajo. I can't remember what it was about. Those are the only two times I know that people have written to the Board in Navajo.

Alan Glass, you know, he doesn't like speaking Navajo, but he can read and write it. When he runs the meetings, somebody'll say something in Navajo. Maybe that person is applying for a job. Alan'll write down what the guy says. He'll take notes like that for his own information. It ain't for me or for the minutes. It's just for himself. [Another administrator who runs the meetings, a Navajo], he writes something in Navajo every now and then, too. One of the Board members will ask a guy, "What's your clan?" The guy'll say, "'Ashííhi." I see him writing down "'Ashííhi." But nothing more than that.

Me, I can't read Navajo. I sound it out, but it takes a long time. If I knew how to read Navajo, I think it would be easier for things to come through the Board. It'd be better to have everything written in Navajo instead of English so they wouldn't need all that translating. Everything would be much faster. If a request were written in Navajo, you could just take it up. It'd be good that way.

Thomas Rush

"The only community that reads and writes Navajo," Thomas Rush says, "is Mesa Valley." He is 27 years old, a member of an Indian tribe from the northwest United States, and the managing editor of the Navajo Tribe's English-language newspaper. Because he is an important political player, but at the tribal level from outside Mesa Valley, he represents a theoretical opposite to the school board's translator. In the interview he describes the imminent threat of Navajo language loss and reasons why his newspaper does not print in Navajo.

If people don't read or write a language, then the danger of language loss is real. That's what happened where I am from on one of the reservations up north. When I was growing up, anyone over the age of 21 used to speak our language. Nobody read or wrote it, but everyone spoke it. No one speaks it now, though, only a few old timers. Here in Window Rock, I see the same thing happening.

This new radio station that the tribe is building, it could really make a difference. It'll be 50,000 watts, clear channel. You'll be able to hear it all over the western United States. If people give it a chance, listen to it, the Navajo language may survive. It might stick around. But otherwise, language loss could happen really, really quick.

We have five reporters here. All of them are Navajo, but only one speaks well enough to converse fluently. None of them read or write Navajo. They never learned it at school, and they have never had to learn it or use it elsewhere.

Seems like the only place people read and write Navajo is with a few church groups, and the only community that uses Navajo literacy is Mesa Valley. No other community does anywhere on the reservation. There's no need to. Outside of church-related materials, there isn't that much to read, anyhow.

One of the biggest problems with Navajo literacy is the spelling. It's so darned hard to spell something "right." With all the diacritics, there is plenty of room for disagreement even among people who supposedly know the written language. Last Christmas, we had a staff party here at the office. We tried to hang up a sign in Navajo saying "Yá'át'ééh Késhmish," you know, "Merry Christmas." We spent half the afternoon arguing over the correct spelling. There were four different versions. We never did decide how the sign should go.

Amos Bahe

Amos Bahe has translated several books of the New Testament and as a teacher and school administrator has worked with Mesa Valley's bilingual program since its inception. In addition, he is a lay preacher at the mission. "He's the best writer of Navajo we have," the pastor's wife said about Amos. "In fact, he's one of the best there is." Although he is recognized as one of the community's best writers of vernacular literacy, he finds limited use for the script. "Why teach [academic] concepts like 'social stratification' in Navajo?" he asks. "Navajo children," he says, will be judged on their abilities to read and write English.

He also finds prevailing notions of "self-determination," "community-control," and "local-autonomy"—ideas used to describe the school—to be illusionary. "It was one person's theory and conviction to start the bilingual program, and this one person," he says, referring to Alan Glass, "still runs the school."

> When I first learned to read and write Navajo, I was working in the school kitchen. When the school first went contract, most of the BIA teachers quit, and they needed people who can learn to read and write Navajo overnight. They were desperate for trained people. That's when they pulled me out of the kitchen, and I started to work with people that were teaching Navajo literacy. I took composition classes at Navajo Community College, and I began to work with students.

> Since that time, I have used Navajo to study the Bible. I have translated several books of the New Testament, too. All along, I wanted to study the Bible, but time is what I have never had. I was always just waiting for something to happen. Then, all of a sudden, a person from Albuquerque came up here and said, "Would you like to work for us this summer?" I didn't know what it was. "We want to have the Book of Mark translated into modern conversational Navajo." I said I could, as long as I had enough to feed my family. "Don't worry about that," he says. That's how I started translating. Along the way, I have learned to really use written Navajo without relying on English or other languages.

> Now, I use my Bible to check myself. It is the direction I should take. I read the Old Testament, the New Testament, and small pamphlets people put out. I cross-check to see how different people interpret. I use commentary, and I ask Pastor Davis and other pastors from other denominations, too, about their ideas. They all seem to agree on the main emphasis of the Bible. Take the Lord Jesus Christ as your personal savior. The Kingdom of God should rule each person's heart, and we should go according to the teachings of the Bible.

> I do reading and translating for personal meaning—to learn and to study the Bible. I found out that translating in particular, using the translators guide, gives out more thorough information than just

reading the Bible, just interpreting it on your own. And in this way, reading and writing in Navajo is good. But, I see classes at school where students would do better if they would go halfway or most of the way in English rather than trying to learn in Navajo. That's why I have doubts about teaching Navajo literacy.

When the school first went contract and first developed the bilingual program, we were saying that our children are Navajo dominant and that, if we turned them completely to English, we would be asking them to learn a new language and new concepts all at the same time. We said that we can help the kids by using the language they already know. That way, they can grow in their cognitive development. Later, they will progress faster in English. They will be able to understand more if they already have the basic concepts.

But when the kids get to a certain grade level, somewhere around ninth or tenth grade, that's when the Navajo language begins to hold them back. Instead of progressing, kids got to figure out the meaning of difficult English words. Take sociology, [taught as Navajo Sociology in Mesa Valley's tenth grade]. What is "social stratification" in Navajo? What do you call "personality trait"? When you insist on teaching these concepts in Navajo, the language begins to hold them back. That's why I have some doubts about it.

With my experience in translating, I can understand Navajo literacy if there is a need for it. On my part, I want to be very sure that I am getting a message across. I want to get this message from English into Navajo so it can be understood without any loss of the true meaning. I think about the material I transcribe as something others need to have. I want to get that idea across.

Transcription is a good way to learn Navajo reading and writing. It forces you to really understand the language. But if a student has the job of transcribing and nothing else, there is no meaning. You got to ask first, where is the need? I see it like that.

At church, Navajo reading and writing is necessary because some people who didn't go to school and get a formal education, who don't speak English, they can still read. My mother can. My aunts, grandmother, and cousins can all read in Navajo even though they can't read in English. With church, that need and importance of using written Navajo is there.

But for students, I can't say whether they will need it, other than for just maintaining their identity so they can say they speak the Navajo language. Children can spend a lot of time doing literacy activities. What they learn can carry across to English. But somewhere along the line, Navajo becomes a hindrance. When they go to Farmington, Flagstaff, and other places off the reservation, all talk is in English. All reading and writing is in English.

It's probably true that Navajo reading and writing is important for the survival of the oral language, but real maintenance must come from the group that wants it. It must be devised by that group. And the people should run it. Outside people can force things on the group, but if there's no need, then you can't force anyone to do anything.

There was a guy who said, "Education is a battlefield. The opposing forces are teachers, parents, and school boards on one side and the administrators on the other, with the children caught in the middle." That's true. All the parents do is elect Board members. And Board members, all they do is agree to what comes before them. They can't say one way or another about things. Something like Navajo literacy comes along and sounds good. "OK, no objections," they say. "We go along with you."

But you know, it was one person's idea to start the bilingual program at Mesa Valley. One person. And he still runs the school. Just one guy. Because he so strongly believed in bilingual education and believed that he couldn't create a bilingual program under the BIA, he told the Board to move away from Washington. Otherwise, the BIA would still control us. He is the reason why Mesa Valley went contract. "If we can take care of the BIA problem," he was thinking, "then the theories about bilingual education and Navajo literacy can be put into practice." He is the only reason the program got started. I'm pretty certain because I was around. I was a part of it. It was this one person's strong intuition, or whatever you want to call it, to get rid of the opposing forces so we could do the program on our own.

But there's been real few people who have really gone along. Most don't say, "Mesa Valley School." They call it "this person's" school. They even say our school buses are "this person's" buses going down the road. People know this, but they don't say it because there's no way that they can come out on top. But that is how Navajo reading and writing and the whole bilingual program got started. It was one person's theory and conviction. "Test out my theory," he said. "We'll keep testing it as we go along." Deleting, adding certain things, we have been going like that for some time.

But most of the people here, they'd say, "We already speak Navajo. We already think Navajo. Now we want our children to learn English so they can find jobs." That's all they can say. When somebody comes along and says, "Teaching and learning isn't all necessary in English," well, that's true to some extent. Sure, we can learn in Navajo or Chinese or Russian or whatever. But there are real shortcomings. What we learn may not be of any use. And if it isn't, what's the point of learning it?

VOICE IN THEORY AND PRACTICE

In this chapter we have heard Mesa Valley people speak about uses for Navajo literacy. The former School Board president uses lists to organize the gathering of medicine for Navajo ceremonies. Mesa Valley's secondary principal uses a journal to record traditional knowledge and songs. These uses are in addition to testimonies and Bible reading promoted by the church, newspaper reading and homework promoted by the school, and letters and notes that individuals write on their own. At the same time, we have heard contradictory arguments for and against the use of written Navajo. The ex-School Board president finds Navajo script useful, but the daughter of one of his fellow Board members does not. The ex-councilman believes in Navajo literacy instruction, but his younger colleague, the chapter vice president, does not. The secondary principal uses Navajo print for heuristic purposes unconnected to school life and deems it important to the survival of Navajo language and culture, but one of his secondary students does not. The contradictions are summed up by the mission's translator of religious texts. Recognized throughout the community as an accomplished practitioner of Navajo literacy skills, this individual finds Navajo script of limited value and believes the school, especially at the secondary level, should stress the acquisition of mainstream literacy.

Thus, beliefs for and against using vernacular literacy mark how Mesa Valley inhabitants view literacy. Individuals who find Navajo script useful voice strands of several arguments: Navajo literacy helps people know more about traditional Navajo culture; it promotes self-understanding; it helps people comprehend Christian truths; and it is good for teaching young children initial reading, writing, and mathematics. People who find the script of no use argue that Mesa Valley people need to read and write English, not Navajo, in order to find work, and that few nonreligious reading materials exist in the vernacular.

All of these beliefs exist in circular relation with practices and ideologies that characterize what goes on at the local church and school. At the church, Christian dogma surrounds and supports practices, whereby individuals, through intensive reflection, analyze how the printed word applies to real-life circumstances. At the school, much talk about local control and self-affirmation surrounds and supports pedagogy, whereby students prepare for the world of higher education and the world of work. Churchgoers celebrate Christian knowledge, whereas community school students celebrate knowledge of Navajo language and traditional culture, and to the extent that the two sets of doctrine differ, the two groups approach the meanings of vernacular texts in quite different ways. Both the church and the school configurations are alike, however, in that each exists as a powerful tool of self-awareness, and each directs the individual to translate ideology into practice. One important way for students and churchgoers to act is to read and write Navajo for indigenous purposes in settings unconnected to church and school domains and for reasons identified by individuals such as Emmis Largo, the chapter president; Lorena Tso, the Navajo literacy teacher; Annie Jones, the elderly student of Navajo script; Howard Benally, the Roadman and school principal; and Bernice Benally, in the opening vignette of this chapter, as "useful," "crucial to the survival of Navajo language and culture," "important for Navajos' self-esteem and self-awareness," and "being for the Navajos."

The point here is not so much to rethink the sociolinguistics of Navajo language and literacy, although this aspect of the research has not been insignificant. The point is to recognize that literacy is fundamentally a social phenomenon. It is not autonomous from social structure. Rather, the forms, functions, and meanings of print are framed by local institutions and ideologies in substantive ways, as the interviews with Mesa Valley residents reveal. We hear and see these framing processes through an understanding of voice.

Viewing literacy through voice, the analysis of print in any community must document the kinds of interaction and account for the web of personalities, biographies, attitudes, and events that underpin uses for language. Then, at a broader level, it must connect to the social system that specifies certain kinds of communicative tasks for particular kinds of purposes. To account for the twin processes requires an understanding of the community constraints that organize a constellation of beliefs and behaviors made manifest through voice—in what people believe, say, and do.

If voice is significant as a descriptive lens, it is also important in a prescriptive sense. In place of "banking" instruction that emphasizes the accurate transmission of presequenced, contextually disembedded knowledge, teachers need to apply dialogical, advocacy-oriented strategies that adhere to a body of overlapping educational theories. Central is the idea that concept formation happens twice: first as an intersubjective process between individuals, then as an intrapsychological process that characterizes the development of inner speech. Psycholinguistic principles of initial reading instruction follow, as do emphases on expressive writing across the K-12 curriculum. The development of advanced literacy and language skills may then proceed as a function of the individual's careful scrutiny of dominant truths and power relations in society. The task is one of establishing dialogue. In so doing, teachers serve to give voice. Instructional strategies that do this are diverse, but a basic purpose remains. The goal is to problematize student and teacher roles and to position political realities, inevitably charged where colonized minorities come together with colonizing forms of power and legitimacy, as starting places for classroom teaching and curriculum development.[10]

As the establishment of voice is important for pedagogy, so it is with research. In opposition to objective models of knowledge, ones that allow an educational researcher, in the name of scientific objectivity, to enter the field, collect data, and return to the safety and distance of the writing desk in the pursuit of publications and career advancement with little commitment to transformative social action, is the fundamental need for helping people solve problems.[11] That research should solve problems dictates a relationship between theory and data. The two must be grounded. The relationship between them must illuminate the lived experiences of the researched and must be illuminated by their struggles. In this way, research represents a fundamentally dialogical process of meaning building. It represents the naming of lives, the rendering of voice. Voice informs theory which in turn positions the researcher and the researched to scrutinize and change, rather than merely serve the wider social order.

CONCLUSION

In this chapter, I sought to explicate a dialogical understanding of literacy. We looked at the case of Navajo print. I tried to show how concepts such as language function, domain, and attitude by themselves are inadequate for describing English and Navajo literacy. The need is to understand print and how individuals view its use as sets of concepts and practices that operate within a cultural context. Rather than view culture a politically, we have seen culture in terms of the individual's interactions with dominant truths and power relations in society. Insofar as literacy is concerned, the need is to examine communicative functions in relation to institutions and literacy-related beliefs in relation to ideology. The need is

[10]For a critique of "banking" pedagogy and an analysis of an opposite dialogical stance, see Freire (1968, 1970a, 1970b). In contrast to "banking" approaches are dialogical notions of teaching and learning that stem primarily from the notion that concept formation happens twice: first between people, then intrapsychologically inside the head of the individual learner (Vygotsky, 1962, 1978). Goodman (1986) summarizes the psycholinguistic principles of initial literacy instruction, and Clay (1979, 1981) and Graves (1983, 1988a, 1988b) summarize the linkages between dialogical pedagogy and writing instruction across the K-12 curriculum. See McLaughlin (1989b, 1991) for detailed analyses of dialogically oriented literacy program development at Mesa Valley School.

[11]See Reinharz (1979), Lather (1986), and Gitlin (1990) for a critique of supposedly "objective" research practices and for analyses of openly ideological research measures that give voice.

fundamentally to understand voice. As I have attempted to show, the full meanings of literacy derive from individuals' struggles for voice within politically charged contexts in which forms, functions, and beliefs about oral and written communication are embedded.

REFERENCES

Aberle, D. (1966). *The peyote religion among the Navaho.* Chicago: Aldine Press.
Agar, M. (1980). *The professional stranger.* New York: Academic Press.
Apple, M.W. (1982). *Education and power: Reproduction and contradiction in education.* New York: Routledge.
Apple, M.W. (1987). *Teachers and texts: A political economy of class and gender relations in education.* New York: Routledge.
Apple, M.W. (1990). *Ideology and curriculum* (2nd ed.). New York: Routledge.
Aronowitz, S., & Giroux, H.A. (1985). *Education under siege: The conservative, liberal, and radical debate over schooling.* North Hadley, MA: Bergin & Garvey Publishers, Inc.
Clay, M. (1979). *Reading: The patterning of complex behaviour.* Portsmouth, NH: Heinemann Educational Books.
Clay, M. (1981). *What did I write?* Portsmouth, NH: Heinemann Educational Books.
Cook-Gumpertz, J. (1986). *The social construction of literacy.* Cambridge: Cambridge University Press.
Cummins, J. (1986). Empowering minority students: A framework for intervention. *Harvard Educational Review, 56*(1), 18-36.
Foucault, M. (1980). *Power/knowledge: Selected interviews and other writings* (C. Gordan, Ed.) New York: Pantheon Books.
Freire, P. (1968). *Pedagogy of the oppressed.* New York: Continuum Books.
Freire, P. (1970a). The adult literacy process as cultural action for freedom. *Harvard Educational Review, 40*(2), 205-225
Freire, P. (1970b). Cultural action and conscientization. *Harvard Educational Review, 40*(3), 452-477
Freire, P., & Macedo, D. (1987). *Literacy: Reading the word and the world.* South Hadley, MA: Bergin & Garvey.
Giroux, H.A. & McLaren, P. (1986). Teacher education and the politics of engagement: The case for democratic schooling. *Harvard Educational Review, 56*(3), 213-238.
Gitlin, A. (1990). Educative research, voice, and school change. *Harvard Educational Review, 60*(4), 443-466.
Goodman, K. (1986). *What's whole in whole language?* Portsmouth, NH: Heinemann Educational Books.

Graves, D. (1983). *Writing: Teachers and children at work*. Portsmouth, NH: Heinemann Educational Books, Inc.

Graves, D. (1988a). *Experiment with fiction*. Portsmouth, NH: Heinemann Educational Books, Inc.

Graves, D. (1988b). *Investigate nonfiction*. Portsmouth, NH: Heinemann Educational Books, Inc.

Heath, S.B. (1983). *Ways with words*. New York: Cambridge University Press.

Holm, W. (1971). *Some aspects of Navajo orthography*. Unpublished doctoral dissertation, University of New Mexico.

Lather, P. (1986). Research as praxis. *Harvard Educational Review, 56*(3), 257-277.

Leap, W. (1993). *American Indian English*. Salt Lake City: University of Utah Press.

McDermott, R. (1987). Achieving school failure: An anthropological approach to literacy and social stratification. In G. Spindler (Ed.), *Education and Cultural Process: Anthropological Approaches* (2nd ed., pp. 173-209). New York: Holt, Rinehart, and Winston.

McLaren, P. (1988). Culture or canon? Critical pedagogy and the politics of literacy. *Harvard Educational Review, 58*(2), 213-234.

McLaughlin, D. (1989a). The sociolinguistics of Navajo literacy. *Anthropology & Education Quarterly, 20*(4), 275-290.

McLaughlin, D. (1989b). Power and the politics of knowledge: Transformative leadership and curriculum development for minority language learners. *Peabody Journal of Education, 66*(3), 41-60.

McLaughlin, D. (1991). Curriculum for cultural politics: Language program development in a navajo setting. In C.D. Martin & R. Blomeyer (Eds.), *Case Studies in Computer Assisted Instruction* (pp. 151-164). London: Falmer Press.

McLaughlin, D. (1992). *When literacy empowers: Navajo language in print*. Albuquerque, NM: University of New Mexico Press.

Ogbu, J. (1987). Opportunity structure, cultural boundaries, and literacy. In J. Langer (Ed.), *Language, Literacy, and Culture: Issues of Schooling and Society* (pp. 149-177). Norwood, NJ: Ablex Publishing.

Reinharz, S. (1979). *On becoming a social scientist*. San Francisco: Jossey-Bass.

Reyhner, J., & Eder, J. (1989). *History of Indian education*. Billings, MT: Eastern Montana College Press.

Scribner, S., & Cole, M. (1981). *The psychology of literacy*. Cambridge, MA: Harvard University Press.

Spolsky, B., & Boomer, L. (1979, April 29-May 1). *The modernization of navajo*. Paper presented at the Conference on Language Planning in North America, William Paterson College, Paterson, NJ.

Spolsky, B., & Irvine, P. (1982). Sociolinguistic aspects of the acceptance of literacy in the vernacular. In F. Barkin, E. Brandt, & J. Ornstein-Galicia (Eds.), *Bilingualism and Language Contact: Spanish, English, and Native American Languages*, (pp. 73-79). New York: Teachers College Press.

Street, B. (1984). *Literacy in theory and practice.* Cambridge: Cambridge University Press.

Szasz, M. (1974). *Education and the American Indian.* Albuquerque, NM: University of New Mexico Press.

Thompson, H. (1975). *The Navajos' long walk for education: Diné Nizaagóó Iiná Bíhoo'aah Yíkanaaskai.* Tsaile, AZ: Navajo Community College Press.

Vygotsky, L. (1962). *Thought and language.* Cambridge, MA: MIT Press.

Vygotsky, L. (1978). *Mind in society.* Cambridge, MA: Harvard University Press.

Young, R.W. (1977). A history of written Navajo. In J. Fishman (Ed.), *Advances in the creation and revision of writing systems*, (pp. 459-470). The Hague: Mouton Press.

4

Reading Rites and Sports: Motivation for Adaptive Literacy of Young African-American Males

Jabari Mahiri
University of California at Berkeley

INTRODUCTION

In *The Right to Literacy* (1990), a work that grew out of the Modern Language Association's "Right to Literacy Conference," editors Lunsford, Moglen, and Slevin identified nine sets of questions raised by essays in the book that were central to the on-going national debate on literacy. This chapter addresses one set of those questions: "Are there literacies we do not see: What alternative varieties exist in communities, schools, and workplaces, and how are these being supported or discouraged" (p. 4): These editors further noted that the word "empowerment" was one of the key terms that emerged through repetition in the titles and arguments of the essays in the volume. The issue of empowerment is also important to this chapter's focus.

The findings of this chapter are based on research conducted on the literacy practices of 10-12-year-old-African-American males revealed during their participation in the Youth Basketball Association (YBA) program of a neighborhood-based organization (NBO), the South side YMCA in Chicago. The data were collected for two and a half years using ethnographic methodology (Hymes, 1974; Labov, 1973; Milroy, 1987;

Saville-Troike, 1989; Spradley, 1979a, 1979b). This researcher volunteered as one of the assistant coaches for two YBA teams (one each year). The informants were the team members, their coaches and parents, and the volunteers and administrators of the YBA program. Three players who reflected a pervasive profile in the YBA by coming from single-parent, female-headed households were selected for more intensive observations that went outside the NBO and into these players' homes.

The initial findings were presented in an earlier article on discourse in sports which discussed several unique language and literacy features associated with the participation of these preadolescents in the YBA program. It showed that these children demonstrated proficiency in *black language styles* that were complex in structure and highly performative. It also showed that these youths in this out-of-school setting revealed significant competence and high motivation in a variety of literacy practices. It concluded that "basketball has such high motivational value that it inspires [these] young boys to engage in a number of collateral activities, some of which have strong implications or consequences for literacy" (Mahiri, 1991, p. 312).

This chapter further substantiates this conclusion by focusing more intensively on the wide array of literacy practices taking place in this sports setting. Identification and description of these literacy practices indicates some of the "literacies we do not see." Analysis of several distinctive literacy practices tied directly to *sports discourse* indicates some of the "alternative varieties [that] exist in communities." Discussion of the goals and structure of the YBA program and the roles of its "conscious" volunteers indicates some of the ways these literacy practices are being encouraged and supported. Youths in the YBA program often expressed a right to literacy through novel and sometimes elaborate literacy rites—"reading rites" that were rites of passage into an empowering realm of sports discourse.

TENSIONS OF LITERACY

The national debate on literacy is more intense now than ever. Yet, test scores in reading and writing on the National Assessment of Educational Progress, verbal scores on the Scholastic Aptitude Test and The American College Testing Program, school drop-out rates, and public dissatisfaction with schools primarily mark failures in the area of literacy (Dyson & Freedman, 1991). For example, in a *Chicago Sun Times* editorial on the dismal SAT scores from 1990, the writer acknowledged that explanations abound but "Americans must still confront the reality that the only national aptitude test that exists shows students at a record low in verbal reasoning" ("Dismal SAT scores," 1991, p. 27). A continuation of these trends, noted Donald M. Stewart, president of the College Board, could result in "a nation divided between a small class of educational elite and an underclass of students ill-prepared for the demands of college or the workplace" (p. 27).

If the educational system in this country is producing dismal results generally, for African American males the results are often seen as deplorable. In Chicago, for example, black males currently experience a school dropout rate of close to 50%, which is significantly higher than any other school group with the exception of Hispanic males (Chicago Urban League, 1989). On standardized tests such as the SAT and ACT, dramatic disparities can be shown between the achievement of blacks and other groups.

Yet, many researchers and educators see these problems as symptomatic of the failure of educational systems (which have social, economic, and political dimensions) rather than as solely the failure of specific groups. On the one hand, there have been serious challenges to the priority and validity given to tests that attempt to standardize measurements of aptitude and/or achievement (Gardner, 1983). On the other hand, a growing body of research demonstrates how the cultural and class foundations of American schools often work against the academic success of culturally diverse students (Apple, 1986; Aronowitz & Giroux, 1991; Farr & Daniels, 1986; Heath, 1983; Kochman, 1981; Ogbu, 1983; Taylor & Dorsey-Gaines, 1988).

By mirroring and reinforcing the power and economic conditions of the larger society and by narrowly focusing on limited measures of aptitude and achievement, American schools are not adequately serving the student populations that they have marginalized. In fact, a strong case can be made that these students are actually victims of schooling. Taylor and Dorsey-Gaines noted in their work on inner-city families that "there are lessons to be learned from these families about schools...and how they can be so disconnected from and potentially destructive of the lives of the children they are supposed to be educating. The description of a child's day at school is heartbreaking" (1988, p. ix). Kochman characterized the problem as one in which "members of minority groups today must still confront a public view that sees their distinctive racial, cultural, and linguistic features as a source of public embarrassment" (1981, p. 11). Farr and Daniels suggested that members of minority groups may actually choose to fail because they perceive that becoming members of a school culture extracts too high a cost in personal terms (1986, p. 25). These views were concisely stated by the guest editors of an issue of Literacy Matters who noted that "we need to begin to take seriously the notion that education is not neutral; that it privileges the knowledge of the white, Anglo Saxon, Protestant, middle class above the knowledge of all other cultures and classes" (Rogers & McLean, 1991, p. 1).

These issues reflect some of the tensions of literacy in America today. If this situation is to change, it will not be enough for the dominant culture to merely acknowledge that there are cultural differences. It must be made to incorporate multiple perspectives and practices that work and are valuable because they are reflective of diverse, colorful patterns that make up the fabric of American life. Perhaps this begins with educators starting to see personal and professional growth in efforts to understand and incorporate the literacy and language experiences that their students bring to classrooms from an array of social practices that take place outside of schools.

CONTENTIONS OF LITERACY

There is no simple definition of literacy. As research on literacy continues, the meaning of the term itself continues to evolve, suggesting a variety of potential and often conflicting meanings. One issue that has been central to attempts at defining literacy is the *relationship between oral and written texts*. Views have ranged between two poles—that there are many sharp distinctions between speech and writing, or that speech and writing are intrinsically linked—a dichotomous model versus a continuum model.

In earlier conceptualizations of literacy, the term referred primarily to the British-essayist tradition. In this tradition the relationship of the written word to thought processes was claimed to be different from that of the spoken word. This argument was that the transition from oral to literate society was a developmental one characterized by writing becoming increasingly explicit, complex, and representative of the capability for abstract thought (Goody & Watt, 1963; Olson, 1977). Scribner and Cole addressed the positions of Olson, Goody and Watt, Strauss, Lerner, and others by attempting to answer through their research whether literacy was a *precondition for abstract thinking* and whether writing and logical thinking were always mutually dependent. A key result of their study of the Vai people was that they "did not find that literacy in the Vai script was associated in any way with generalized competencies such as abstraction, verbal reasoning, or metalinguistic skills" (1981, p. 457). Like the Scribner and Cole study, a number of subsequent studies (for example, Heath, 1983; Shuman, 1986; Tannen, 1982; Taylor, 1983) have challenged rather than confirmed a dichotomous relationship between oral and written texts.

Scollon and Scollon argued that essayist literacy had been

embraced so enthusiastically because it was being made into a paradigm that attempted to explain everything (1980, p. 26). They discussed the need to recognize several types of literacy. Similarly , Heath (1980) described seven types of uses of literacy and suggested that actually very little was known about specific literacy features. These ideas along with Scribner and Cole's distinction between literacy as development and literacy as practice (1981, p. 449) helped to lay the foundation for a new conception of literacy, or literacies, viewed in conjunction with specific practices and functions of language use inside a particular social context.

Conceptually, this "stretching" of our understanding of literacy has opened up the ideas of text and context and has pointed to novel categories for literacy investigation. One example of this is a study in progress by Conquergood on the "street literacy" of Latino gangs in Chicago. Conquergood (1991) identifies at least three kinds of literacy along with an interesting kind of interaction among them. There is alphabetic literacy in tension with iconographic literacy along with a kind of literacy of corporal inscriptions which was the way the gang member's body was made to mirror and become a mobile extension of the graffiti literacy one sees inscribed on buildings and the like marking gang territory.

Another example of how our understanding of literacy is being stretched is in the area of computer literacy. Scribner and Cole correctly projected that "as the technology of any society becomes more complex, the number and variety of tasks to which literacy skills must be applied increases as well" (1981, p. 458). Because an interesting aspect of the investigation for this chapter deals with some of the informants' interactions with computers, an examination of computer literacy concerns is also necessary. From research already completed in this area, "the evidence is very clear that the impact of microelectronics and computing generally make more rather than fewer demands upon literacy, and the definitions of literacy will have to be extended" (Adams, 1985, p. x). Interestingly, some of the claims being made for the relationship between computers and thinking are reminiscent of earlier claims regarding the relationship between writing and thinking. According to Chandler and Marcus, "using computers involves not only a different kind of use of language but also a different kind of thinking" (1985, p. 8).

The contentions of literacy are varied, controversial, sometimes contradictory, and often incomplete. Clearly, concepts of literacy are still in the process of being defined. At the end of their pivotal study, Scribner and Cole (1981) suggested that we need to know a great deal more about just how literacy is practiced and what people in various communities and walks of life do with literacy. The study of literacy in more and more diverse contexts will enhance our understanding and defining of it more fully.

SPORTS AND LEARNING

It is widely felt that participation in sports is linked to the learning of a number of attitudes, values, and skills. For example, some statistics indicate that "participation in sports boosts attendance, graduation rates and grade-point averages and reduces the number of disciplinary problems" (Bell, 1990, p. 84).

Education and sports have traditional links that go back to the early years of this century when decisions were made to include sports in the school curriculum. Originally this inclusion reflected all age groups. However, in the 1930s, the philosophies of professional physical educators changed, and "they dropped any sponsorship of children's sport they had previously provided and refused to condone high level competition for preadolescents" (Smoll, Magill, & Ash, 1982, p. 4). By the end of the 1940s, organizations such as the Society of State directors of Physical and Health Educators actively advocated policy statements directed to school administrators and board members suggesting that interscholastic athletics had no place in elementary schools. Ironically, "the very aspects of the competitive sport they were condemning were the interesting and unique features which were attracting the young. . . . Leagues, championships, tournaments, travel, spectators, and commercial sponsors" (p. 8). The exodus of children's sports programs from the educational context created the opportunity for various voluntary youth groups to attract large numbers of elementary-aged children to their organized sports programs.

Yet, little is known about the current or potential contributions that neighborhood agencies that serve youth through programs such as the YBA can make to academic and social development. Most of the research that has been done on various aspects of the involvement of youth in sports programs like the YBA has been descriptive of issues such as the number of participants and their attitudes about involvement, the number and types of injuries, and the reasons for children dropping out of sports programs (Smoll et al. 1982). Heath and McLaughlin (in a 1987 proposal to the Spenser Foundation) noted that although some attention has been given to the kinds of after-school activities in which young people are engaged, very little qualitative research has been done specifically on NBO's. It is assumed that they contribute to language development and socialization because they provide environments for language use, learning, and skill development reflective of some of the situations in the larger society. But little is known about the nature and contributions of specific agencies with respect to how they influence language and literacy development.

YBA PROMOTION OF LITERACY

Research for this chapter identified a number of ways that the YBA sports program of the South side YMCA influenced not just physical development but also the literacy development of preadolescent African-American males. In addition to surveying some of the literacies that we often do not see, an intensive treatment of several alternative varieties and uses of literacy in this setting are presented. It is also useful to describe the structure and goals of the YBA program and the roles of its adult participants to indicate some of the ways these literacy practices are being encouraged and supported.

The coordination, participation, and influences on this NBO came from a number of sectors-socially conscious volunteers, some to the adults in the players' homes, and a variety of professional educators with vested interests in the YBA program. These interlocking interests were motivated by a pervasive belief by most of the adults associated with the program that the YBA players needed and could get much more from this environment than mere athletic skill development.

To this end, three key entities of the YBA program exhibited remarkably high integration of purpose and participation. These were the YBA director who worked for the NBO along with the volunteers he got to help with the day-to-day coordination of the program, the YBA parents council, which supplied a number of critical supportive services, and the YBA coaches council, which was composed entirely of volunteers. Each entity had its own structure with scheduled meetings and developmental activities for its members. These entities also met together in attempts to jointly shape or revise the program's goals and activities, that made this YBA's character highly reflective of their interests and beliefs. This was especially true of those volunteers who had a long-standing relationship with this YBA. There were a number of key adult volunteers who had been involved for more than a decade.

Because volunteering is the most essential characteristic of this YBA PROGRAM, this study looks at the three key entities through which volunteers participate in the YBA. It identifies ways that these entities, separately and in combination, provide a context for communicative events (Hymes, 1974; Saville-Troike, 1989, p. 26) and literacy events (Heath, 1982) that involve preadolescent YBA participants and often promote their use of language and literacy skills.

To make the discussion of literacy practices more reflective of the human concerns of the people who are responsible for the YBA's existence, the role of a principal adult informant is described in two of the three entities of the YBA. All informants, adults and children, in this study have been given pseudonyms.

The YBA Parents Council

Mrs. Amy Chandler, the parents council president, had been a member of the parent council for 11 years. She was also a math teacher at one of the elementary schools in the Chicago Public Schools. In addition to having had her son in the program, she was the homeroom teacher for one of the players on the team that was being observed. Although her son was older and no longer in the YBA, she continued to assume significant responsibilities in the coordination of the program.

The parents council of this YBA program was primarily the province of women. Almost everyone on the council had a college degree, and several members were teachers. Although any parent of a player in the program could be on the parents council, it only had about 15 active members (only two were men). Hence, the parents council's character was not completely representative of the entire parent body. It reflected more a group of conscious volunteers.

The parents council organized a number of activities throughout the season, and literacy events were designed into most of them. A literacy event is defined as "any action sequence, involving one or more persons, in which the production and/or comprehension of print plays a role" (Heath, 1982, p. 92). The following are a number of YBA activities which were sponsored or coordinated by the parent council. Each one incorporated or necessitated literacy events for the players:

- fundraisers
- academic achievement awards programs
- all-star and honorable mention games
- special team events
- coaches' game
- coaches appreciation dinner
- the end of the season banquet.

Also, the way that the parents council communicated with the general parent body incorporated a continuous stream of literacy events for the players. Leaflets were the key way that the parents council communicated with the players and their families. Because the players were on site at least twice a week for practices and games, they were the key contact points between the parents council and the parents. They were encouraged to not merely transport announcements of upcoming events and activities to the parents, but to read the information themselves and both inform and remind parents of the times, places, dates, and the requested or expected roles for parents and/or players in the activities. Examples of the kinds of materials that made up these literacy events were:

- announcements of the rules of the YBA program
- announcements of practice schedules, league schedules play-off schedules, and holiday schedules
- announcements relating to the above mentioned parent council-coordinated activities.

The role of the players in these activities and events was often such that they were encouraged or required to exhibit and/or practice both *literacy skills* and *literate behaviors*. Heath (1987) defined literacy skills as *"skills* that promote only basic reading and writing" (p. vii). Whereas literate behaviors were defined as *"behaviors* that instill problem-solving abilities and knowledge-creating resources" (p. vii). A description of one of these parents council coordinated activities—the coaches appreciation dinner—provides an example of their nature and significance as literacy practices.

At the end of the 1989/90 season, the parent council hosted a coaches appreciation dinner and served homemade food prepared by parents council members. Along with the parents council members, 10 coaches and about 25 players attended. As the eating and relaxed conversation came to a close, Mrs. Chandler handed out copies of a sheet with 21 short verbal puzzles or mind bogglers that everyone was asked to solve. They were asked to work in groups of three or four. Each group, however, was structured to include a mixture of children and adults. There was much discussion in the 10 or 11 groups before the answers were written, at Mrs. Chandler's request, by a child in each of the groups. There were prizes for each child group member after a group finished. Eventually, Mrs. Chandler went over the answers orally with the entire group; then, everyone had dessert. The following are examples of three of the questions:

- Why is it illegal for a person living in Chicago to be buried west of the Mississippi River?
- An archaeologist claimed he found two gold coins dated 46 B.C. Can you disprove his claim?
- You are given two U.S. coins that total $.30 in value. One is not a nickel. What are the coins?

Solving these word problems required the application of literacy skills and in some cases literate behaviors. Answering the first question, for example, required more than comprehension of its meaning on the level of vocabulary. It also required recognition of an incongruity between the semantic and grammatical relationships of "living" in the present (and in the present tense) and being "buried" in the past. The point is that this exercise was one in a continual stream of literacy events built into YBA parents council-sponsored activities consciously designed to reinforce the literacy instruction these players received in school.

Yet, there were observed differences in the way this literacy practice was organized and carried out when contrasted to methods of literacy instruction in traditional school settings. Because players, coaches, and parents found themselves working together in groups to solve puzzles that did not require much background in specific content areas, there was a sense that everyone was on an equal footing rather than the traditional hierarchy of teachers over students or adults over children. In fact, some of the children were first to come up with answers in their groups. When individuals could not solve specific problems, they did not experience a sense of failure or frustration because they were carried by other members of the group. There was also a mild sense of competition between the groups which gave the activity more of a game quality. Both the children and the adults had considerable fun as they raced toward completion of the exercise.

In addition to infusing literacy events into many YBA activities, the parents council also did a number of overt things to reinforce and promote literacy and schooling. For example, a lot of attention was given throughout the YBA season to the players' academic achievements in school. Honor roll students were given special recognition in several ways. For the second half of the season, once players' grades had been validated, they had honor student patches sewn onto their uniforms. Additional awards were given to honor students by the parents council at the end-of-the-year awards banquet which included calling them up to the stage for visual and verbal recognition.

Like the parents council, the other two entities of the YBA also emphasized academic as well as physical development. A brief look at the role of the YBA director in this endeavor concludes this section on ways that the YBA promoted literacy.

The YBA Director

Mr. Mosi Carter was the only NBO employee with a principal, day-to-day role in coordinating the YBA program. The YBA served more than 200 participants with three separate leagues that practiced or played league games six days a week for the 7-month season. One of Mosi's key attributes was his ability to inspire and coordinate adult male volunteers in the administration of the YBA program.

Mosi's involvement with the YBA began 13 years ago when his oldest son became a participant. For years he volunteered as a game official and a team coach before becoming the YBA director. The following excerpt from his orientation to the new and returning participants during the first practice of the 1989/90 season showed his emphasis on academic versus athletic development.

> Today shows that all of you have lots of work to do on your skill development. Most of Y'all not in any kind of physical shape. The exercises show that. I want y'all to work on your exercises every day at home so you can get stronger, and I want you to work on your basic basketball skills. But do that after you finish your homework. In fact, if you don't get to work on these skills because of homework then that's all right. The order should be when you get home from school that first you do your homework. Then you do your housework, and I know all you all have housework. Then, if there's any time left you work on your basketball skills. . . . Basketball is not mandatory. This is just somethin' you do for fun. If you want to stay in this program then you better git organized on the things that are mandatory, your homework and your housework.

In addition to his frequent verbal support of academic skills, the YBA director, like the parents council, coordinated a number of activities that incorporated and/or gave strong reinforcement to mental as well as physical development. For example, he networked with other youth services organizations and brought in speakers such as the executive director of Big Buddies Youth Services, an organization with ties to the University of Chicago, to help orient members of the parents council and the coaches council to novel ways that education and sports could be linked. Big Buddies' mission was to offer options for youth to street life, and one of its programs was to publish a magazine titled *School Sports and Education* through its Institute of Athletics and Education. The YBA director would use resource people from organizations such as Big Buddies to inform and inspire YBA adult volunteers.

Similarly, the YBA director would bring in sports heroes and other role models to inform and inspire the YBA players. After one Saturday practice, for example, a former All-American basketball player from a Chicago high school who went on to become a well-known star for a Big Ten college team spoke to the assembled YBA players. He used his own career after basketball to highlight the value of excelling in school over excelling in sports as illustrated in the following excerpt from his presentation:

> I'm more proud of what I do as a college administrator helping people get in school, helping people stay in school . . . than I am of anything I did on the courts. I had a good time playin' in school but I thought I better get more from school than just a good time. Why? 'Cause not everybody's gonna make it in professional sports. Why? Because there's only about twelve hundred professional black athletes in this country. . . . And that's for all sports combined.

Like the YBA director and the parents council, the YBA coaches council also promoted literacy development in the players in a number of ways. The communicative interaction between coaches and players was the most pervasive discourse that adults had with youths in the YBA program. The specific nature of this discourse is detailed in a subsequent paper by this researcher titled "African American Males and Learning: What Discourse in Sports can Offer to Discourse in Schools" (1992). It extends the teacher-as-coach, student-as-worker school reform model by assessing an actual framework (the "discourse of basketball," or "register" in sociolinguistic terms) that facilitates language and literacy development in the YBA in a communicative style that is culturally based.

The character of adult participation in the YBA program, therefore, was such that many activities for the youths were structured or coordinated in ways that promoted literacy. Many adults who assumed responsibility for various aspects of the YBA program were "conscious" volunteers. They were educated, sometimes educators themselves, and they were motivated by the perception that the energy and excitement that young people brought to the game of basketball could be channeled toward literacy. Many of these occasions for literacy practices are not seen outside of the YBA context.

Although literacy development in general was promoted extensively, actual literacy events initiated by adult volunteers correlated primarily to what Heath (1987) defined as literacy skills-mechanistic linguistic abilities that focus on manipulating discrete elements of a text. However, a more comprehensive kind of literacy development was initiated primarily by the players themselves. Interestingly, these literacy events were more reflective of those higher order literacy abilities "to analyze, discuss, interpret, and create extended chunks of language" that Heath (1987) defined as literate behavior. Spontaneous or adaptive readings of a variety of sports-related texts were the foundations of widely occurring literacy events that were markedly different from the ways these players encountered literacy outside of this sports context. Analysis of these literacy events revealed subtle codes for participation that have been characterized in this chapter as "reading rites." In the remainder of this chapter, several significant reading rites are presented and analyzed as indications of alternative ways that literacy is practiced in this community and sports setting.

FOLLOWING THE YBA, NBA, AND NCAA TOURNAMENTS

The YBA to a high degree was modeled on the National Basketball Association (NBA). For example, every team in the YBA league was named for one of the NBA teams. Players received numerous handouts and announcements throughout the season, but they gave particularly close readings to information that had to do with the rules and/or structure of YBA tournaments. One reason for this was that they would often argue the application of the rules in a given regular season or playoff game situation. For example, one rule was that "participants must play a minimum of seven regular season games to be eligible for the playoffs." As the regular season moved toward the playoffs, players would sometimes debate the merit of that rule among themselves or with their coaches. Also, they would request to read the official scoring sheets for the entire season to try and catch particular players (usually the better players) who they thought were in violation of that rule in order to challenge eligibility to play in the playoffs. Of importance here was the value given to comprehension and interpretation of the written text and the priority of the written text as a source for the generation and validation of oral texts, especially arguments.

Another rule to which players would call attention, either to challenge that it was being violated by their coach or the coach of the opposing team, stated that "all participants that have played the first quarter must sit out the second quarter." One of the most difficult decisions for coaches was to attempt to give all the players on the team adequate playing time regardless of their skills yet at the same time attempt to win. Players were extremely sensitive to any perceived imbalances, and their first line of challenge was often to cite the rules. Players often demonstrated that they had not only read and comprehended the meaning of the extensive rules covering all aspects of participation and play in the YBA, but that they had also interpreted the intent behind the meaning when it was appropriate. For example, when one player was asked to explain why the YBA had a rule like the one just cited that was so different from regular basketball rules, he gave the following interpretation to the rule:

> So everybody on the team gets a chance to play. Some coaches have some players they want to leave in for the whole game. That's probably why they made the rule. Like sometimes our coach wouldn't play Marcus because he didn't really like him, he couldn't really dribble or anything, so he didn't really play him some games. If it wasn't for this rule somebody like Marcus might not get to play at all.

This player recognized unstated assumptions in the written text and was able to go beyond the given data to determine their implications. His ability to extrapolate in this manner was a clear expression of literate behavior.

Like the National College Athletic Association (NCAA) and the

NBA, the YBA had a rather complicated playoff structure. Unlike the NCAA and the NBA, however, the YBA playoff was a double elimination tournament—each team had to lose twice to be eliminated. Each player was given a copy of the diagram of the playoff tournament. In order to understand how the playoffs worked, players had to synthesize the connections and interactions between elements of the diagram. The following dialogue illustrated how players struggled to comprehend and even explain these interrelationships. Both players were on one of the teams under observation (the "Bulls"); the dialogue took place while they sat in the stands and watched the end of the game that preceded their game.

> Jason: Bulls number one. Bulls number one
>
> Kamau: What about all the people who don't lose?
>
> Jason: Nobody will not lose. Everybody, in order to get eliminated you have to lose twice.
>
> Kamau: I know but what if somebody does not lose? They gon' play somebody that already lost.
>
> Jason: I know that, but what I'm sayin' is if they do then the team that has not lost [if it] loses the first game they play they have to play another game. Then the other team . . . it'll be two playoff games and the other team will have to beat 'em twice. If they haven't lost. Everybody gets . . . it's a double elimination.
>
> Kamau: Oh, oh! Okay!
>
> Jason: In other words if we go through and win three straight and we play a team that's lost one
>
> Kamau: Yeah Jason: And they beat us. Then they still gotta beat us again to win the championship.
>
> Kamau: Awh. Alright. Even the Lakers?
>
> Jason: Anybody, you gotta lose twice to be out.

The YBA players, however, went much further in demonstrating analysis skills within both written and oral texts and in transferring ideas between written and oral texts. In addition to comprehending interrelationships between elements in a schematic text, players frequently analyzed the characteristics of individual teams, compared the various teams to each other, and formed and debated hypotheses of which teams could beat other teams or which team would win the entire tournament. Interestingly this activity carried over to other activities such as the analyses of teams competing in tournaments of the NCAA, the NBA, and in the simulated basketball tournaments of computer games. In order to do these analyses they read significant amounts of rather complex print material in the form of newspaper articles and diagrams, basketball cards, and computer game booklets.

As a prelude to the NCAA tournament, for example, both major Chicago newspapers printed diagrams similar to the YBA playoff diagram under the headings of "The Race to Indianapolis" or "The Road to the Final Four." These newspaper diagrams, however, were much more detailed. They had brackets for 64 teams, rather than just 8, with 16 teams spread across four divisions aligned according to division seeds based on season records. In each division the number 1 seed played the number 16 seed, 2 played 15, and so forth. On other pages the sports writers provided about a paragraph of analysis on each of the 64 teams. Additionally, there were full-length articles on several of the more dominant teams and players.

Two members of one team under observation were brothers. On one evening when an observation took place in their home, their older brother, who was a senior in high school, was also present. All three were watching a Chicago Bulls regular season game on television and simultaneously filling in their picks in the blank diagrams printed in the newspapers for teams to win each of the 32 games of the NCAA tournament all the way to the championship game. They had made a bet with each other as to which one could choose the highest number of correct picks based on an elaborate scoring system which assessed successively higher points for each correct pick in each of the successive rounds of the playoffs. In addition to bets with each other, they all also had bets going on in their schools in large pools in which the potential winnings were as high as $200.

To arrive at their picks, they went back and forth between the *Chicago Sun Times* and the *Chicago Tribune*, read and reread the 128 analysis paragraphs by the sports writers, evaluated and compared the strengths and weaknesses of each of the teams, and debated the validity of their various choices as they filled in their picks. This process went on for about three hours and still was not complete at the end of the evening.

Their use of both written and oral texts showed significant literate behavior. Again, written texts were used as a basis for generating and validating oral texts. These youths delighted in the discussions and debates associated with the tournaments, and they saw connections between the reading rites in which they engaged and the possibility of earning bragging rights (as well as money) for coming up with the best picks. These were intensive and extensive literacy practices during which players were highly motivated to analyze, synthesize, and evaluate significant quantities of written and visual material as a pretext to oral discussion and debate. It all took place outside of and relatively independent of school settings. A little later in the spring, these youths engaged in similar reading rites during the NBA tournament.

COLLECTING BASKETBALL CARDS

Another aspect of these reading rites or what Anzalone and McLaughlin (1982) have termed "specific literacies" (to designate special-interest or special-purpose literacy skills) was apparent in the basketball (and other sports) card collections that many YBA players kept. Four YBA players were interviewed about their card collections by this researcher, and the extent and sophistication of the literacy practices associated with collecting, trading, and selling cards was significant. They read successive editions of a publication that assessed the value of cards, and two of these players had gotten their parents to take them to a card-trading convention. All four were quite comprehensive in talking about the relative merits of almost every player in the NBA in terms of how valuable certain basketball cards would become. The amount of data that these children read and discussed was significant. Just to stay abreast of the active players in the NBA in any given year entailed knowledge of 12 players on 28 teams or 336 individual players in the league.

Considerable data are contained on each card. In addition to giving the birthdate, birthplace, height, weight, college attended, draft pick, and professional team of each NBA player, a card also gives four years of college career statistics in five categories and professional career statistics in nine categories for every year that the player has been in the NBA. Usually, there is also about a paragraph of narrative highlights in the player's career.

In addition to speculating on the potential value of an individual NBA player's card, these youths also had to make judgments about which brand of basketball cards to buy. The basketball card market has mushroomed, and some brands of cards are more valuable than others. A partial list of basketball card brands includes NBA Hoops, Upper Deck, Sky Box, Fleer, and Star Picks. Even McDonald's attempted to cash in on the enthusiasm by offering its own brand of basketball cards—"for a limited time only." They aired commercials timed to correspond with the 1992 NBA All-Star game. These commercials depicted two NBA coaches haggling over a "high-level" trade that involved Michael Jordan. Only when the camera turned to a cute African-American boy sitting at the head of the table was it clear that they were trading McDonald's basketball cards. The boy smiled and said, "I got two Jordans!" It ended with one coach saying in frustration, "Gee, I wish I had two Jordans."

In order to facilitate their decisions regarding collecting, trading, and selling basketball cards, the youths interviewed by this researcher regularly purchased and read *Becket's Basketball Monthly,* an approximately 40-page guidebook. One youth described how he determined the value of cards:

> Each card has a number. All you have to do is find that number in the price guide and it'll tell you how much the card is worth that month. It has a arrow to show if the price is going up or down.

According to an article in *Worth*, the guidebooks published by Dr. Beckett have a combined circulation of over 2 million. Additionally, the maturing of the card trade has resulted in the printing of 7 billion new sport and hobby cards a year, and 15,000 card shops have sprung up across the country (Rothchild, 1992).

The YBA youths kept their cards in thick notebooks with pages of plastic pockets. They had different styles for organizing their collection and different strategies for how they were going to corner the card market. One youth explained one of the personal touches he had added to the organization of his collection.

> I put this David Robinson card in the top pocket on this page with Larry Nance guardin' him 'cause when you turn the page you got this card right behind it with Larry Nance being guarded by David Robinson. They must'a took the pictures at the same game.

The same youth explained how his collection strategy was different from his step-brother's.

> First, we were both collecting the same year. . . but he lost some of his. So, during Kwanzaa his mother bought him a whole box of 91/92. I had 90/91 he had 91/92. We would trade so I could get all the 90/91 and he could get all 91/92. Now we both have the whole set of Hoops for our year. Mine's worth more than his.

Like their bets on the NCAA tournament, the prospect of winning or earning money was part of their motivation to engage in literacy practices associated with collecting and trading basketball cards. There may be ethical considerations regarding this motivation, but it also indicated the extent of adaptive learning in which these youth engaged when they saw possibilities for real-world consequences, in this case renumeration. This kind of learning was more reflective of their direct needs and experiences than many of the more artificial situations they encountered in schools.

But there was another side to their motivation in addition to the monetary considerations and their enthusiasm for sports discourse. All of the statistics, personalities, predictions, and endless considerations associated with college and professional basketball added up to a knowledge base (a discipline) that these youths had mastered to a higher degree than just about every adult they knew. Rothchild (1992) noted this motivation in his own experiences as a child collecting baseball cards, and it still holds for basketball card collecting today.

"When I was a child, the greatest thing about baseball cards was that grown-ups had nothing to do with them, and wouldn't have known whether two Duke Sniders were worth one Sandy Koufax" (p. 61).

As these youths sought out and consumed the various forms of written texts that had information they desired, they entwined these written texts with oral texts in spontaneous and adaptive literacy events. They extended their mastery by challenging each other orally and using either written texts or the outcomes of sports events for validation. In short, through their readings of newspaper accounts of sports events, basketball cards and guidebooks, and computer sports game booklets (addressed in the final section of this chapter), these youths felt empowered in the realm of sports discourse. Their reading rites were rites of power.

Heath (1982) noted that "examination of the contexts and uses of literacy in communities today may show that there are more literacy events which call for appropriate knowledge of forms and uses of speech events than there are actual occasions for extended reading or writing" (p. 94). But the reading rites associated with this community-sports context showed "occasions for extended reading" activity as central in the discourse. This activity went beyond mere functional literacy and reflected a unique twist on what Scribner (1988, p. 75) has termed "literacy as power". Scribner suggests that literacy as power emphasizes a relationship between literacy and group or community advancement. There were certainly elements of this metaphor of literacy at work in the YBA director and parents council's overall attempts to facilitate the players' literacy development. However, the spontaneous or adaptive literate behaviors these youths exhibited on their own empowered the individual players directly, in addition to the less immediate notion of group advancement.

PLAYING COMPUTER SPORT GAMES

If, as suggested earlier in this chapter, there is no simple definition of literacy, then concepts of *computer literacy* further stretch notions of literacy. Computers are already used extensively in Western society with new and far-reaching applications that are being continually developed. Dillon suggested that "while computer applications in schools range through the whole curriculum, their impact has been greatest in maths and in our area of concern, literacy" (1985, p. 86). It is generally thought that computers have a number of positive, although not fully understood, impacts on literacy development. But Dillon and others have outlined many potential dangers to literacy development that hinge specifically on how computers are used to enhance literacy. Perhaps the key question is "who is in charge of learning: machine or machine user"? (p. 86).

Dillon argues that if the application of computer technology is toward developing "software that structures knowledge, including knowledge about literacy, in a particular way and leads pupils rather passively on a predetermined path through material—and evaluates them—in the same way" (p. 94), then this application of technology further empowers teachers to control not only instruction but also behavior. On the other hand, "software that allows pupils to program, record, compose, and retrieve seems to have the potential for empowering learners, and for facilitating growth in authentic literacy" (p. 94).

These concerns about the impacts of computers on literacy in school settings also have an out-of-schooi correlation. Programmers for computer sport games recognized that the "highly directive and controlling instructional patterns in most Language Arts software in use in schools" (Dillon, 1985, p. 93), which required an interaction with the machine not unlike the teacher initiates—student responds—teacher evaluates pattern, would not work in settings such as the home or the video arcade where neither the authority of the teacher to enforce nor the motivation of the player to facilitate this kind of interaction was present. Consequently, computer sport games that were played in the home by YBA participants gave the children both a sense of unlimited challenge (competition) and a sense of empowerment. They were also occasions for literacy practices that operated on several levels.

As with the players' experiences with tracking and predicting the performance of NCAA and NBA teams in playoff tournaments and in collecting basketball cards, their experiences with computer sport games revealed literate behaviors in conjunction with both oral and written texts. Some of the oral discourse generated within this framework reflected interesting ways of learning as well as the operation of literate behaviors. Playing computer sport games also intensively engaged these youths with written texts.

Part of their motivation to play these games came from their extremely high interest in sports. But part of their motivation also came from the fact that these games were designed in such a way as to give players a sense of both challenge and empowerment that was significantly different from the majority of their experiences at school or in other sectors of their lives. For example, one player on the team, Kamau, gave the following response:

> In sport games there is always another level, a higher level to go to. Plus you get to play other people. And it might be in the control that you get. Did you read the book? You like, have you read the book all the way through? You own the team. You control when the players go in. . .when they come out. You control when they shoot, you know. . . when they pass the ball, who gets to dribble. You also control what

person they stick on defense, what person they guard on the floor. You control the team, you are the team.

Kamau kept emphasizing the need to read the book. He was referring to the booklet that explained one of the computer sport games, *TV Sports: Basketball* (1990) by Cinemaware. The booklet was 24 pages of single-spaced text with only four small pictures that combined would not take up a complete page. Assessing the reading level of this booklet was of interest because it was clear that Kamau, who was in seventh grade at the time, had read it with enough comprehension to set up and play what appeared to be a very complex computer game. His mother had no interest in the game and, in fact, could not play the game on the computer, so he had to decode and apply the instructions in the booklet himself. That he was capable of doing this is clearly indicated in his discussion of how to play the game that is provided later in this section.

A passage from the booklet on "Loading the Game" (p. 1) was selected, and the Gunning Fog Index was used to measure the grade equivalent of the text. The Gunning Fog Index applies two equations to relationships among the number of words, the number of sentences, and the number of difficult works in a text to determine the readability level. The actual passage is included here because there are additional aspects of difficulty reflected in the computer jargon that were not apprehended by the Gunning Fog Index formula.

Boot you computer with DOS 2.11 or higher. At the "A" prompt, insert Disk 1 into drive A: Now type BBV (for VGA) and press "Enter". If you are playing with a joystick, center it during this load; the game will calibrate your joystick. If you are playing on an EGA or Tandy machine, type BBE or BBT respectively. Note: If you are using 5.25" disks and have one disk drive, only exchange disks when the program requests it. Any additional instructions will be in the file, README.DOC on Disk 1. To read this document, type the following command after a prompt: TYPE README.DOC

The readability level of this passage is 9.016 or ninth grade. Kamau, as mentioned earlier, was in seventh grade, but he demonstrated that he had comprehended this text rated two grades higher than the grade he was in, a text that arguably could be rated higher still if terms that are difficult, not because they have three or more syllables but because they have computer jargon-specific meanings, are factored in. Examples of these terms are: "Boot," "prompt," "joystick," "load," "disk," "program," and "file."

When Kamau was interviewed about *TV Sports: Basketball* he spoke entirely from memory. His explanation for how to play this game was extremely detailed and significantly longer than the portion reported here. It does, however, illustrate several key considerations regarding levels of computer literacy motivated by discourse surrounding sports that took place in settings outside of schools. This interview appeared in an earlier article (Mahiri, 1991), but it is given more extensive discussion here.

> *Researcher:* If I didn't know anything about the game, which I don't, what can you tell me from start to finish about how to play?
>
> *Kamau:* Get into A drive, then type BBE. Switch disks. Then you go to disk two. First screen comes up after you switch and then you have three choices: exhibition, league play, clipboard statistics.
>
> *Researcher:* What happens with the three choices?
>
> *Kamau:* In exhibition you practice playing a game when you're not ready for league play. When you play in the league you have up to 28 teams controlled by humans players. Clipboard gives you statistics on the league leaders, lets you view the teams' main menu, all on a sheet of paper like a clipboard. [Kamau goes on in minute detail for three more transcript pages and then ends with the following persuasive narrative.] Everybody likes to play the game. It's real fun. It's almost like the real NBA. There's nothing you can't do in the game that they don't do in the NBA except it doesn't have all the calls. It also has the statistics, so that's nice. It also has the buzzer beater shots, steals. I even hit a buzzer beater once. So, that's fun. And they have like fans and stuff in the crowd. I even saw a sweeper come out once when someone dunked and broke the backboard. They also have a commentator. It's not just words on the screen. He's like a black guy. He's like a regular person. His hair is nice, low cut. He has a nice tie, blue suit. He has a pen in his hand. He's sitting at a desk and there's like a TV screen that he looks at. He has a pen and paper. I mean, it's nice. You really have to see it to get the full effect. You have to come over one day when we're playing it. You have to actually watch it 'cause it's really exciting. It's hard to believe what they're doing with computers now.

The complete transcript of the interview revealed that Kamau had produced an exceptional amount of detail from memory that corresponded closely to the actual written text. For example, in the first part of Kamau's explanation he said, "Get into A drive, then type BBE." The booklet said, "insert Disk 1 into drive A: Now type *BBV.*" The researcher assumed that a mistake had been made in not distinguishing the "V" sound from the "E" sound during. When Kamau was asked about this he said he had definitely said "BBE," because that was the command change needed for the type of computer he had in his home.

In addition to detailed recall and comprehension of a relatively complex text, playing computer sport games involved literate behaviors and aspects of computer literacy at higher levels of abstraction. Dillon has suggested that the computer software that most facilitated growth in literacy was the kind that empowered learners by allowing them not only to record and retrieve but also to program and compose on the computer (1985, p. 94).

Playing *TV Sports: Basketball* at the level of Kamau and his siblings and friends required these players to not only comprehend a text, but also to analyze, synthesize, and make evaluations about data presented within the game situation—behaviors that are also central to academic discourse.

Literate behaviors were evidenced in the way Kamau described aspects of the game. His recall and presentation of exact details of the commentator reflected descriptive discourse with a systematic spatial organization pattern. His description followed the pattern of a wide angle lens zooming in on more and more specific details right down to the pen that the commentator was holding in his hand. Persuasive elements were also apparent and related to the themes of fun and excitement. In other words, fun and excitement were key themes used to get the researcher to want to do more than just learn about the game.

The introduction to *TV Sports: Basketball* stated that it was the most realistic and exciting basketball simulation ever created. A brief survey of the knowledge and skills a player needed to play this game illustrates why Cinemaware made this claim. The league had 28 teams divided into two conferences and four divisions. Because each team could have either a human or computer owner, there could be up to 28 human competitors in a season of league play that ended with the playoffs. The ability of a team to perform in the league was partially determined by the owner's choice of players and by the characteristics chosen for each player on the team as well as for the coach. The owner had to decide how to accentuate or balance the skills of passing, shooting, rebounding, dribbling, and defending for all of the team's players with considerations of what would be most effective for their positions of point guard, shooting guard, small forward, power forward, or center. The possibilities were almost endless, so these youths had to constantly analyze the game's "Clipboard" file with its complete statistics on every aspect of the computer game's league. For example, in choosing the characteristics for a particular player, Clipboard gave the best and worst performances in the league in 69 categories and in 24 combinations. Clipboard also allowed each owner to analyze the record of every team in the league, and it also provided detailed statistics on each member of every team.

The above features of the game give a brief sketch of the data available to owners who analyze, synthesize, and evaluate these data in order to structure their teams to give them the highest probability of winning before they actually engage in playing the game. The element of human competition, the opportunity to program and compose, and the realistic nature of the game ("There's nothing you can't do in the game that they don't do in the NBA...") served as motivating factors for the players to apply literacy skills and literate behaviors at the highest levels of their capabilities because that was what was required in order to win.

CONCLUSION

Learning and literacy practices observed in these literacy events taking place outside of school settings contrasted markedly with the top-down transmission process of learning present in so many educational environments in which teachers do the vast majority of analyzing, synthesizing, and evaluating to which students get brief opportunities to respond. Many educational settings rarely utilize some of the obvious, inherent, concrete, and personal interests of African-American males to enhance their learning and literacy development.

Aronowitz and Giroux (1991) suggested that central questions in education today have to do with relationships "between power and knowledge, learning and empowerment, and authority and human dignity" (p. 109). These central questions have important implications for what counts as legitimate academic knowledge and what teaching styles, learning environments, and content areas best facilitate learners in becoming knowledgeable. They further suggested a consideration for the types of knowledge that are tied to electronically mediated popular culture:

Popular knowledge, even if it does not possess the same apparatus of inquiry that has marked legitimate academic knowledge, is nevertheless a form of intellectual knowledge. Jazz buffs, rock music fans, and those who closely follow various professional and college sports are required to abstract from the particular to find commensurable and incommensurable features. . .within their fields. (p. 18)

Basketball has high motivational value for the YBA players. It inspires them to engage in a wide array of literacy practices that often "we do not see." Yet, many are novel and "alternative" literate behaviors. The practice of specific literacy skills are generally supported and encouraged by conscious adults associated with the YBA, but more sophisticated literate behaviors are adapted by the youths themselves as part of the rites of participation in a dynamic realm of sports discourse. In other words, participation in much of the sports discourse generated by these children is dependent on close and extensive readings of certain required texts-newspaper accounts of sports events, basketball card collections and associated guidebooks, and computer sport game screen texts and instruction books. If there is a continuum, its direction is often from written to oral for these youths. Therefore, these rites of participation are termed *reading rites*.

These findings relate to the ongoing discussion and research on literacy as adaptation, or functional literacies, which takes the goals and settings of people's use of written language into account. They also suggest an additional consideration for the formulation of literacy as power that emphasizes literacy acquisition for group advancement (Scribner, 1984). In this case, however, it is the empowerment of individual players that is enhanced through literate behaviors which are reinforced and rewarded in a number of ways. These findings illustrate how African-American males, who are usually seen as at-risk students, initiate and sustain frequent engagements with a variety of written texts when they are motivated by the content. The findings must be considered with reference to the specific age, gender, and racial group that was observed . But for purposes of literacy development, they suggest that a better link must be made between what schools hold as important and meaningful and what these youths find to be meaningful in their daily lives.

REFERENCES

Adams, A. (1985). Foreword. *Computers and Literacy* D. Chandler & S. Marcus, Eds. Philadelphia: Open University Press.

Anzalone, S. & McLaughlin, S. (1982). *Literacy for specific situations.* Amherst: University of Massachusetts, Center for International Education.

Apple, M. (1986). *Teachers and texts: A political economy of class and gender relations in education.* New York: Routledge.

Aronowitz, S., & Giroux, H.S. (1991). *Postmodern education: Politics, culture, and social criticism.* Minneapolis: The University of Minnesota Press.

Bell, T. (1990, July 13). Julian poorer without Smith. *Chicago Sun-Times*, p. 84.

Chandler, D., & Marcus, S. (Eds.). (1985). *Computers and Literacy.* Philadelphia: Open University Press.

Chicago Urban League. (1989). *Basic facts about blacks.* Chicago: Chicago Urban League.

Conquergood, D. (1991, May). *Street literacy.* Paper presented at the meeting of the Chicago Language and Literacy Network, Chicago.

Dillon, D. (1985). The dangers of computers in literacy education: Who's in charge here? In D. Chandler & S. Marcus (Eds.), *Computers and Literacy.* Philadelphia: Open University Press.

Dismal SAT scores test nation's resolve. (1991, August 28). *The Chicago Sun-Times*, p. 27.

Dyson, A. H., & Freedman, S. W. (1991). *Critical challenges for research on writing and literacy: 1990-1995* (Tech. Rep. 1-B). Berkeley, CA: University of California, Center for the Study of Writing.

Farr, M., & Daniels, H. (1986). *Language diversity and writing instruction.* Urbana, IL: National Council of Teachers of English.

Gardner, H. (1983). *Frames of mind.* New York: Basic Books.

Goody, J., & Watt, I. (1963). The consequences of literacy. *Comparative Studies in Society and History,* 5. [Reprinted in P. P. Giglioli (Ed.). (1972). *Language and social context* (pp. 311-357). New York: Penguin Books.]

Heath, S. B. (1980). The functions and uses of literacy. *Journal of Communication,* 30, 123-133.

Heath, S. B, (1982). Protean shapes in literacy events: Ever-shifting oral and literate traditions. In D. Tannen (Ed.), *Spoken and written language: Exploring orality and literacy.* Norwood, NJ: Ablex.

Heath, S. B. (1983). *Ways with words: Language, life, and work in communities and classrooms.* Cambridge: Cambridge University Press.

Heath, S. B. (1987). Foreword. In H. Graff, The *labyrinths of literacy: Reflections on literacy past and present.* London: The Falmer Press.

Heath, S. B. & McLaughlin, M. W. (1987). *Language, socialization, and neighborhood-based organizations: Moving youth beyond dependency on school and family.* A proposal submitted to the Spenser Foundation.

Hymes, D. (1974). *Foundations in sociolinguistics: An ethnographic approach.* Philadelphia: University of Pennsylvania Press.

Kochman, T. (1981). *Black and white styles in conflict.* Chicago: University of Chicago Press.

Lunsford, A., Moglen, H., & Slevin, J. (Eds.) (1990). Introduction. *The right to literacy.* New York: The Modern Language Association.

Labov, W. (1973). *Sociolinguistic patterns.* Philadelphia: University of Pennsylvania Press.

Mahiri, J. (1991). Discourse in sports: Language and literacy features of preadolescent African American males in a youth basketball program. *Journal of Negro Education,* 60, 305-313.

Mahiri, J. (1992, November). *African American males and learning: What discourse in sports can offer to discourse in schools.* Paper presented at the meeting of the National Council of Teachers of English, Louisville, KY.

Milroy, L. (1987). *Observing and analyzing natural language.* New York: Basil Blackwell.

Ogbu, J. U. (1983). Literacy and schooling in subordinate cultures: The case of black Americans. In D. Resnick (Ed.), *Literacy in historical perspective.* Washington, DC: Library of Congress.

Olson, D. R. (1977). From utterance to text: The bias of language in speech and writing. *Harvard Educational Review, 47*, 257-281.

Rogers, T. & McLean, M. (1991). Message from the guest editors. *Literacy Matters, 3*(2), 1-3.

Rothchild, J. (1992, March). Sleaze play. *Worth*, pp. 61-62.

Saville-Troike, M. (1989). *The ethnography of communication: An introduction*. New York: Basil Blackwell.

Scollon, S., & Scollon, R. (1980). Literacy as focused interaction. *The Quarterly Newsletter of the Laboratory of Comparative Human Cognition, 2*(2), 26-29.

Scribner, S. (1988). Literacy in three metaphors. In E. R. Kintgen, B. M. Kroll, & M. Rose (Eds.), *Perspectives on literacy* (pp. 71-81). Carbondale: Southern Illinois University Press.

Scribner, S., & Cole, M. (1981). *The psychology of literacy*. Cambridge, MA: Harvard University Press.

Shuman, A. (1986). *Storytelling rights: The uses of oral and written texts by urban adolescents*. Cambridge: Cambridge University Press.

Smoll, F. Magill, R. & Ash, M. (1982). *Children in sport*. Champaign, IL: Human Kinetics Books.

Spradley, J. (1979a). *The ethnographic interview*. New York: Holt, Rinehart, and Winston.

Spradley, J. (1979b). *Participant observation*. New York: Holt, Rinehart, and Winston.

Tannen, D. (1982). The oral/literate continuum in discourse. In D. Tannen (Ed.) *Spoken and written language: Exploring Orality and Literacy*. Norwood, NJ: Ablex.

Taylor, D. (1983). *Family literacy: Young children learning to read and write*. Exeter, NH: Heinemann Educational Books.

Taylor, D., & Dorsey-Gaines, C. (1988). *Growing up literate: Learning from inner-city families*. Portsmouth, NH: Heinemann-Boynton/Cook.

TV sports: Basketball. (1990). [Computer software manual]. Cinemaware Corporation.

5

Creating a Community: Literacy Events in African-American Churches

Beverly J. Moss
The Ohio State University

INTRODUCTION

Background

This chapter, like other chapters in this volume, examines literacy in a social institution or community other than the mainstream academy—the African-American church. In examining a literacy event to which most members in the African-American community have been exposed, I use Heath's (1982) definition of a literacy event: "Any action sequence, involving one or more persons, in which the production and/or comprehension of print plays a role" (p. 92). The African-American sermon fits this definition, and it is the major literacy event that most African Americans have been exposed to in their communities, including those African Americans who do not attend church.

Over the past few years our discussions about literacy have taken a new direction, one long overdue—looking at literacy in nonacademic communities. A major tension in the discussion of literacy centers on the way literacy is defined or, more accurately, how people who are perceived to be literate and people who are perceived to be not literate are characterized. This issue relates to how we characterize literate behavior, literate texts, and literacy events. At the core of much of the dissension is the assumption on the part of many educators that there is one definition of literacy, a standard list of features of literate behavior, literate texts, and consequently literate peoples.

It seems, then, impossible to talk about literacy without discussing the social practices of literacy. Yet, that is precisely what happens when we ignore the cultural environment from which children come and in which children learn language outside of school. Szwed (1981) suggests that to define literacy we must examine "the social context in which writing occurs, the participants (the writer and intended readers), the function the writer serves, and the motivation for writing" (p. 14). Street (1984) labels this model of literacy the "ideological" model, a model that stresses the specific social practices of reading and writing. Those supporting the ideological model argue that language does not occur in a vacuum and that we cannot separate our language from its social and physical environment, be it oral or written language. The view that there are various kinds of literacies that are defined by various cultures and communities deserves closer examination because of its potential impact on education, and particularly on writing instruction.

When researchers examine literacy in nonschool settings, we focus on crucial questions: How do we determine what is valued in different cultures or in different communities within a society such as the United States? Do these values affect the way language is learned? How is language being used in particular communities or cultures? What roles do reading, writing, and speaking play in these communities? Heath (1983) addressed many of these questions in *Ways With Words*. Heath's study focused on three communities in the Piedmont Carolinas: Trackton, a small black working-class community; Roadville, a small white working-class community; and the Townspeople, a middle-class integrated community.

Even though Heath (1983) notes that all the communities were literate communities, there were varying degrees of "literacy" in each community; that is, reading and writing were used differently in each community. What is important to note here is that even though children in Trackton and Roadville were not very successful in school (the Trackton children were least successful), they were quite successful communicating within their respective communities.

Heath's research and other similar studies point to the importance of discovering the uses and functions of language, oral and written, in the community as well as in the classroom, and to the importance of exploring expanding definitions of literacy. This view has prompted many scholars, before and after Heath, to explore the notion of multiple definitions of literacy in various communities (Fishman, 1988; Philips, 1972; Scollon & Scollon, 1981; Scribner & Cole, 1982; Taylor & Dorsey Gaines, 1988; Weinstein-Shr, 1986). This view also helped shape my thinking about my previous research on literacy in the African-American church (Moss, 1988).

Data Sources

The major data in this study consist of sermons from three Chicago area African-American ministers. To compare and contrast the impact of writing on the shape of the sermon as a literacy event, I chose a minister who writes his sermons, one who does not write his sermons, and a minister who writes only a portion of his sermons.

I spent approximately 10 Sundays in each minister's church observing and collecting data through ethnographic methods. The major sources of data are the five sermons I collected from each minister. From the minister who writes a complete manuscript from which to preach sermons, I collected copies of written sermons as well as the cassette tapes of the oral performances of those written sermons. From the minister who writes only parts of his sermons, I collected the partially written manuscripts and tapes of those sermons. And from the minister who writes very little of his sermons, I collected audiotapes of the sermons along with any notes the preacher may have written.

As in most studies done from an ethnographic perspective, participant observation was a standard means of collecting data (Spradley, 1980). I was a participant observer in each of the church's Sunday services, so I kept field notes on the services as I participated in them. Although most of these notes deal with the sermons, many of them concern other aspects of the service such as what actions during the service made use of written sources, what actions drew the most audience response, and so on. I also conducted ethnographic interviews (see Spradley, 1979, for details about how to conduct an ethnographic interview) with each minister. I interviewed each minister before I began to collect the sermons and during the sermon collections and in some cases after the field work was completed. The field notes and interviews provide insight and support for issues arising out of the analysis of the actual written sermons and/or transcripts of the oral sermons.

The African-American Church and Worship Service

This chapter explores seemingly simple questions: (a) What are the major literacy events and their functions in these three churches? (b) What features characterize these events, particularly the major literacy event—the sermon? (c) How does literacy in this community compare and contrast with academic literacy? Before addressing these questions, it is necessary to provide some background information on the African-American church and preaching tradition and to introduce the three churches in which the highlighted literacy events take place.

The role of the church in the African-American community has been unsurpassed by any other institution (Hamilton, 1972; Smitherman, 1977). Smitherman (1977) states that "the traditional African-American church is the oldest and perhaps still the most powerful and influential black institution" (p. 90). Theologian C. Eric Lincoln (1974), emphasizing the impact of the church on African-American people, states that "[their] church was [their] school, [their] forum, [their] political arena" (p. 6). Lincoln (1974) also asserts that "whether one is a church member or not is beside the point in any assessment of the importance and meaning of the Black church" (p. 115), and Mays and Nicholson (1933) assert that the "Negro church is one of the greatest perhaps the greatest channel through which the masses of the Negro race receive adult education. . . . It becomes the center of religious, moral, and intellectual teaching" (p. 58). This role of the African-American church is not a new one. Many reports focus on the role of the church and religion in helping African Americans survive slavery in America in the 18th and 19th centuries. Blassingame (1979) states that "slaves found [in religion] some hope of escape from the brutalities of daily life" (p. 130). Frazier (1974) points to Christianity as the force that bonded slaves from many diverse backgrounds (p. 16).

Features of African-American preaching. The characteristics which are the core of African-American preaching are the very features that make the sermon a literacy event worthy of study and that provide more insight into literacy acquisition and functions in African-American communities. These essential characteristics of African-American preaching can, I believe, lead us to think more complexly about literacy, literate behaviors, and literate texts.

Mitchell's *Black Preaching* (1970) is probably one of the most complete explorations of African-American preaching. Mitchell suggests that African-American preaching takes place only in dialogue, and he credits the congregation with "making the dialogue a normal part of the black preacher's sermon" (p. 95). Mitchell (1970) characterizes the dialogue as that which occurs when a member of the congregation responds "because he identifies with something the preacher has said . . . he is at home, he is interested in what the preacher is saying because he is involved, crucially involved in the issues as the preacher shapes them with scriptural reference and skillful allegory" (p. 97). In other words, as the typical African-American sermon is being shaped by the preacher, he or she depends on the participation of the congregation in completing that sermon.

This dialogic quality contributes to another essential characteristic in African-American preaching: African-American preachers must create a sense of community between themselves and their congregations. Mitchell (1970) states that through the sermon "one has to establish a kind of intimate fellowship" (p. 185). It is this task of creating a sense of community or "intimate fellowship" and its connection to the sermon that I concern myself with in my discussion of features of the sermon. That is, one of the major features of the sermons in the churches that I studied is that the texts are used to create and maintain a sense of community. This feature sets this literacy event apart from the essay—the major academic literacy event—because of the sermon's dependence on both participants, preacher and congregation, to be considered a successful text in the community. African-American preachers, like other rhetoricians, can only be successful at setting up this dialogue if they know their audience and their needs.

Mitchell's (1970) characterizations of African-American preaching can be condensed to two major points:

1. Black preachers must preach in the language and culture of their people no matter how educated the preachers are.
2. The preacher must address the contemporary man and his needs. (p. 29)

The first point is similar to one raised by St. Augustine (1958) who argues that preaching is a rhetorical act and that the preacher/rhetor must, if necessary, speak the language of the people to reach them. One key difference between Augustine and Mitchell is that Mitchell sees this role as a necessity for being successful in the African-American church, whereas St. Augustine views it somewhat as a last resort. The second point stresses knowing enough about the congregation, being connected enough with them, to know what's important to them. This kind of knowledge and skill, prerequisites for building a community, makes African-American preachers quite effective in reaching their congregation. The dialogic quality of the text and the creation of a community through the text make the African-American sermon a distinctive text.

THE MINISTERS AND THEIR CHURCHES

Each minister in the study held a bachelor's degree, had seminary training, and currently held the position of pastor in a mainstream African-American church. With the inclusion of the term *mainstream*, I excluded storefront churches where memberships are generally small, and there is less likelihood that the preachers have gone through formal training. Even though each church in the study belongs to a different denomination, each denomination falls within the reformed tradition in which the sermon is the key part of the service. Also, the Sunday services are similar in format and follow in the tradition of the African-American church, and even though each preacher is marked by fairly different individual styles, each is firmly within the tradition of African-American preaching discussed earlier in the chapter.

G. Davis (1985) argues that in spite of differences among denominations and preaching styles "the sermon structure identified . . . as African-American describes sermons preached from hundreds of Black pulpits across America without regard to denominational affiliation. That sermon structure is cultural" (p. 30). The only noted exception to Davis's statement may be seen in African-American Catholic churches, where the structure of the service does not permit or invite the kind of sermons that are commonplace in most other African-American churches.

Meeting the Manuscript Minister

The most important distinction among the three preachers for the purposes of this study is the amount of writing they do in preparing their sermons. The minister who writes and uses a full manuscript from which he delivers his sermon is referred to hereafter as the *manuscript minister*, a term used by the manuscript minister himself. The manuscript minister pastors a church located on the South Side of Chicago, which in 1992 celebrated its 30th anniversary. This church has approximately 5,500 members and an annual budget of approximately $2,000,000. It is the largest church in the study, and to accommodate the large numbers of people who attend this church, the minister normally preaches at two services, one at 8 a.m. and one at 11 a.m. This congregation will be moving into a newly built worship center within a year.

Licensed to preach at 17 years old, and ordained eight years later, this minister has been a pastor since 1972. He has a B.A. in English, an M.A. in literature, an M.A. in the History of Religions, and a doctoral degree in Divinity. This minister's seminary training focused on academic scholarship rather than preparation to preach. He explains that this kind of training has an influence on what he preaches, specifically his understanding of the African-American religious tradition in the context of world religions. In addition, he serves as an adjunct professor with the Seminary Consortium for Urban Pastoral Education.

This manuscript minister's biographical sketch gives evidence of his deep commitment to education. Also, he is deeply committed to addressing political and social issues as well as religious issues. His sermons contain many illustrations that concern politics from the local level to the global level such as criticisms of Chicago politician Ed Vrdolyak, former U.S. President Ronald Reagan, and former South African President P.W. Botha. He does not shy away from relating Biblical politics to world politics nor does he shy away from criticizing politicians from the pulpit. Some of these references to politics are impromptu, but most of them are parts of the written sermons. This minister also educates his congregation about different cultures, telling them about the cultures of the people in the countries he visits, particularly the cultures of peoples of color. He constantly introduces Hebrew and African concepts to the congregation in the context of a particular sermon's message. His focus on the bonds between peoples of color was evident to me after two months of observation. In short, he is a well-educated, charismatic man whose command of language and knowledge of the Bible and religions of the world are displayed in his sermons.

Meeting the Manuscript Minister's Congregation

Some churches reflect their denomination's teachings, some reflect the congregations' wishes, and other churches reflect their ministers' visions. This church falls into the latter category. Many of the programs that exist in this church are a result of the manuscript minister's philosophy and ideas brought to fruition. His effectiveness as a pastor can be measured by the growth of the congregation and the church's programs since his arrival over 20 years ago. The membership has grown from less than 100 members to approximately 5,500 members. The church now has a federally approved credit union, a reading, writing, and math tutorial program, a day care center, a legal counseling service, a large pastoral counseling staff, an educational program that concentrates on educating the church membership about their religious and cultural roots as an African people, broadcast ministries, and much more.

The manuscript minister stresses to his congregation that they should be "unashamedly Black and unapologetically Christian." This statement is part of the oath that the congregation takes when accepting new members into the church. During the time that the data were collected, this church was always full, with standing room only. Worshippers arrive 50 minutes before the service starts so that they can get seats in the sanctuary.

The congregation of this church is viewed as middle-class by many members of Chicago's African-American community. However, the minister views his congregation as a mixed group. He takes pride in the diversity of the congregation. Yet, although the members of this church represent a range on the socioeconomic ladder, there are a large number of people who are professionals: judges, lawyers, doctors, educators, businessmen and women, entertainers, and so on. A TV documentary which aired nationally addressed the perceived "middle classness" of this church ("Keeping the faith," 1987). It is a church that stresses education, yet it does not make the less formally educated feel uncomfortable. Its apparent upward mobility makes this church appealing to those who identify with the upwardly mobile. In fact, many members of the congregation drive to Chicago's South Side from Chicago suburbs.

Despite its middle-class identification, this church is rooted in the tradition of the African-American church, and the minister is rooted in the tradition of African-American preachers. My interviews with this minister confirmed what I had observed previously: that this manuscript minister takes great pride in being identified as "in the tradition of black preachers." He believes in making connections between the traditional African-American church and the contemporary African-American church, and in using the language of the African-American community in his sermons. This use of the language is much more than just speaking; it is also establishing a sense of community, communicating ideas and attitudes about African-American people, and promoting certain community values.

Meeting the Nonmanuscript Minister

The second preacher in the study prepares no manuscript from which to preach and usually no written notes. He pastors a church, located in a North suburb of Chicago, that has approximately 800 members. Even though the church is in a Chicago suburb, it is located just across the northern border of Chicago and has very strong ties to the city. Many of its members live in Chicago. Like the manuscript minister, the nonmanuscript minister also preaches at two Sunday morning services, at 8:00 and at 11:00. This church, rich in history, celebrated its 122nd anniversary in 1992.

This preacher initially came to this area as a faculty member at a nearby well-known seminary. He was on the faculty at this seminary for 15 years. During the latter years of his faculty appointment, he also served as senior pastor of this church, probably one of the few professors who also pastored a church full time. In his church he is addressed by his academic title "Dr_____" rather than "Reverend_____." This minister brings to this church not only a traditional training of years of preaching experience mostly in smaller churches, but also a scholarly foundation. And although this scholarship includes the study of noted Western philosophers such as Heidegger and Kant, this minister has devoted much of his scholarship and his ministry to African-American theological issues.

Like the manuscript preacher, the nonmanuscript preacher has a basic philosophy that guides his ministry. That philosophy, which is printed on the church bulletins, is "faith and freedom for African-American people." He says that he is "unapologetically a race preacher." Committed to his people, this minister's philosophy and commitment affects his sermon preparation and consequently his sermons. Through my interviews with this minister I learned that his experiences as a preacher at a southern church and at divinity school in the South played a major role in his training to be a pastor to African-American people. Born in a midwestern, white-collar city, it was his experiences in the South that introduced him to the traditional African-American worship patterns that so many African-American preachers exemplify. He now describes the congregations of many urban churches as full of transplanted Southerners who are used to the Southern African-American tradition of worship, a sentiment echoed by Davis (1985) who notes the important influence of the Southern African-American church tradition on African-American churches in general.

When discussing methods of communicating with his congregation, the nonmanuscript minister focused on verbal and nonverbal language. He relies on gestures to communicate as well as words. The nonmanuscript preacher explains that in the African-American church he reaches some people with words; he states, for instance that, "celestial skies means heaven for some, but those words mean nothing to people ruled by emotions. A gesture, however, pointing upward and looking upward has the meaning of heaven for those people who attach less meaning to words." This raises the issue of how much value some people attach to words in this setting. It also raises the issue of how this minister and others identify and communicate with the multiple levels of audience that make up their congregations. This minister, as evidenced by his identification of the different kinds of language use to which people respond, has a special awareness of this multiple audience issue. More importantly, he seems to meet the needs of his congregation.

Finally, of great importance when discussing this nonmanuscript minister is his commitment to political and social issues. It is very obvious that he sees the pulpit as the perfect place to discuss politics. During the time that I attended services and collected data, I noted that this minister regularly discussed local, state, national, and international politics. Many times, issues of politics were used as illustrations in a sermon. Tied to political issues raised in the pulpit are social and economic issues. One sermon began with a discussion of the impact of AIDS on the African-American community. The politically centered discussions focus on their impact on African-American people, in keeping with this minister's identification of himself as a race preacher.

Meeting the Nonmanuscript Minister's Congregation

The oldest of the three churches in this study and located in a middle-class suburb, this church's location suggests that it serves a predominantly middle-class African-American population. Indeed, many of its members fit that label. Like the congregation in the manuscript minister's church, this church has a large number of African-American professionals. There are teachers, judges, lawyers, doctors, businesspersons, and corporate executives in this congregation. In addition, because this church is located very near a major university, there are a large number of African-American college students, both at the undergraduate and graduate level, who attend this church.

This church, unlike the other two churches in the study, is not located in an African-American neighborhood; people drive from various distances to get to Sunday morning service. In spite of these facts, the minister indicated that he does not really see his church as middle class, although he recognizes that there are a large number of professionals and what he calls intellectuals in his congregation. His perception does assist him in not preaching above the heads of those who are limited in their vocabulary and educational levels or who do not respond as enthusiastically to verbal stimuli.

This church's organizations are concerned not only with the operation of the church but also with education and community fellowship. This church has an administrative staff consisting of the senior pastor, executive assistant pastor, and assistant pastors in charge of special ministries, educational ministries, and youth ministries. There are the traditional deacon, trustee, and usher boards. There is also a library committee and a group that runs a precollege seminar for church members who are going off to college. The focus on education reflects one of the priorities of the minister, who promotes the value of higher education in his sermons.

In addition, this church has numerous organizations that promote fellowship among the congregation such as the singles' ministry, the widows' and widowers' club, the bowling league, and the softball team. There is also a church-run marriage counseling program. These organizations and programs show how many diverse groups the church tries to serve. It also emphasizes the church as the center of not only religious and political activities but social activities as well.

Meeting the Partial Manuscript Minister

The third preacher in the study, hereafter referred to as the partial-manuscript minister, writes approximately 25% of his sermons. He brings into the pulpit with him a written text that physically resembles a sentence outline but that seems to include far more information than an outline usually does. The partial-manuscript preacher pastors a 78-year-old church on the far South Side of Chicago. This church, with approximately 550 members on roll (only half attend regularly), has one morning service at 11 a.m.

I learned of the partial-manuscript minister's church through an acquaintance who is a member of that church. This acquaintance described his minister as one who did not write his sermons. So it was the search for a nonmanuscript minister that brought me to this church. What I found, when I talked with the minister, was that he wrote too much to be considered a nonmanuscript minister (approximately one-fourth of his sermon was written), and he wrote too little to be considered a manuscript minister. However, this minister placed himself more on the nonmanuscript end than the manuscript one. I refer to him as a partial-manuscript minister to distinguish him from the nonmanuscript minister.

This minister is the youngest of the three ministers in this study. After leaving the military he became pastor of his first church in 1974, and he has been a minister for 25 years and pastoring over 18 years. He has the least amount of education of the three ministers in that he was completing his graduate work (master's level) at the time of this study. However, he has studied in several seminary programs which, although they do not offer graduate degrees, prepare ministers to preach and pastor a church. He even stated in one of his sermons I collected that he goes to seminars and takes courses on preaching and the ministry to become a better communicator. What this congregation has is a model, the minister, who is constantly trying to improve himself as a preacher and pastor, mostly through education.

This minister's effectiveness is measured by his congregation's admiration of him, admiration which seems to cover the preacher and the man. When discussing his preaching, he said his sermons were arranged a certain way because he wasn't good at other kinds of arrangements, particularly topical arrangements. Yet, he also questioned the legitimacy of preaching topical sermons. He describes himself as being more of an exegetical preacher, which he views as the most legitimate type of preaching. Many works on preaching support him (H.G. Davis, 1958; W. Thompson, 1981). Exegesis involves close reading of the scripture as a basis for the sermon. It deemphasizes choosing a sermon from outside the Bible as the other two ministers often do. This minister's sermons closely resemble line-by-line literary explications of text. He is by far the more conservative in personality and philosophy of the three preachers.

He rarely included any political statements in his sermons

during the time that I was in his church. The extent of his political statements was to urge people to vote in the upcoming election, a statement he made during the announcements, not during the sermon. His style is not to mix politics and religion in the pulpit, even though he does think that African-American preachers characteristically feel perfectly free to discuss social and political issues in the pulpit. Although the partial-manuscript minister discusses few social and political issues in the pulpit, on one occasion he did use the pulpit to tell women not to wear pants to any function held at the church because some members had complained. This policy suggests the conservative nature of this church. The partial-manuscript minister basically sees the pulpit as the place to expound on the word of God. This is reflected in his sermons and interviews. This minister believes that sermons should be explanations of the Bible. His goal is to explain the Bible to his congregation as best as he can.

Meeting the Partial-manuscript Minister's Congregation

The congregation, like their minister, can be described as low key. Holiness churches generally have the reputation, in the African-American church community, as being even more active and expressive than most African-American churches. Congregants also have the reputation of "staying in church all day." I even asked my acquaintance how long the service was when he first suggested that I visit his church. He said, "it's never more than two hours, unlike most holiness churches." This congregation and its service did not fit the image I had of how their service was supposed to be, an image which was shaped by my experiences with holiness churches in the rural South.

The low-key nature of the congregation is evident in many ways, most notably in how the congregation proceeds through the service. As in the other churches, the congregation is more active in some parts of the service than they are in others. Yet, their participation is not as intense or perhaps as verbal as in the other two churches. For example, when the senior choir sings, the congregation generally listens fairly quietly rather than standing or clapping to indicate that they are moved by the song. This could be because the choir sings anthems and spirituals more so than gospel music, and anthems and spirituals, which sometimes move people to tears, do not seem to invite the same kind of vocal responses from the congregation as do gospel songs.

The partial-manuscript minister's congregation is most vocal during the sermon and after the sermon. During the sermon, the congregation participates in the call-and-response patterns that are traditional in the African-American church, but the response seems limited to a few verbal statements. I noted that the congregation rarely showed their excitement by standing or clapping during the sermon, even during the climax. Yet, many members, especially men, answer the preacher during the sermon with "amen" and "umm hmm" or an affirmative nod of the head, and the congregation consistently answers [the minister] as a group "yes," "that's right," and "Lord." In addition, individual voices can be heard over the group responding "preach" along with other comments. As in the other churches, the more excited the minister becomes (when he raises his voice), the more vocal the congregation becomes. The more low key this minister is during the sermon, the quieter the congregation. Unlike the other two ministers, this minister seems to "wind down" during his climax, and his congregation "winds down" with him. The congregation's response reflects the minister's preaching style—straightforward and reserved, but not so low key that the service does not resemble a traditionally expressive African-American church service. However, I saw few people outwardly carried away by emotion in this church as I did in the other two churches.

Because this church is smaller than the other two churches, more members of the congregation know each other; consequently, they know when there are visitors, even when the visitors do not stand to identify themselves. I was recognized right away as new, and members of the congregation came up to me after the services each Sunday to greet and welcome me, treatment that other visitors and new members also received. Because few members knew about my research, they saw me as a potential member. I was constantly asked if or when I would join their church. I was surprised that more of the congregation's outgoing personality did not appear during the service.

Differences and Similarities

Although the three churches are similar in the format of their service, the manuscript minister's church and the nonmanuscript minister's church are more similar to each other than they are to the partial-manuscript minister's church. In a sense the partial-manuscript minister's church is a very traditional church. There are the normal organizations: deacon board, board of trustees, usher board, choirs, Sunday schools, youth groups, and so on. With the exception of the usher board and the choirs, most of these organizations are traditionally dominated by men, especially the leadership positions.

The usher board and choirs, traditionally female dominated, are organizations that have almost no role in the decision-making process of the church. In this particular church, men hold the leadership positions of almost all of the organizations. During my weeks of observation, I never saw a woman in the pulpit of this church. In contrast, the churches of the manuscript and nonmanuscript ministers have large ministerial staffs including women, who also have roles in other phases of the church. Both churches also have nontraditional organizations, such as singles groups. The manuscript preacher's church has African-American men's and women's organizations, and the nonmanuscript preacher's church has a widow(er)'s organization.

I note these differences in church organizations and the role of women because they reflect not only different philosophies of denomination but also of preachers and that affects how the preachers view their congregations. Consequently, their sermons are affected.

Although I have noted some differences, one major similarity which should be noted is the active youth groups and youth programs of each church. Each church has regular Youth Sundays when the youth run the entire worship service, including preaching. The youth also have organizations and other programs which are integral parts of the church. Because the youth at each church are so active, they are vitally involved in their churches, constantly exposed to and, indeed, deeply entrenched in the tradition of the African-American church and, therefore, its literacy traditions. This exposure to the sermon may have important consequences for how these youth and other members of the congregation view formal discourse, written and oral.

LITERACY EVENTS AND LITERACY PRACTICES

This chapter focuses mostly on the sermon, but that is not the only literacy event that exists in the African-American church. Therefore, this chapter includes a brief discussion of other literacy events in these three churches which occur during Sunday worship services. It is these other literacy events that provide the context from which the sermon takes place.

Literacy Practices in the Manuscript Minister's Church

At first, one might think that the typical worship service at this church revolves around oral language use. And indeed, the sermon, which is the major activity of the service, is an orally performed event, as are the various prayers throughout the service. However, before the congregation hears this sermon, they most likely have participated in several reading acts. Upon entering the sanctuary, worshippers are given bulletins by the ushers. These bulletins average 12 pages of written material.

The bulletin, used to present the order of worship and to make churchwide announcements, is the method that this church uses to provide non-sermon-related information to its congregation. Although many of the same announcements are read orally by one of the associate pastors each Sunday, it is this bulletin that lets the congregation know what activities are occurring in the church from week to week. Also included in this bulletin are a list of the sick and shut-in members of the church, apartment advertisements, employment opportunities, and sometimes editorial essays from the desk of the pastor. This is by far the most effective method of disseminating information to the congregation. Usually before each service officially starts, most members of the congregation are using the time to read their bulletins. The information in these bulletins also becomes the basis of the talk by the pastor who highlights important information. In this case the congregation uses writing as a source of information.

The bulletin also contains the order of worship for each service. This is a church that rarely deviates from the printed order of worship in the bulletin. This order of worship appears almost ritualistic. Every Sunday the service opens with the choral introit, an opening choral number, and the Lord's Prayer. The next two acts are reading acts. The congregation sings an assigned hymn which can be found printed on an insert in the bulletin or in the hymnal. Then they participate in the responsive reading which is also printed in the bulletin and in the back of the hymnal. These two acts are performed every Sunday, and at the center of these acts is a written text. It is clear that the written Order of Worship provides structure to the service, serving the function for which it is named. Using writing as an ordering device then becomes one use of literacy in this church.

The elements in the worship service that change from Sunday to Sunday are the songs and the sermon. Because of the ritualistic nature of the service, the written Order of Worship may be more a tradition than a necessity, and if so, what kind of message is sent to the congregation about the value of writing in this situation? In African-American churches in which the Order of Worship is not consistently written, the services generally proceed in an orderly fashion but are far longer than in the churches in which the Order of Worship is written.

If one looks only at the Order of Worship, one may be puzzled by its seeming rigidity in what has been traditionally seen as the spontaneous nature of the African-American church. However, by attending the services of the manuscript minister's church, I found that within this structured service is opportunity for spontaneity by the preacher(s) and the congregation, particularly when the choir sings, during prayer time, or during the sermon. It is during these three times, when the congregation has no written text to guide them through these acts, that they seem most involved as measured through their verbal and physical responses. They are attentive through other parts of the service, but their responses are rather mechanical. Anytime the congregation reads a text, they become more passive participants as if they are listening to a lecture. However, during the times when there is no written text such as the choir's musical selections, the invocation, altar call prayer, and the sermon, the congregation becomes more active by responding vocally, clapping, standing, or some combination of the three. In short, the congregation becomes part of a dialogue.

In the sermon, the manuscript minister invites these responses. He believes that the sermon is a dialogue, not a lecture, and that the congregation should be actively involved. He sees this practice as marking a major difference between the African-American worship service and most white worship services. This practice, referred to as "call and response" (Holt, 1972) is a mainstay of the sermon event. Therefore, in this particular setting, reading is a passive act, but listening, which is normally viewed as a more passive act than reading, is far more active.

Listening to the sermon, the songs, and the prayers means answering the minister when he "hits home," or singing along or calling on Jesus to "help me," encouraging the preacher with "come on preacher" or "I know that's right," and saying "Amen" or countless other responses to let the preacher or the singer or the person praying know that you are participating in the act. Two of the more popular responses during the sermons are "preach" and "come on minister." Whether the speaker has a written text or not is not an issue for this congregation. So whatever the congregation may learn about language from a sermon or a prayer, they learn through the oral/aural mode. This is the norm (of interaction) in this church as well as in most other African-American churches I have attended over the past 25 years. And this norm is attached to an oral performance just as there are norms attached to the reading act. For the congregation these acts, prayers, and sermons are speech events that are detached from whatever written text from which they may have originated. Yet, this minister's sermons are based on written texts.

Just as the channels of language change throughout the order of service, that is, oral and written language are both used alternately throughout the service, the many acts within the Order of Worship (Lord's Prayer, invocation, ritual of friendship, altar call, sermon, hymn of invitation, etc.) result in different "keys" (Hymes, 1972). Hymes uses "key" to refer to the tone or manner of a particular act. The tone during the ritual of friendship is upbeat and lively, whereas the tone during the altar call is very serious and intense, and during the sermon the "key" may change many times. In this particular setting, there are many elements that may signal "key" from how loud the congregation is singing to how much feedback they give the preacher to how stationery the manuscript minister is during his sermon to the intonation patterns of this minister. During the services of this church, key is tied to the Order of Worship as well as to what is said and done. Because the congregation generally knows what should happen next in the service, they also know the appropriate tone and manner in which to perform an act. During my period of observation, neither the minister nor the congregation gave any indication of any inappropriate responses.

The manuscript minister best signals the key through his intonation patterns in his sermons and his physical gestures as he preaches. This minister's use of intonation and rhythm not only signals his feelings and emotions but also guides the congregation's responses to the sermon. For instance, in every sermon the manuscript minister establishes a pattern of repetition with words and intonation. As he moves toward the end of this pattern, his voice rises and along with it the congregation's responses become more vocal, louder; the clapping becomes more intense. In short, the response level rises with the minister's rise in intonation.

Literacy Practices in the Nonmanuscript Minister's Church

The nonmanuscript minister's church resembles the manuscript minister's in the way that written texts are used in the service. As in the manuscript minister's church, this church has a printed Sunday bulletin that includes the order of service, announcements, names of the sick and shut-in, and sometimes forms to fill out (e.g., Vacation Bible school registration). The bulletin averages approximately 7 pages per Sunday. Although most of the announcements are in the bulletin, there are a few that are not and therefore must be read to the congregation. Every Sunday, someone, usually the same person, highlights many of the announcements in and out of the bulletin. This printed bulletin, combined with the oral reading of announcements, seems to be an effective means of disseminating information. And as stated earlier, it provides the order of service.

This order of service includes two reading acts in addition to reading the bulletin—the responsive reading, which is a part of most church services, and the hymn of celebration, both of which are found in the hymnal. No other reading acts are read by the congregation; instead, someone reads to the congregation. These reading acts tend to occur early in the service before the sermon. The scripture, however, is generally read by one of the assistant pastors. Many members read along (silently) in their own Bibles, as does the congregation in the manuscript minister's church. Most of the service proceeds according to the program. The congregation is generally low key during this part of the service, participating when they are supposed to.

The only time that feedback occurs before the sermon is when the choir sings a particularly moving arrangement of a song or when some announcements are read that invite feedback. For example, one Sunday, members of the singles ministry performed a brief commercial to advertise the church picnic which was to occur in the near future. It drew great responses from the audience. There are several occasions when the choir sings songs that have many members of the congregation singing along, standing and clapping, and a few times physically feeling the spirit and shouting, although shouting is rare in this church. For the congregation, everything in the service is an oral speech event except the two previously mentioned reading acts. Again, as in the manuscript minister's church, in this church, language is predominantly oral; therefore, one must deduce that most of what the people in this congregation learn about language use in this setting, they learn from and through the oral mode.

Literacy Practices in the Partial-Manuscript Minister's Church

The services in his church are similar to the services of the other two churches in that they also follow a written Order of Service printed in the Sunday bulletin. This bulletin averages four to five pages (front and back) per Sunday. Much smaller than the bulletins of the other two churches, this bulletin has on its cover a picture of the church and the biblical statement, "I was glad when they said unto me, Let us go into the house of the Lord." This cover statement illustrates the differences between this church and the other two churches, namely, that the first two churches explicitly combine their religious and social missions for the world to see. The partial-manuscript minister's church, in contrast, pushes social (and political) missions into the background and pushes its religious mission to the front. This is not to say that the other churches do not place their religious missions at the top of their priorities. Indeed, they do. However, they seem to consider their social mission as part of their religious mission.

Usually, the bulletin at the partial-manuscript minister's church includes one page devoted to the Order of Service, another devoted to a list of the sick and shut-in, a page or two that lists announcements, and finally a page which lists church officers and regular weekly church activities. Also, on the last page of each bulletin is a space called "sermon notes" where parishioners can take notes on the sermon. That is unique to this church. The other two churches provide no space in the bulletin to take notes on the sermon. This space is very small, but by virtue of its existence, one may assume that the idea of taking written notes is not an alien idea. My acquaintance in this church even told me that many people including himself take notes during the sermon. As I looked for this during my observation, I found that the people I noticed taking notes were the younger, more educated members who had been introduced to me by my acquaintance, then a doctoral candidate in biomedical engineering, and his wife, a medical doctor. Very few of the other members of the congregation take any kind of notes during the sermon.

This church's order of worship only deviates from what is printed in the bulletin when there is a guest speaker, and even then, the deviation is slight. The congregation moves through the order of worship in a very straightforward manner. The services open with the same hymn each week and a scripture which is printed in the bulletin. This call-to-worship scripture was the same three times out of the five weeks of services for which I have tapes. The congregation reads this call to worship aloud as a group, but there is no responsive reading as it is done in the other two churches. However, as in the other two churches, there are musical selections, announcements, scriptural readings, and as in the manuscript minister's church, an altar call in each service.

Also like the other churches, this church adds to the bulletin communion-related concerns on every first Sunday when they celebrate communion. In addition, during the time of my observation, a memory verse was assigned in the bulletin each week. The congregation was given the book, chapter, and verse of the passage which they were to look up and memorize. This verse changes each week, unlike in the manuscript minister's church, where a memory verse is assigned every month and is printed in the weekly bulletin. For both these churches, assigning a memory verse encourages the congregation to learn the Bible. In African-American churches there is great value attached to being able to recite Bible verses from memory because it indicates that you know the Bible.

As in the other two churches, in the partial-manuscript minister's church, oral language dominates the service, particularly for the congregation. For them the most important part of the service, the sermon, is oral and aural, whereas for the minister, it is oral and written. Written texts are the basis for his sermons. The written texts that the congregation regularly uses during the service are the bulletins, the hymnal, and for a brief 60 seconds or so, the Bible.

THE SERMON AS A LITERACY EVENT: THE TIES THAT BIND

One of the more well-known facts about African-American sermons is that they are characterized by a call-and-response pattern, in which the congregation provides feedback to the minister throughout the sermon. This audience participation pattern is always prevalent in the minds of the three ministers in this study. It is this pattern that prompts each minister to characterize the sermon as a dialogue and because of this characterization to distinguish African-American sermons from most other American protestant sermons (there are some exceptions) which more closely resemble a monologue. This dialogic pattern is the rhetorical device that acts as the foundation for the other three devices I focus on in this section.

In the ministers' discussions of their sermon preparation, each seems acutely aware of the role of the congregation in the construction of a successful sermon. Even the manuscript minister who writes practically all of his sermons speaks of making room for the congregation to participate in the sermon. What these ministers do in their "texts" is to invite audience participation by using the sermon to create and maintain a community. In a sense, viewing the sermon as a dialogue between minister and congregation makes the sermon a community text that is written (or created) through a collaboration between minister and congregation. What I examine in the remainder of this chapter are the features used by the ministers in the sermons that contribute to this sense of community and create space for the dialogue.

Much of the success and/or effectiveness of the three ministers depends on their creating a bond between themselves and their congregations. Also, because part of people's identities are linked with the communities in which they hold memberships, when these preachers use sermons to construct communities, they are also constructing not only their identities, but also the identities of the members of the congregation.

Why is it important to create this sense of community? According to the ministers, placing themselves in the congregation and seeing themselves as part of the group, helps them keep their sermons relevant to the congregation, helps build trust between the minister and the congregation, and therefore, makes it easier for the congregation to hear and accept the message that the minister is preaching. Ultimately, these three ministers try to eliminate distance between them and the congregation through the sermon; yet, they must maintain the "proper" distance because of their leadership positions. Already we can see the multiple functions of this literacy event as well as its multidimensional nature.

The rhetorical strategies that the ministers use to construct and maintain community range from the seemingly simple reliance on first person plural pronouns to the more complex reliance on personal narratives and shared information. Various rhetorical devices are used by these ministers to construct community. It is also important to note that the theme of community also pervades the sermons as a mechanism for emphasis.

"We, The People"

One of the most obvious strategies that each minister consistently uses to help establish a sense of community is the employing of the collective pronouns *we, our,* and *us.* This strategy is a favorite of these ministers, and although it is not unique to African-American sermons (see Jellema, 1988), it is a feature that they use effectively. When the ministers use this strategy, they are tapping into the multiple levels of community represented in their churches as well as establishing their relationships with those communities. Consider the following examples from two different sermons in which the manuscript minister invokes at least three communities: his specific church community, the community of Christians, and society at large. As he taps into these three communities, his membership in these communities is also emphasized:

> Example 1: Some of the meanest most miserable ungodly people I know got more degrees behind they names and make more money than most of us will ever see in a lifetime.

> Example 2: We not at the pinnacle and we not in the pits. We just in between. Nothing to complain about and nothing to write home about either. We're not on a constant high no matter what kind of rhetoric we spout. And we not continuously in the dumps. Oh we have our moments like everybody else. But for the most part we find ourselves hanging around that gray area called in between.

In the first example, the pronoun *us* is so subtly used that we almost miss it. Based on its linguistic context, we can reasonably deduce that the community that the manuscript minister is tapping into is the specific church community. More interesting than the community that he taps into is that he includes himself in this community with the rest of the congregation. He is constructing his identity as a "regular guy" out there in the pew with little money just like everyone else in the church. Yet, he has a BA, two MAs, and was working toward a doctorate (which he has obtained since the study). He drives an expensive car, makes a most respectable if not enviable salary, and lives in an upper middle class Chicago neighborhood (in the church parsonage). But he constructs an identity that downplays his credentials and status.

It's important to this minister that he not separate himself from the congregation based on socioeconomic issues. That is seen even more clearly in the second example taken from the first few minutes of one of the manuscript minister's sermons. In this example, *we* can have at least three referents—the church community, the Christian community, and the community of people in general. The primary audience seems to be the church community; yet, there are no cues that signal a specific community. Again, the minister establishes himself as a member of all of these communities, constructing his identity and contributing to the construction of their identities as a group. The congregation's apparent acceptance of their identities as shaped in this example (through nods of the head, amens, and other comments) marks their contribution to the dialogue that constructs their identities.

Another prominent community which the ministers, particularly the manuscript and nonmanuscript ministers, reference consistently is the African-American community. This is no surprise given the philosophies of those two ministers. They constantly emphasize their identities as African Americans and try to get their congregation to do so as well. Therefore, many times, the collective pronouns refer to the African-American community to which the ministers and their congregations belong. Consider the following example from the manuscript minister and a later example from the nonmanuscript minister:

> *Example:* The God of Harriet Tubman is an *us* God—Community
>
> The God of Martin Delaney is an *us* God—Community
>
> The God of Ida B. Wells is an *us* God—Community

These names refer to famous African Americans from the past. One reading of this passage is that the God of these noteworthy African Americans who struggled yet accomplished much is a God of the people—a God who embraces African Americans. He is not a *them* God—a God for the rich and powerful only, or a God for whites only. African Americans are part of the community too. Here, the theme of community is intertwined with constructing the community. This passage is also one of those examples, which I address later, of using an assumed shared knowledge between minister and congregation to construct and maintain community.

An example of the nonmanuscript minister using collective pronouns to emphasize the African-American community occurs in statements such as the following:

> Example: We can no longer stand in this world as second class in the economic world, but we got to think big.

Previous statements in the sermon signal that we refers to African Americans. The nonmanuscript minister implies that he, along with his other sisters and brothers, needs to think big. Of course, after being in this church for only a couple of weeks, it is clear that this minister thinks big consistently and that he is really trying to get African Americans in general, and his African-American congregation in particular, to think big. In this case, the minister is trying to change the perceived identity of the community. Yet, he has chosen not to place himself apart from the community he is addressing.

"I Can Witness"

This strategy of using collective pronouns to bind the ministers with their congregations seems obvious and simple, but its functions, as shown above, are subtle and complex. A less obvious strategy in creating and maintaining a community in the sermon is the use of personal narratives and testimonial-like statements. Again, this pattern is prevalent in both the manuscript and nonmanuscript ministers' sermons. These ministers' references to themselves as individuals in the sermons most often take the form of personal stories, testimonies, and testimonial-like statements. In these churches there appears to be an implied distinction between testimonies and what I refer to as testimonial-like statements. A person who testifies, who gives a testimony, usually gives a detailed account of some tragedy or down time in his or her life. The account ends with how God brought him or her through this bad time. The testimony is usually quite specific. A testimonial-like statement is a more general version of "testifying;" for example, "God has lifted me up when I was down." Yet, we do not know what the down period was. My field notes contain several entries concerning how excited and vocal the congregations become in the midst of these ministers' stories or testimonies.

During interviews, each minister commented on how African-American churches value personal stories from the ministers. The partial-manuscript minister explains this value most succinctly: "In black churches, the people want to know what God has done for you [the minister]. What can you testify to?" The ministers gain more credibility and authority when they can show their congregations that they know what they are preaching about because they have been down and survived, they have been scared and conquered the fear, they have had experiences which have paralleled those of the people in the pew, and they have persevered and prospered. These personal stories provide the congregation with a more intimate view of the minister.

In sharing something personal, be it poignant or funny, these ministers forge even stronger bonds between themselves and the congregations; hence, they are strengthening community ties. The following example is a personal narrative that the nonmanuscript minister uses as an illustration in his sermon about Abraham:

> I was in the Marine Corps. I was training in Parris Island. I learned something at Parris Island. It was back in those days in 1954 when they was killing marines down there. Marines died on forced marches. I went down there right after six marines were drowned. When I got there the first thing I heard when I got off the bus, somebody said "move." Then he called me a name that just hurt me to my heart. When he called me he said move it you [blank] and I went to him and said sir,

just a minute. I said I'm "——— " Then he called me another name. I don't care who the [blank] you are. It took me a whole week. My heart just lay bare. I was hurt to the core. But every time in the morning they would get up early when you are tired they would come in and say "move it." We just got in bed. "Move it."

My friend and I were put in swimming. I never swam in my life. I didn't know how to swim. They took us into the pool. One day there we were. I thought we were going in there to learn how to doggy paddle. Stand on the side, put your feet up and down, learn how to swim the normal and intelligent way. There we all were there buck naked standing over the side of the pool. I remember all of us lined up. DIs standing on the side over there. There was a young brother named Logan standing next to me. I said, "Logan guess we're going to learn to swim in a minute. They going to teach us how to do this." Logan said, "Yes I've been waiting for this." Then they told us I want you to bend over just like that (demonstrates to congregation). All of us bent over then I heard this loud crack, "Move it!" I turned and looked back and said, "Do you mean?" "Yes, move it." I looked at Logan and said, "We're on this island out here. We're not going to get out of here. I better move." Logan said, "Are you sure?" I said, "Yes." I jumped in. I took a risk. When I jumped in I went down. There I was swallowing the whole pool. I went up and down again. I started down the third time. They threw something out and pulled me out. . . . Brothers and sisters God is often saying to us and you know something I moved at least four times, almost drowned at least four times. But the fifth time I got out there. I found a way of swimming like nobody has ever seen before. I got out that pool. I was not going to drown out there anymore. Brothers and sisters what I'm saying to you. God said it to Abraham, "Move it."

This lengthy example is actually two smaller stories within one longer one, and it highlights this preacher's skills as a storyteller. Storytelling, be it personal or biblical, is a dominant rhetorical device that this minister uses throughout his sermons. The story above is one of his most successful ones as measured by the large amount and loud volume of feedback he receives from the congregation. In this example, this minister shows himself as a naive, sometimes frightened young man who overcomes these drawbacks by taking a risk, by moving forward. This characterization of him as naive and frightened is in direct conflict with the person that he seemingly is now. He has a confident, self-assured presence. One might view him more as a drill instructor than a naive marine private. Therefore, sharing this story about himself with the congregation shows the congregation a different, more vulnerable side of him.

This minister also uses the testimonial-like examples in his sermons to the same effect as he uses the narrative:

Example: A Jesus that I know lives. He is not a dead Jesus. This Jesus that I serve, this Jesus that I know is alive. The Jesus is at this table right now (inaudible) Jesus, he's alive. He lives. How do I know he lives? Because he walks with me and he talks with me. He tells me I am his own. Jesus is the life of the world. Jesus puts joy in my life. Jesus gives me peace when I'm sorrow . . .

Example: Well what do I get from it? You see these degrees that I've got? Well I see. They're not there just for me. But one is for my father, one is for my grandfather, one is for my great-grandfather, one is for those generations yet unborn. I've come a long way. And don't stop me now. I am what I am Thank God. I am so glad to be (inaudible). thank you Jesus. I am what I am. Don't mess with me. Don't mess with me.

The latter example is fascinating because it relates to the earlier example from this minister of thinking big, and it contributes a new dimension to the issue of constructing an identity through the sermon. Although the manuscript minister emphasizes how he is just like everybody else, this minister emphasizes how he is not like everybody else. The latter example emphasizes his degrees. The earlier narrative emphasizes how he takes risks. He is constructing an identity of himself as a strong-willed, aggressive, upwardly mobile person. He wants his congregation to reach his heights and not accept being "just plain ole folks." He wants them, particularly his African-American congregation, to construct an identity different from that which society has given them. And the implicit message is that he should be the role model for this reconstruction of identity.

Even though the nonmanuscript minister appears to distance himself from his congregation by emphasizing his successes, he, in fact, is trying to decrease the gap by appealing to them to rise to his heights and by showing them that his successes were for those who had come before him and for "generations yet unborn." He emphasizes his dedication to his people and, implicitly, his faith that his risks will pay off. The evidence of the value of his strategy is the positive response of the congregation; their level of feedback increases; they respond vocally, and they applaud with a great deal of energy. Through this focus on himself, this minister skillfully manages to maintain community ties, and he skillfully yet subtly establishes some standards for community behavior: taking risks, thinking big, and so on.

The final example below fits into two categories. It is another example of the testimonial-like statement, and it is an example that introduces the strategy of using shared information between minister and congregation to emphasize community ties.

Example: I don't sing . . . because of thunderous ovations and grand audiences. I don't sing . . . because I've got a voice like James Cleveland, Dave Peaceton, or Teddy Pendergrass. I don't sing because I

> think I got a solo voice, and I might get discovered by some record
> company. I sing to praise him. I sing to my little light shine. I sing . . .
> because God has been good to me. I sing because I'm happy and I
> praise him and I say thank you Lord. I sing because I'm free. And I
> praise him. I sing because I know he watches over me

As the manuscript minister delivers this part of his sermon, much of the congregation stands and applauds, waves their hands, and responds with encouragements such as "preach," "yes," "amen," "thank you, Jesus," and other phrases. As they are responding to the minister's words about himself and his relationship with God, there also seems to be a kind of transformation which takes place. The congregation is moved by the witnessing of the minister, but they also identify with him. That is, the "I" in the example becomes a collective "I" that refers not only to the minister but also to the community of believers in that congregation. The minister is no longer speaking for himself but for the community as well. This takes the personal testimony to a new dimension in which the minister's story becomes the people's story.

The manuscript minister says that one of his goals when he prepares his sermons is to seek this collective voice. He views himself as part of the congregation and asks himself, "What do I need to hear today?" He is successful only if he is so much a part of the congregation that he sees himself in them, and they see themselves in him; hence, the "I" becomes representational. When the minister and congregation identify with each other so strongly, the community ties are more deeply embedded, the minister is more firmly entrenched as a role model, and his or her use of language and literacy is more influential.

"The Knowledge We Share"

The previous example provides a segue into the final feature of the literacy event on which this chapter focuses—relying on shared knowledge. These ministers relied on shared knowledge between themselves and their congregation to signal community identification. That is, the ministers assume that their congregation, by virtue of their membership in various communities, has a body of knowledge about certain topics, and that this knowledge is part of their culture. Therefore, these ministers assume that they do not need to explain certain references that come under the auspices of these topics. Many of the examples in the sermons point to an assumed shared knowledge of popular culture, of the Bible, and most often, of African-American culture and history. The previous example emphasizes a knowledge of African-American music, both secular and gospel. James Cleveland was a well-known African-American contemporary gospel singer. David Peaceton is most recently known as a rhythm and blues singer, and Teddy Pendergrass is noted for being a soul singer. All of these singers are popular in the African-American community and noted for their great voices. The manuscript minister assumes that this information is knowledge that the community shares, therefore, there is no need to explain.

In addition to the three references that rely on shared or given information, this example also taps into the community knowledge of music in a different way. Included in the minister's example are lyrics from the popular gospel song "His Eye Is On the Sparrow." This song is not unique to the African-American community, and it is a very popular song. "I sing because I'm happy/I sing because I'm free/I know that he watches over me" are lyrics found in this song. Never in the sermon does the minister make mention of the song title. Again, he assumes that the congregation knows the song. Using song lyrics as examples, either gospel or secular, is a common device for the manuscript and nonmanuscript ministers. In interviews each minister emphasized how important music is in the African-American community, particularly in the African-American worship tradition. Music is so important that it becomes part of the text and, therefore, part of the literacy event. Neither of these ministers make clear distinctions between secular and sacred music.

As I mentioned earlier, the ministers also assume a shared knowledge of African-American history. Earlier in this chapter, I discussed an example from the manuscript minister that employed collective pronouns and focused thematically on community: "the God of Harriet Tubman is an *us* God . . .community/the God of Martin Delaney is an *us* God . . . community/the God of Ida B. Wells is an *us* God . . . community." The minister mentioned other famous African-American historical figures. Again, he offers no explanation of who these people were. His assumption is that people in the community know these people, and if they do not, they should know and better find out about their history and culture, or that those who do not know are not in the community. Being in the community and not having the shared knowledge becomes, for some, a motivation to learn—a subtle teaching device like many of the strategies discussed earlier.

Using examples from the culture of his congregation not only emphasizes the value of the culture but also signals that the minister knows the music, history, literature, and ways of the community. He understands and is part of the community. When we assume memberships in the same communities, then we feel comfortable assuming that other members of that community are familiar with much of the same information. Tapping into that familiarity, that common ground, through the text is a major function of the sermon. Tapping into that familiarity also allows the ministers to move their congregations from the familiar to the unfamiliar, by beginning with what people know—a sound pedagogical strategy.

CONCLUSION

I had three major goals in this chapter: (a) to describe the major literacy events and their functions in three African-American churches; (b) to describe and analyze the features and functions of the African-American sermon, the major literacy event in African-American churches; and (c) to compare and contrast models of literacy in three African-American churches with models of literacy in the academy. The discussion of the first goal provides a context for discussing the second goal, a description and analysis of the African-American sermon, which in turn provides the basis for the third goal. All of the literacy events discussed meet Heath's (1982) definition of a literacy event: "Any action sequence, involving one or more persons, in which the production and/or comprehension of print plays a role" (p. 92).

Even though each of the three churches represents a different denomination and has ministers with different styles, there was some consistency in the kinds of literacy events which took place in each church. The most obvious literacy event in each church beyond the sermon was represented in the church bulletin. The bulletin's major function was to disseminate information, but it also served as a structuring device by providing the Order of Worship for the service and as a mnemonic device, reminding the congregations of the verse they were to memorize weekly or monthly.

Other literacy events in both the manuscript and nonmanuscript minister's churches included responsive readings of the scriptures from either the bulletin or the hymnal. And one of the more interesting yet overlooked literacy events in each church was the songs assigned. At least one song in each church functioned as a reading act. That is, the song was either printed in the bulletin or in the hymnal. The literacy events mentioned above are typical kinds of literacy events recognized and/or used in the academy because they involve reading print. They are, as this chapter demonstrates, part of the ritualistic services at most African-American churches and many protestant churches in general.

The atypical literacy event in this institution is the major one—the African-American sermon. The description of the features of the sermon has shown its uniqueness both as a literacy event—an ongoing process—and as a literate text. The textual features of the sermon which I have focused on are (a) use of collective pronouns in the sermon, (b) use of personal narratives and testimony, (c) reliance on shared cultural knowledge, and (d) the dialogic quality of African-American sermons. Because of its foundational role, the fourth feature—the dialogic quality—could not be treated separately; instead, it is shown to be an integral part of each textual feature. The ministers use these prominent sermonic features to create a community in their churches. The text—the sermon—becomes the major instrument by which to construct and maintain community ties and identities.

As the analysis has shown, the first three features are rhetorical devices that the ministers use in their sermons to draw them closer together with their congregation. The ministers use collective pronouns and personal narratives to show their congregations that they are no different than the people sitting in the pews, that they [the ministers] can identify with their congregation. The third device calls for the ministers to display their understanding of cultural knowledge, thus establishing community insider/outsider status. These are all devices that encourage the congregation to involve themselves in the making of the text. Seeing themselves as part of the text, as being able to provide feedback and respond to the minister as part of the sermon, is a traditional characteristic of African-American sermons, and it is this process that is the essence of the fourth device—the dialogic quality.

The final goal—comparing and contrasting literacy in these African-American churches with literacy in the academy—is best understood by examining the implications of this study. First, this study suggests that because of the dialogic quality of African-American sermons and the focus on constructing community identities through the sermon, no fixed boundary between speaker and audience exists. Instead, participant roles constantly switch back and forth during the sermon. Even when a minister writes his sermon, as the manuscript minister does, he understands, allows, and, in fact, needs audience participation to complete the text. Audience participation in performance events, such as the sermon, is an Afrocentric concept characteristic of many African-American communities' performance-oriented events (R.F. Thompson, 1983).

The dialogic nature of the text also suggests, because of the lack of fixed boundaries, that the sermon can realistically be viewed as a community text. As he conceives of and shapes the sermon, the minister has no real ownership of the text. The ministers in this study argue that once a sermon is preached, it is no longer their sermon. There appears to be no concept such as ownership of text or intellectual property. Yet, academic literacy holds as one of its most sacred principles the ownership of words. These ministers also suggest that even if they preach the same sermon twice, it really is not the same sermon. Once the audience changes, the dialogue changes, and, therefore, the sermon changes. In other words, the sermon can never be decontextualized. Much of its meaning is determined by the participants.

As the boundaries are blurred between speaker and audience, so too are the boundaries between oral and written patterns in the sermons. Even though the sermon is an orally performed event, it also represents a literate text, one that uses varying degrees of writing and speech. This integration of speech and writing is part of the text of the sermon and once more points to the blurred boundaries and seamlessness that surround the sermons. This seamlessness can be found not only within the sermons, but also within the service that surrounds the sermon (see Mountford, 1991). That is, neither the sermons nor the service can be easily segmented into discreet sections.

The blurred boundaries between speech and writing are most evident when one considers how many devices the manuscript and nonmanuscript ministers' texts have in common, even though one minister wrote everything down and preached verbatim from his written text, and the other wrote nothing. Because the sermon is an orally performed event, one is inclined to think of it as only an oral text, but the sermons are generally rooted in biblical scriptures—a written text. In addition, these ministers are highly literate men (as defined by the academy) whose lives are deeply influenced by written words. Yet, clearly, they do not view writing and speaking as an either/or dichotomy; in their communities, writing and speaking are intertwined and interdependent. The boundaries blur.

The nonfixed and blurred boundaries which characterize these ministers' sermons point toward a model of a literate text that is far different from the model that most quickly comes to mind when one thinks of the kind of literate text that dominates in school—the academic essay. The academic essay is generally characterized by its fixed boundaries between media and genres, its radical individualism and monologic quality, its decontextualized meaning, and its traditional definitions of intellectual property. These are features of the essayist tradition.

Although some argue that this is an ideal rather than a real model of the academic essay, it is still the model from which we operate in the academy and which we use to measure most other models and to measure students. Even though collaboratively written texts are acceptable texts in the academy, the text is still one that uses the monologic model. No matter how many writers a collaborative text may have, the writers strive for only one voice to be heard, as if there were only one writer and there were no audience involvement in the text.

Thus, the African-American sermon stands as a model of a literate text which in many ways is the antithesis of the academic essay and promotes a type of literacy which is the antithesis of the most popular academic notion of literacy. Like those who point to electronic and hypertextual forms of literacy, this study suggests that the academy must broaden its definition of literacy and, in addition, its conceptualization of the literate text and the "writer" or "owner" of that text. Privileging the essayist tradition of literacy leaves the academy unable and unwilling to recognize and validate types of literacies from other communities. One powerful consequence of this weakness is that we ignore the richness of literacies that our students from nonmainstream communities bring to the academy, literacies that could be used to help many of these students to more easily expand their knowledge base to include academic literacies. Most seriously, we also close ourselves off from opportunities to learn more about the diverse cultures and literacies represented in our classrooms. If multiculturalism and diversity are the future of the academy, then so is multiliteracy.

REFERENCES

Blassingame, J. (1979). *The slave community: Plantation life in the antebellum south.* New York: Oxford University Press.

Davis, G. (1985). *I got the word in me, and I can sing it, you know.* Philadelphia: University of Pennsylvania Press.

Davis, H.G. (1958). *Design for preaching.* Philadelphia: Fortress Press.

Fishman, A. (1988). *Amish literacy: What and how it means.* Portsmouth, NH: Heinemann.

Frazier, E.F. (1974). *The Negro church in America.* New York: Shoeken Books.

Hamilton, C. (1972). *The black preacher in America.* New York: William Morrow.

Heath, S. (1982). Protean shapes in literacy events: evershifting oral and literate traditions. In D. Tannen (Ed.), *Spoken and written language: Exploring orality and literacy* (pp. 91-117). Norwood, NJ: Ablex.

Heath, S. (1983). *Ways with words.* Cambridge: Cambridge University Press.

Holt, G.S. (1972). Stylin' outta the black pulpit. In T. Kochman (Ed.), *Rappin' and stylin' out* (pp. 189-204). Chicago: University of Chicago Press.

Hymes, D. (1972). Models of the interaction of language and social life. In J.J. Gumperz & D. Hymes (Eds.), *Directions in sociolinguistics: The ethnography of communication* (pp. 35-71). New York: Holt, Rinehart and Winston, Inc.

Jellema, L. (1988). *Rhetoric and economics in television evangelism: What evangelists say and do to bring in money.* Unpublished doctoral dissertation, University of Illinois at Chicago.

Keeping the Faith. (1987, February). *Frontline* [television program]. Chicago: PBS, WTTW.

Lincoln, C.E. (1974). *The black experience in religion.* Garden City, NY: Doubleday.

Mays, B., & Nicholson, J. (1933). *The negro's church.* New York: Negro Universities Press.

Mitchell, H. (1970). *Black preaching.* Philadelphia: Lippincott.

Moss, B. (1988). *The black sermon as a literacy event.* Unpublished doctoral dissertation, University of Illinois at Chicago.

Mountford, R. (1991). *The feminization of the Ars Praedicandi.* Unpublished doctoral dissertation, The Ohio State University, Columbus, OH.

Philips, S. (1972). Participant structures and communicative competence: Warm Springs children in community and classroom. In C. Cazden, V. John, & D. Hymes (Eds.), *Functions of language in the classroom* (pp. 370-392).

St. Augustine. (1958). *On christian doctrine* (D.W. Robertson, Trans.). New York: Bobbs-Merrill Company.

Scollon, R., & Scollon, S. (1981). *Narrative, literacy and face in interethnic communication.* Norwood, NJ: Ablex.

Scribner, S., & Cole, M. (1981). *The psychology of literacy.* Cambridge, MA: Harvard University Press.

Smitherman, G. (1977). *Talkin' and testifying'.* Boston: Houghton-Mifflin.

Spradley, J.P. (1979). *The ethnographic interview.* New York: Holt, Rinehart and Winston.

Spradley, J.P. (1980). *Participant observation.* New York: Holt, Rinehart and Winston.

Street, B.V. (1984). *Literacy in theory and practice.* Cambridge: Cambridge University Press.

Szwed, J.F. (1981). The ethnography of literacy. In M. Farr (Ed.), *Writing: The nature, development, and teaching of written communication* (pp. 13-23). Hillsdale, NJ: Erlbaum.

Taylor, D., & Dorsey-Gaines, C. (1988). *Growing up literate.* Portsmouth, NH: Heinemann.

Thompson, R.F. (1983). *Flash of the spirit.* New York: Random House.

Thompson, W. (1981). *Preaching Biblically.* Nashville: Abingdon.

Weinstein-Shr, G. (1986). *From mountaintops to city streets: An ethnographic investigation of literacy and social process among the Hmong of Philadelphia.* Unpublished doctoral dissertation, University of Pennsylvania, Philadelphia.

World Travelling: Enlarging Our Understanding of Nonmainstream Literacies

Elizabeth Chiseri-Strater
University of North Carolina–Greensboro

In these chapters we have travelled to worlds we might never have experienced on our own and learned about literacies that would be inaccessible, even invisible, to outsiders to these nonmainstream communities. These ethnographers positioned themselves as teachers, coaches, and participant-observers in ways that allowed them, and consequently us, entry into extended families and kinship groups, school board policy-making committees, out-of-school recreational activities, and African-American church services. We have moved across diverse geographical and language communities, overhearing dialogues about vernacular literacy from the Navajo Indians of the Southwest, listening to the problems of reading and writing a second language for the immigrant Hmong of Philadelphia; observing Chicago Mexicanos learning literacy *lirico*, or informally; sharing in the communal and dialogic practices of the African-American sermon; and learning about the "reading rites" of a literacy-based basketball program for young African-American males. "World travelling" as it is described by feminist Maria Lugones (1987), invites participation in diverse cultural settings, yielding an understanding of both others and ourselves. Lugones describes the value of world travelling this way: "The reason I think that travelling to someone's 'world' is a way of identifying with them is

179

because by travelling to their 'world' we can understand *what it is to be them and what it is to be ourselves in their eyes*" (p. 17; emphasis in original).

For teachers of nonmainstream students, research on culturally defined literacy practices reflects back onto our own classrooms, our students, and ourselves in an attempt to improve pedagogy. Educators now recognize that pedagogy embraces more than what is called teaching; it includes curriculum and classroom strategies, student development, and learning styles, as well as methods of evaluation. Moreover, as Farr points out in her chapter, pedagogical approaches are never neutral; rather there are political, economic, and ideological issues at stake over the defining, labeling, and categorizing of what is and what is not considered as mainstream literacy. Those interested in teaching nonmainstream students have begun to enlarge their definitions of literacy to include skills and behaviors beyond those traditionally valued in schools and to realize that language and literacy are best observed within the community and its "close and intricate interplay with social life and social structure" (Shannon, 1992, p. 3). The collected insights of these chapters, then, offer approaches and perspectives for teachers who want to travel to their students' worlds and learn from them about literacy practices and literacy events that might be incorporated into classroom pedagogies.

In order for classroom teachers to "open spaces" (Greene, 1988) for new literacies to enter schools, they might follow the examples of these field researchers by first recording how literacy is used within the communities they are serving. As other ethnographers of nonmainstream communities have shown (Fishman, 1988; Heath, 1983; Taylor & Dorsey-Gaines, 1988), all cultures have specific literacy practices or events that support daily reading and writing for the participants within them, yet many of these are unfamiliar to educators. In these studies, for example, there are surprising ways that second language learners negotiate literacy socially by pooling linguistic resources and working collaboratively within their community networks. Some of these studies involve new ways of envisioning literacy such as the computer skills involved in playing sports games documented by Mahiri. Other literacy practices or events that have implications for school curriculum are mainstream within the culture but not well known by outsiders, such as the rhetorical aspects of the African-American sermon discussed by Moss. Schools cannot build on the strengths students bring into their classrooms if teachers are ignorant of what these literacies are.

If the first step for teachers is to travel to the worlds of their students and watch "what goes on there," the second step involves listening, interviewing, and recording a plurality of voices on educational issues within any given setting. McLaughlin's research on the Navajos provides a model of dialectic engagement among a range of informants in order to get at the contradictions and complications that surround literacy issues. Weinstein-Shr's research offers an awareness that different community members value and need English literacy for very different purposes. One of the more complex issues that comes out of this set of chapters focuses on bilingual education: how, when, and why English should be introduced to second language learners. From the research on the Navajos and the Hmong (and to a lesser extent, the Mexicanos), we discover that second language learners are often not literate in their native languages, due to either a lack of opportunity or need for school literacy in their home cultures. For some participants in these studies, then, becoming print literate in their native languages represents a way of preserving cultures which might otherwise be lost. One Navajo informant summarizes the danger of abandoning one's native language: "Forgetting your language is like forgetting your mother." And yet for other participants within the same community, acquisition of English literacy is equated with access to social and economic mobility. In McLaughin's study, this debate over bilingual education is played out between two Navajo school children of different ages. The third grader who values learning to read and write in her native language says, "Navajo is for the Navajos," substantiating the position that language is culture. A high school student from the same Mesa school system, however, questions the overall usefulness of Navajo print literacy in an open letter published in the school newspaper. This student supports learning English over Navajo because "Students are more likely to get jobs off the reservation than on because there are more jobs off the reservation." Like ethnographers, teachers need to listen to a range of informants' voices in order to understand the different positions held by community members before changing classroom practices or policies.

If there is some debate over classroom instruction for bilingual students, there is complete agreement among the researchers in this collection that schools must become more sensitive to the cultural traditions of nonmainstream groups and build literacy programs around them. When introducing Navajo literacy within the Mesa school system, children were also taught Navajo songs, dances, and clanship traditions so that they would not only become bilingual but bicultural as well. The Hmong community so valued their native traditions that they held schoollike classes in their homes for young men to learn the songs and customs for courtship, marriage, and funerals in order to carry on these customs.

As an ethnographer, Farr was witness to religious ceremonies such as *lavantamiento* and religious practices such as the *doctrina* classes held within the Mexicano homes that she studied. She notes that these religious events and practices included the reading and writing of extended texts that were not only culturally significant but might hold curricular implications for teachers working with such students. Understanding the register used in sports discourse or the rhetorical devices used by African-American ministers to create a communal text might help teachers connect culturally-specific speech events with curriculum for the African-American students in their classrooms. Shirley Brice Heath (1992) has suggested that educators have not taken much notice of the flexible linguistic repertory of African-American students: "The school has seemed unable to recognize and take up the potentially positive interactive and adaptive verbal and interpretive habits learned by Black Americans (as well as other non-mainstream groups), rural and urban, within their families and on the streets" (p. 35).

The research considered here—literacies across communities—indicates that outsiders to nonmainstream communities often have little awareness of the resources available to individuals in such settings from kinship ties, extended families, or church and after-school activities. Weinstein-Shr, who originally taught English classes to the students she eventually studied, shares the insight that as a classroom teacher she could not begin to uncover the support network that was operating or not operating for her students based on their facility with English in her classroom. She relates that the student she felt was her "star pupil" was revealed to have very few networking resources available to him, whereas two other students, who could not master the technology of the English language, were supported by extensive kinship ties within the immigrant community. One informant she discovered to be a respected leader for his history-recording and news-keeping abilities and another for her ability as a cultural broker for Hmong crafts. Among Farr's extended Mexicano community, members supported one another's literacy needs with respect to locating housing and filing tax information and citizenship applications in ways that would be invisible to an outsider to that extended group of *compadrazgo*. Teachers' awareness and understanding of athletic programs such as the Youth Basketball Association might help strengthen and extend the literacy goals inherent in this out-of-school program. All of the African-American churches observed by Moss had extensive youth programs; one offered math and literacy tutoring and another a college preparatory program for its youth. Again, awareness of the literacy goals of both religious and nonreligious institutions outside of school and their considerable resources, along with an understanding of family and kinship support systems, could help teachers connect with students' literacies and lives beyond their classrooms.

Although teachers are not ethnographers, they can position

themselves to become teacher-researchers of language use in their classrooms and in the communities of their students (see Heath's (1983) *Ways With Words* for a model of how teachers and students can become language researchers in their communities). Teachers who follow the path of these ethnographers—holding no preformed judgments on the language and literacies of nonmainstream communities, observing and listening to a wide range of community informants, discovering how the social network patterns of specific cultures work as well as the literacy-related resources available there—will be ready to rebuild the classroom curriculum based on the cultures of the students in them. What follows are some specific pedagogical changes for teaching and learning literacy that emerge not only from the combined data of these studies but from other studies on nonmainstream communities as well.

1. Changes in the teacher's role from that of an authority figure to that of a well-trained coach who supports both his or her individual players and his or her whole team toward success. Mahiri's chapter on the adaptive literacy of adolescent males playing basketball and another of his articles on sports discourse (1991) make similar suggestions about the value of this teacher/coach model and its potential for encouraging literacy and language development. In writing instruction, both Murray (1968) and Elbow (1973) have relied extensively on this metaphor for describing how the writing workshop can help students rely on one another for feedback rather than only on the teacher. Coaches, of course, do wield authority, but their power is based on wanting the whole team to succeed, not just individual players, and is manifest in a different speech register, that of a supportive rather than an authoritarian voice.

2. Changes that help classrooms function as collaborative communities, working together in some of the same ways that extended families and kinship groups operate, trading literacy resources and sharing linguistic knowledge. Because all of the studies in this collection have shown that literacy is most often motivated through social and personal relationships, classroom literacy instruction must also be viewed as oral, not merely textual. Among those pedagogies that reinforce collaborative learning are group work and peer tutoring. Peer and cross-age tutoring allows students to take advantage of the linguistic resources of others by learning in dialogue with one another. Classrooms that emphasize group work and tutoring acknowledge cultural differences in the ways of displaying knowledge. Farr's example of the Mexicano who read English

within his family network but not within a larger setting suggests that many cultures do not value the individualism which is so much the focus of our educational system. Mahiri also noted in his example of the games played at the coaches appreciation dinner that the groups were comprised of different ability levels, working together as teams to answer the word problems.

In her chapter, Moss has critiqued collaborative writing projects when the goal is to produce a single essay voice. She suggests that this reinforces the essayist literacy of the academy at the expense of the diversity of voices inherent in group work. The goal of collaborative writing projects or any group activity need not be to reproduce the same kind of product that might be done individually, but rather to discover a wider range of textual or presentational options—videos, plays, dialogues, newspapers, and scripts, just to mention a few forms—that easily incorporate a range of voices. Diversity of both form and style should be a goal for collaborative writing projects.

3. Changes in the communication system between schools and the communities they serve. Rather than the current unidirectional model, communication about literacy should become bidirectional, going out from schools but also coming back from parents as well. As Farr's chapter indicates, many nonmainstream communities hold education in high regard and are grossly disappointed when their children do not succeed at school. Farr suggests that school routines such as homework sheets are not well explained or even thoughtfully constructed for that matter. She locates the school rather than the home as the source of communicative difficulty for the Mexicano families with whom she worked.

CONCLUSION

Teachers facing the challenges of multicultural classrooms have begun to devise ways of communicating with the nonmainstream families they serve. Following the example of the Mesa school system, which invited parents into classrooms to talk about the cultural traditions of Navajos, any classroom can draw on the cultural heritage of parents by asking them to share holiday traditions, religious ceremonies, particular foods, or crafts from their cultures. It is not difficult to imagine having Bao Xiong stage a Hmong crafts fair in a classroom. And, as Voss (1992) has recently pointed out in her study on home-school literacies, nonmainstream parents can be asked to contribute their everyday knowledge and skills as well by demonstrating how to fix a bike, or how to cut hair. All such contacts between home and school help forge better literacy partnerships.

There are many strategies for communicating about classroom activities and learning philosophies with nonmainstream parents. Some of these which involve print make use of the student as a cultural broker between the home and school by asking them to translate classroom fliers, newsletters, and notices to their parents because teachers themselves are often not literate in many of the languages of their students. In order to find out more about the literacy practices of their students at home, teachers have devised literacy questionnaires or interest inventories for use in subsequent meetings with parents. One of the easiest ways to attract parents to come into schools is to hold classroom meetings that involve their own children reading from their writing, sharing ongoing class projects, or demonstrating new skills. These evening meetings can become occasions for celebrating the work of all the children in the classroom as well as providing time for discussing the individual progress of children.

Pedagogical changes that draw on the coaching model of teaching and involve collaborative learning projects and increased communication with parents about school activities and home literacy move toward improved classrooms for nonmainstream students. More than anything else, educators who take the time to travel to their students' worlds outside the classroom and observe the particularities of language use there will become more sensitive to how the literacies of home and community differ from those currently valued in our classrooms. In order to empower students from cultures different than our own, educators need to merge the worlds of community and school by enacting pedagogies which draw on the language, literacies, and learning resources of these nonmainstream students.

REFERENCES

Elbow, P. (1973). *Writing without teachers.* New York: Oxford University Press.

Greene, M. (1988). *The dialectic of freedom.* New York: Teachers College Press.

Fishman, A. (1988). *Amish literacy: What and how it means.* Portsmouth, NH: Heinemann.

Heath, S.H. (1983). *Ways with words: Language, life and work in communities and classrooms.* New York: Cambridge University Press.

Heath, S.H. (1992). Oral and literate traditions among Black Americans living in poverty. In P. Shannon (Ed.), *Becoming political.* Portsmouth, NH: Heinemann.

Lugones, M. (1987). Playfulness, 'world'-travelling, and loving perception. *Hypatia, 2*(2), 3-19.

Mahiri, J. (1991). Discourse in sports: Language and literacy features of preadolescent African American males in a youth basketball program. *Journal of Negro Education, 60,* 305-313.

Murray, D. (1968). *A writer teaches writing.* Boston: Houghton-Mifflin.

Shannon, P. (1992). Introduction, why become political? In P. Shannon (Ed.),*Becoming political.* Portsmouth, NH: Heinemann.

Taylor, D., & Dorsey-Gaines, C. (1988). *Growing up literate.* Portsmouth, NH: Heinemann.

Voss, M. (1992). *More than print: The home and school literacies of three fourth-graders.* Unpublished doctoral dissertation, University of New Hampshire, Durham, NH.

Author Index

Subject Index

A

African American churches, 147-151
  literacy practices in, 160-165
    music as literacy event, 173
    reading and writing acts, 160-164, 174
  organizations, 156, 159-160
  role in community, 150

African American congregations, 153-154, 156, 158-160
  nature of worship services, 149, 153-154, 156, 158-160
    audience response, 151-166
    key, 162
    singing, 158

African American ministers, 151-159
  manuscript minister, 152-153, 159-160, 167-173
  nonmanuscript minister, 154-155, 159-160, 167-173
  partial manuscript minister, 156-158, 159-160, 167-168, 172-173
  preparation and education of, 152-153, 154-155, 156-158

African American preaching, 150-151

sermons, 152-158, 162, 165
  collective pronouns in, 167-168, 172
  community identity, 151, 166, 168, 172-173
  dialogic nature, 150-151, 174-175
  non-verbal language in, 155
  personal narrative, 169, 171
  political foci, 152-153, 155, 157-158
  relation to academic essays, 175-177
  shared knowledge, 172-173
  structure, 152

B

Bahe, Amos, 112-114
Begay, Ruth, 107-108
Begaye, Roy, 98-100
Benito Juarez High School, 12-13
Bennally, Howard, 105-107
Bilingualism, 2, 32-36, 42-43, 180-181
  bilingual education, 87-92, 181
Biliteracy, 32-36, 42-43
Black language styles, 122